Cairo
&
Nile
Delta

Vanessa Betts

DBI
6/13
12.95

Credits

Footprint credits

Editor: Felicity Laughton
Maps: Kevin Feeney

Managing Director: Andy Riddle
Content Director: Patrick Dawson
Publisher: Alan Murphy
Publishing Managers: Felicity Laughton, Jo Williams, Nicola Gibbs
Marketing and Partnerships Director: Liz Harper
Marketing Executive: Liz Eyles
Trade Product Manager: Diane McEntee
Accounts Managers: Paul Bew, Tania Ross
Advertising: Renu Sibal, Elizabeth Taylor

Photography credits

Front cover: Dreamstime
Back cover: Dreamstime

Printed in Great Britain by CPI Antony Rowe, Chippenham, Wiltshire

Every effort has been made to ensure that the facts in this guidebook are accurate. However, travellers should still obtain advice from consulates, airlines, etc about travel and visa requirements before travelling. The authors and publishers cannot accept responsibility for any loss, injury or inconvenience however caused.

Publishing information

Footprint *Focus Cairo & Nile Delta*
1st edition
© Footprint Handbooks Ltd
May 2012

ISBN: 978 1 908206 69 5
CIP DATA: A catalogue record for this book is available from the British Library

® Footprint Handbooks and the Footprint mark are a registered trademark of Footprint Handbooks Ltd

Published by Footprint
6 Riverside Court
Lower Bristol Road
Bath BA2 3DZ, UK
T +44 (0)1225 469141
F +44 (0)1225 469461
www.footprintbooks.com

Distributed in the USA by Globe Pequot Press, Guilford, Connecticut

The content of Footprint *Focus Cairo & Nile Delta* has been taken directly from Footprint's *Egypt Handbook*, which was researched and written by Vanessa Betts.

Contents

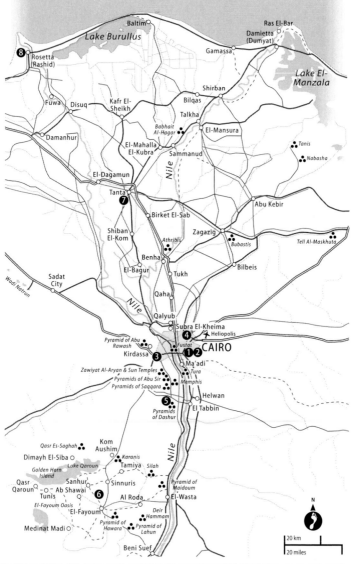

Mediterranean Sea

Lake Burullus

Lake El-Manzala

Ras El-Bar
Damietta (Dumyat)
Baltim
Gamassa

8 Rosetta (Rashid)

Shirban
Bilqas
Talkha
El-Mansura
Tanis
Nabasha

Fuwa
Disuq
Kafr El-Sheikh
Babhait Al-Hagar
Sammanud

Damanhur
El-Mahalla El-Kubra

El-Dagamun

Tanta **7**
Abu Kebir
Birket El-Sab
Zagazig
Bubastis
Tell Al-Maskhuta

Shiban El-Kom
Athribis

Sadat City
Benha
El-Bagur
Tukh
Bilbeis

Wadi Natrun
Qaha

Qalyub

Subra El-Kheima
Heliopolis
4

Pyramid of Abu Rawash
Kirdassa
Fustat
3
1 **2** CAIRO
Ma'adi

Zawiyat Al-Aryan & Sun Temples
Pyramids of Abu Sir
Pyramids of Saqqara
Tura
Memphis

Helwan

5
Pyramids of Dashur
El Tabbin

Qasr Es-Saghah
Kom Aushim
Dimayh El-Siba
Karanis
Lake Qaroun
Tamiya
Silah

Golden Horn Island
Sanhur
Ab Shawai
Sinnuris
Pyramid of Maidoum

Qasr Qaroun
Tunis
6
Al Roda
El-Wasta

El-Fayoum Oasis
El-Fayoum
Deir Hammam

Medinat Madi
Pyramid of Hawara
Pyramid of Lahun

Beni Suef

N

20 km
20 miles

At the crossroads of Asia, Africa and Europe stands the metropolis of Cairo, the largest city in the Middle East and Africa and one of the most populous in the world. The Nile runs like a vein through the centre. On either bank extraordinary remains of civilizations past – thousands of years of pharaonic, Coptic and Islamic history – mingle with the dwellings and lives of modern Egyptians. A walk around Cairo is a walk through thousands of years: from the colossal Pyramids of Giza at the edge of the Western Desert to the Old Coptic Quarter on the east bank; along the alleys of Islamic Cairo, gushing with life and hundreds of ancient monuments, to the downtown quarter where the stunning façades of 19th-century buildings tell of the profound influence of European occupiers. And in between, the ancient monuments and modern buildings, *souks* and *ahwas* (coffee houses), bazaars and *felafel* stalls fill every crevice.

Pyramids in romantically ruinous state are scattered to the south of Cairo, while the north is dotted with the desolate remains of pharaonic cities. The famous Step Pyramid of Saqqara in the vast necropolis of the early pharaohs is worth visiting before going on to Giza, to see the development from the simple underground tomb to the audacious concept of the Pyramid of Cheops. Further south, the harsh desert gives way to the beautiful pseudo-oasis of El-Fayoum, a lush expanse of fields and palms offering sanctuary to some of the richest birdlife in Egypt. Ptolemaic temples, the artists' enclave of Tunis and the ultramarine waters of Lake Qaroun all nestle on the edge of the arid western desert only 90 minutes from the city.

Beyond Cairo, the two main tributaries of the Nile continue northwards to meet the Mediterranean near Damietta and Rosetta, where Ottoman houses, winding medieval lanes and the picturesque expanses of the Nile are a pleasant surprise. On either side, and between the two branches, the green and fertile plains fan out to create – with the help of some of the world's oldest and most efficient irrigation systems – Egypt's agricultural heartland.

Planning your trip

Getting to Cairo and the Nile Delta

It is possible to fly direct to Egypt from Europe, the Middle East, the USA and most adjacent African countries. Airfares vary according to season. They peak from June to September and around other holiday times (Christmas and New Year). The cheapest times to travel are during November and January. As a rule, the earlier you buy a ticket, the cheaper it will be. It's worth checking in with a few travel agents to see if any special promotions are available and sometimes tour companies offer cheaper fares. Return tickets are usually a lot cheaper than buying two one-way tickets or opting for an open-ended return, unless you fly with a charter airline. Round-the-World tickets don't include Cairo on their standard itineraries.

From Europe From London, BMI, www.flybmi.com, British Airways, www.ba.com, and EgyptAir, www.egyptair.com, offer daily flights to Cairo International airport. Flight time is about five hours and ticket prices range from £350 in the off-season to £450 during peak tourist season. You can save a bit of money if you fly indirect via a European capital (see below), usually in Eastern Europe, Germany or Greece. Have a look at www.thomsonfly.com, www.firstchoice.co.uk, www.jet2.com and www.fly thomascook.com, as there are some great deals (as low as £50 one way if you get lucky) if you don't mind starting your journey outside Cairo.

There are no direct flights from Ireland and most people fly via London. **Air France**, www.airfrance.com, offers direct flights to Cairo via Paris. From Germany, **Lufthansa**, www.lufthansa.com, via Frankfurt, and **TUIfly**, www.TUIfly.com, are a good budget choice from Berlin, Munich and Cologne. **KLM**, www.klm.com, flies to Cairo from Amsterdam. **Austrian Airlines**, www.aua.com, **Czech Airlines**, www.czechairlines.com, **Malev**, www.malev.hu, and **Olympic Airways**, www.olympic-airways.com, have services too, often at competitive prices.

From North America From New York EgyptAir offers an 11-hour daily direct flight to Cairo, ticket prices range from US$1000 in the off-season up to US$1500 during peak travel times. Most European carriers offer flights from major North American cities to Cairo via their European hubs. **British Airways** and KLM serve the bigger cities on the west coast. From Canada, there are direct flights with **EgyptAir** from Montreal two or three times a week, taking about 11 hours. Some European airlines also have connecting services from Montreal and Toronto that do not necessitate overnight stays in Europe.

From Australia and New Zealand There are no direct flights from Australia or New Zealand, but many Asian and European airlines offer services to Cairo via their hub cities. Tickets can be expensive, so it may be worth opting for a Round-the-World ticket, which could be comparable in price or even cheaper than a round-trip flight. From Australia to Egypt tickets range from about AUS$1750 during the off-season to AUS$2500 in the peak season. **Qantas**, www.qantas.com, **Austrian Airlines**, www.aua.com, and **Alitalia**, www.alitalia.com, in addition to a few Asian carriers, offer competitive prices.

Don't miss ...

1 **Egyptian Museum**, page 40.
2 **Islamic Cairo**, page 48.
3 **Pyramids of Giza**, page 94.
4 **Fishawi's**, page 112.
5 **Saqqara and Dahshur**, pages 134 and 141.
6 **El-Fayoum** and **Lake Qaroun**, pages 143 and 147.
7 **Tanta's eight-day moulid**, page 155.
8 **Rosetta**, page 157.

Numbers refer to map on page 4.

Airport information Departure tax is included in the price of airline tickets. Confirm airline flights at least 48 hours in advance. Most airports require that travellers arrive at least two hours before international departure times. Have all currency exchange receipts easily available, though it is unlikely you will be asked for them. Before passing into the departure lounge it is necessary to fill in an embarkation card. Only a limited amount of currency can be reconverted before you leave, which is a tedious process. Sometimes suitable foreign currency is not available. It is better to budget with care, have no excess cash and save all the trouble.

Baggage allowance General airline restrictions apply with regard to luggage weight allowances before a surcharge is added; normally 30 kg for first class and 20 kg for business and economy class. If you are travelling with a charter flight or budget airline, you might have to pay for even one item of luggage to go in the hold. Carry laptops in your hand luggage, and check the airline's website to see what the restrictions are on hand luggage as this varies between different carriers.

Transport in Cairo and the Nile Delta

From camel to plane to *felucca*, Egypt is equipped with numerous transport options. Congestion and chaos can be a bit anxiety-inducing on long road ventures, but with a bit of courage and flexibility, you can access most areas without too much effort. As for timetables and infrastructure, the country seems to run on magic. There are few regulations and little consistency, but somehow, people always seem to get where they want to go.

Air
The national airline is EgyptAir, www.egyptair.com, who have rebranded and became the first Middle Eastern member of Star Alliance in July 2008. In the past, foreigners paid a different (and much more expensive) price for internal flights than Egyptian residents or nationals, but now there is one ticket price for all and flying has become an affordable option for many travellers. In peak seasons, demand can be high and booking ahead is essential. You can buy E-tickets on the EgyptAir website, though it doesn't always accept the final payment. In this case, you'll have to go to an EgyptAir office or travel agent.

There are daily flights from Cairo to Alexandria, Luxor, Aswan, Abu Simbel, Sharm El-Sheikh and Hurghada and less frequently to Marsa Matruh (in season) and Taba.

Rail

Rail networks are limited, but travel by train can be delightful, especially to a few key destinations along the Nile. First class is most comfortable in that it tends to be the quietest with air conditioning and a waiter service, but second-class air-conditioned is very similar and almost half the price. Third class never has air conditioning and can be quite cramped and dirty, and a foreigner travelling on main routes would not be sold a ticket anyway. There are daily sleeper trains to Luxor and Aswan, which are pricey but mean you can actually lie horizontally. A 33% discount is given to those with an ISIC student card on all trains, except the sleeper cars to Aswan and Luxor. Carriages are non-smoking but people tend to collect and smoke in the corridor by the toilets. Long-distance trains generally have food and beverages available.

The rail network extends west to Salloum on the Libyan border, south along the Nile from Alexandria and Cairo to Luxor and Aswan. There are links to Port Said and Suez. For detailed train information, contact the **Cairo information office**, T02-2575 3555, or check their useful website, www.egyptrail.gov.eg. Approximate journey times from Cairo by train: Alexandria two hours; Aswan 12 hours; Luxor nine hours; Port Said four hours.

Restricted travel Though there are a dozen daily trains travelling south from Cairo to Middle and Upper Egypt, foreigners are technically only permitted to ride on one, which is guarded by policemen. For train travel once in Upper Egypt, the tickets visitors can purchase are still restricted, but it's sometimes possible to board the train and pay the conductor once in motion. It's highly unlikely you will be kicked off.

River

Nile cruises, feluccas and dahabiyas Heading up the Nile on a cruise boat, *felucca* or *dahabiya* is one of the quintessential Egyptian experiences. The actual distance covered depends on the wind. River trips are a great way to get around Egypt and see some wonderful sights along the way. For more information, see page 101.

Road

Bicycle and motorcycle Bicycle hire is available in any town where there are tourists, but the mechanical fitness of the machines is often dubious. Take a bike for a test ride first to check the brakes and tyres are OK. It is feasible to cycle long-distance through Egypt but the heat is punishing, and in between towns and cities along the Nile Valley, cyclists find they are accompanied by their own personal police convoy. In urban areas, traffic conditions make cycling a very dangerous sport. Motorcycles can also be hired, though it's less common. The problems regarding cycles apply also to motorcycles – only more so.

Bus Buses, the main mode and cheapest means of transport, link nearly all towns in Egypt. Air-conditioned coaches ply the major routes and keep to a timetable. It's advisable to book tickets 24 hours in advance, though this is not possible in some oasis towns or from Aswan. **Upper Egypt, East Delta** and **West Delta** are the three main operators covering the whole country and are cheapest, usually with air conditioning and assigned seats. **Superjet**

Hazardous journeys

Bear in mind that Egypt currently tops the statistic charts for the highest mortality rate due to motor accidents in the world. You are taking your life in your hands on many road journeys and this is particularly true at night, when driving without headlights is the norm and buses seem to career wildly into the unknown blackness. Long-distance service taxis are the most dangerous, at any time of day, and should be taken only when there are no other options. Drivers push all limits to get there as fast as they can, so as to be able to start filling up with passengers again and complete as many return journeys as possible per day.

and **GoBus** also offer buses to/from most towns to Cairo, with newer and more luxurious buses that are about 30% more expensive. The downside is they play videos half the night. There are usually night buses that can save you losing a day on long journeys, and drivers always make a couple of tea-and-toilet stops at roadside coffee shops. Inner-city buses are usually dirty and crowded, and there's a jostle when the bus arrives. In the larger cities, buses often fail to come to complete stops so prepare to run and jump if you do not get on from a route's hub point. Ask a Cairene for an intra-city bus schedule and they'll laugh. The easiest thing to do is ask which bus is going to your desired destination. Using buses to travel from one city to another is a good way to get around but sorting out the routes of most inner-city buses makes taking the tram, subway, or a cheap taxi, a better option. Example fares: Cairo to Dahab E£80, Cairo to Bahariyya E£30.

Note Buses in Middle and Upper Egypt, if carrying more than four foreigners, are a bit wary. It is essential, therefore, if travelling by bus, that you purchase your ticket in advance (where possible) to ensure a seat. Because of these restrictions, travel by train offers the most flexibility and reliability in the region. It's also generally faster, more consistent and comfortable.

Car hire Vehicles drive on the right in Egypt. An international driving licence is required. Petrol (super) is E£2-3 per litre. Road signs are in Arabic, with most offering the English transliteration. Cairo and Alexandria have street signs in Arabic and English on all the major thoroughfares. Road conditions vary from new dual carriageways to rural tracks only one-vehicle wide to far flung roads that are a rough, unsurfaced *piste*. Problems include encroaching sand, roads that end with no warning and lunatic drivers. Driving at night is especially hazardous as people only put their headlights on to flash at oncoming vehicles. Likewise, driving in the major cities can be nightmarish with no margin for error and constant undertaking. If you are going to give driving a shot, make sure that you are well insured as the road accident rate is one of the highest in the world.

Car hire cost varies greatly relative to the quality of the vehicle and the location of the rental agency. The minimum is about US$40 per day, and a large deposit is generally required. Some companies place restrictions on areas that can be visited. Be aware that there are many police check points for cars in Egypt and they often request to see your papers, so have them on hand or be prepared for a hefty fine on the spot. The problems of driving your own or a hired car are twofold – other drivers and pedestrians.

The main car hire firms are **Avis**, www.avis.com, and **Hertz**, www.hertz.com. See listings in each individual town transport section. Approximate **journey times** from Cairo by road: Alexandria three hours; Sharm El-Sheikh six hours; Aswan 16 hours; Luxor 10 hours; Port Said three hours.

Hitchhiking   This is only really a consideration in outlying places not well-served by public transport. Rides are often available on lorries and in small open trucks but payment is often expected. Hitchhiking has a measure of risk attached to it and is not normally recommended, but in out-of-the-way places it is often the only way to travel. Solo women travellers are strongly advised not to hitchhike.

Taxi and service taxi   Private vehicles, often Toyota Hiaces (called microbuses or service taxis, pronounced *servees*), cover the same routes as buses and usually cost less. They and the large stationwagon-like long-distance service taxis (Peugeots), sometimes following routes not covered by buses run on the 'leave when full' principle, which can involve some waiting around. For more space or a quicker departure the unoccupied seats can be purchased. However, the drivers can be some of the most reckless in the country (particularly in the nippier Toyotas) and it is probably only worth taking them if you've missed the bus and are stuck somewhere. Inner-city taxis are smaller, rarely have a working meter, and can also be shared. In Cairo you will immediately note the hordes of aging black and white taxis decorated with tasselled fringes, mirrors, and a Koran on the dash. Newer taxis in Cairo are white with black checks on them. They should have functioning meters which start with E£2.50 on the clock and go up in increments of 25pt. In such urban centres taxis are unquestionably the easiest way to get around, and extraordinarily cheap (particularly outside of Cairo).

Note   Until very recently service taxis in Upper Egypt would not accept foreigners when travelling between towns so they could avoid the confines of the convoys. Though the convoys (with the exception of Aswan to Abu Simbel) no longer function, some drivers remember the problems of the past and are reluctant to take foreigners. Be calmly persistent and you should get on in the end.

Where to stay in Cairo and the Nile Delta

Hotels
As tourism is one of Egypt's major industries, accommodation is widely available at the main sites and in all the major cities. With prices to suit all pockets, this varies from de luxe international hotels to just floor or roof space for your sleeping bag. Most quality hotel chains are represented and offer top-class facilities in their rooms and business centres. There are also many cheap hotels with basic and spartan rooms ranging from the clean to the decidedly grimy. Mid-range accommodation is a bit more limited, though the occasional gem exists. There is a pronounced seasonality to demand for accommodation and in the spring, autumn and winter holiday months the main tourist areas can be very busy and the choicest hotels fully booked. Advanced reservations are recommended, especially for luxury hotels. Finding cheap accommodation is easy throughout the country, even in high season. Make sure you ask to see the room first.

Price codes

Where to stay

€€€€	over €150		€€€	€65-150
€€	€30-65		€	under €30

Price for a double room in high season. During the low season it's often possible to bargain the room rate down.

Restaurants

€€€	over US$20	€€	US$5-20	€ under US$5

Prices for a two-course meal for one person, excluding drinks or service charge.

Prices for the top-class hotels are on a par with prices in Europe while mid-range hotels are generally cheaper in comparison. Note that while price is a reasonable reflection of the type of hotel and service you can expect, some hotels are expensive but very ordinary while others are wonderful and quite cheap. International hotels have an uncomfortable habit of changing owner and name. Be prepared for this and if confused ask for what it was called before.

In almost every case, the advertised room price (that charged to the individual traveller) is higher than that paid by the package tourist. Bargaining is common, especially when tourism is scarce. The categories used in this book are graded as accurately as possible by cost converted to American dollars. Our hotel price range is based on a double room in high season and includes any relevant taxes and service. We try to note when a meal is included. Please be aware that prices for hotels are constantly shifting, sometimes significantly, depending on the season and the political climate. As we have quoted high season prices, expect to find costs equal to, or less than, the prices indicated. When in doubt, always ask as prices can literally be sliced in half in the hot summer months. At hotels of three-stars and higher, credit cards are almost always accepted.

Note Tax and a service charge will be added to your accommodation bill, apart from in budget hotels or unless it is clearly stated as inclusive.

Youth hostels

Information from **Egyptian Youth Hostels Association** ① *1 El-Ibrahimy St, Garden City, Cairo, T02-2796 1448, www.iyhf.org*. There are 17 hostels (in Egypt's main historic and tourist towns) that are open year round. Overnight fees range from US$1.5-9 and often include breakfast. Visitors may stay more than three consecutive nights if there's space. Although cheap meals are available, all the big hostels have a members' kitchen where guests can prepare meals for themselves (use of the kitchen is free). Rules generally include no alcohol or gambling, single-sex dormitories, and lights out between 2300-0600. Booking is recommended during peak travel times. They can be a good way to meet Egyptians, but are generally a couple of kilometres out of the centre of town and are horribly busy during student holidays.

Camping

There are only a few official campsites with good facilities and guards. It's possible to stake out an unofficial campsite in the oases of the Western Desert, but always ask if you appear to be on someone else's land, and offer them a tip before you leave. Beware of veering too far off road in regions that are desolate as landmines are still widely scattered around some regions, especially near El-Alamein, Sinai and along the Red Sea coast. Camping Bedouin-style under unpolluted sky in the pristine Western Desert is a highlight of many travellers' journeys.

Food and drink in Cairo and the Nile Delta

Forget the stories of sheep's eyes and enjoy the selection of filling, spicy and slightly unusual meals. Less adventurous, Western-style food (other than pork) can be found in many restaurants, and high-end hotels have fantastic international cuisine (but for the price you would pay at home). Basic street-stall food can be delicious, but if you are wary or they look a bit grungy, a multitude of cheap restaurants also serve local favourites often brought out *mezze*-style with a basket of bread so you can enjoy tasting a bit of everything. Do bear in mind the suggestions in the Health section on food best avoided in uncertain conditions, see page 22.

Food

Egyptian food is basically a mixture of Mediterranean cuisines, containing elements of Lebanese, Turkish, and Greek cooking, with few authentic local dishes.

Breakfast is usually *fuul*, fava beans simmered slowly overnight, the national dish and a cheap meal at most stalls (see box, page 13). These are served in a thick spicy sauce, sometimes with an egg, and usually in a sandwich. When it's fresh and when it's been done well, it is a mouth-watering savoury delight. Some of the best *fuul* comes from the colourful carts on wheels, which station themselves in the same places every day so hungry customers can gather round. The *fuul* is ladled out of a vast pot, hidden in the depths of the cart and heated from below, before being mashed with spices, oil, lemon, salt and pepper. Tourists rarely stop and sample a plate, but the vendors will be pleased and surprised if you do, while other customers will be highly entertained. It's probably best to avoid the chopped salad that comes with the dish, but the *ai'ish* (bread) is certainly safe enough. Equally cheap and popular is *taamiyya*, deep fried balls of ground fava beans spiced with coriander and garlic, again often served in a sandwich garnished with *tahina* (sesame seed dip) and *torshi* (brightly coloured pickled vegetables such as turnips, carrots, and limes). These constitute Egyptian fast food with the addition of *shawarma*, sliced lamb kebab sandwiches, and *fatir*, which is sold in special *fatatri* cafés, where the thin dough pancake is made to order with either sweet or savoury fillings.

Bread is the staple of the Egyptian diet, its Arabic name *ai'iish* means life. The local *ai'iish baladi*, a brown flat loaf similar to pita, tastes good fresh and should only be eaten on the day of purchase. The white flour *ai'iish shami* is less common.

Lunch is the main meal of the day, eaten anytime between 1300 and 1700. Carbohydrates, usually rice and bread, form the bulk of the meal accompanied by fresh seasonal vegetables and either meat or fish. *Mezzas*, a selection of small salads, are served at the beginning of the meal and include *tahina*, *babaghanoug* (*tahina* with mashed

Fuul for all

Fuul has been an important dish for Egyptians since banqueting scenes were painted on the pharaonic tombs. It is nutritious and cheap and is the staple diet for low-income and strong-stomached locals. In Cairo a meal from one of the 25,000 (illegal) street vendors will start the day. At E£1 per sandwich it fills an empty hole and provides protein and carbohydrates.

Fuul is also considered 'in' by the Cairo smart set, who frequent luxury outlets such as Akher Saa, El-Tabei and El-Omda to buy it with onions, pickles, lemon and fresh bread – to eat in or take away.

The *fuul* bean is grown in most agricultural areas of Egypt, as an accompaniment to a major crop – the best is said to come from Minya. Nevertheless, imports are still necessary to supply consumption demands.

Variants on *fuul* dishes include: *fuul bil zeit el harr* – with oil; *fuul bil samna* – with ghee (clarified butter); *bisara* – with oil, onion, garlic and coriander. *Fuul* is also the main ingredient in *ta'ameya* and *felafel*.

aubergines), olives, local white fetta-style cheese, *warra einab* or stuffed vine leaves, and *kobeiba*, deep fried bulgar wheat stuffed with meat and nuts. Like most Middle Eastern countries, *kebab*, lamb pieces grilled over charcoal on a skewer, and *kofta*, minced lamb, are common main dishes. Chicken and pigeon are also widely available, the latter considered a local delicacy when stuffed with rice and nuts. Fish is commonly eaten in coastal regions and often superb. Try the sea bass or red snapper but watch the bones in the latter. Lobster and shrimp are relatively cheap.

Egyptian **main dishes** include *molokhia*, finely chopped mallow leaves, prepared with garlic, spices and either rabbit or chicken, and a good deal more tasty than its glutinous texture suggests; *fatta*, layers of bread, rice, chunks of lamb or beef, yògurt, raisins and nuts, drenched in a vinegar garlic broth; *koshari*, a poor man's feast that will fill a belly for at least four hours, is composed of macaroni, rice and brown lentils covered with fried onions and a spicy tomato sauce; and *mahshi*, vegetables, typically black or white aubergines, tomatoes, green peppers, cabbage leaves or courgettes, stuffed with rice, herbs and vegetables.

Fruits, like vegetables, are seasonal although there is a wide variety available all year round. Produce is picked when it's ripe and so generally fruit and vegetables are absolutely delicious. Winter offers dates of various colours ranging from yellow to black, citrus fruits, small sweet bananas, pears, apples, and even strawberries. Summer brings plums, peaches, figs, pomegranates, guava, mangoes, grapes, melons and a brief season, for a few weeks in May, of apricots.

Traditional Egyptian **desserts** are sweet, sticky, fattening, and delicious. The best of all is *Om Ali*, or Mother of Ali, a warm pudding of bread or pastry covered with milk, coconut, raisins, and nuts. Also try the oriental pastries including *atayef*, deep fried nut-stuffed pancakes; *baklava*, honey-drenched filo pastry layered with nuts; *basbousa*, a syrupy semolina cake often filled with cream and garnished with pistachio nuts and *konafa*, shredded batter cooked with butter and stuffed with nuts. Cold rice pudding is on offer at most *koshari* restaurants, and is much better than it sounds.

Vegetarianism is not a concept with which Egyptians are familiar. While vegetable dishes are plentiful, and the majority of Egyptians only rarely eat any large quantity of meat, it is difficult to avoid tiny pieces of meat or meat stock in vegetable courses. Even the wonderful lentil soup, like most Egyptian soups a meal on its own, often has the addition of a chicken stock cube. Fortunately, basic staples such as *koshari*, *fuul* and *taamiyya* are omnipresent in any town and true life-savers for vegetarians. In the smaller oases, a diet of rice, salad and potatoes or courgettes stewed in tomato sauce is tasty though repetitive.

Drink

Tea (*shai*) is the essential Egyptian drink, taken strong without milk but with spoonfuls of sugar. Tea is also prepared with mint, *shai bil na'ana*, and said to be good for the digestion. Instant **coffee**, just called 'Nescafé', is available. If you want it with milk, ask for *laban* and if you want sugar separately request *sucre burra*. The thick Turkish coffee known as *ahwa*, which is usually laced with cardamom or occasionally cinnamon, should be ordered either *saada*, with no sugar; *arriha*, with a little sugar; *mazbut*, medium; or *ziyada*, with extra sugar. Leave the thick mud of coffee grains in the bottom half of the cup. The *mazbut* is the most popular.

Other hot drinks include a cinnamon tea, *irfa*, reportedly good for colds; and the less common *sahleb*, a milk drink with powdered arrowroot, coconut, and chopped nuts.

Cold drinks include the usual soft drink options of Coca-Cola, Pepsi, 7-Up, and Fanta. Of more interest are the traditional *ersoos* (liquorice juice); *asir limon*, tangy and delicious but highly sweetened lemon juice; *karkade*, made from the dried petals of the red hibiscus, drunk both hot and cold; and *tamarhindi*, from the tamarind. Freshly squeezed juice stands are located throughout all cities, and mean you can drink seasonal pomegranate, mango, or orange juice for just E£2-3 a glass.

Bottled water is sold widely. Check that the seal is intact and that the bottle has not been refilled. Be prepared for shortage or restriction of water in more rural areas. Tap water in the urban centres is generally safe to drink, but so chlorinated it's intolerable for a lot of travellers. It's better to opt for bottled water which is cheap and easily available.

Although Egypt is a Muslim country, **alcohol** is available in bars and some restaurants. While five-star hotels are beginning to import beer in barrels, the local 'Stella' beer is the most popular sold, with the better-quality 'Stella Export', in half litre bottles. There are a few local wines, the reds and rosés are very drinkable and the whites less so. Most commonly found are Omar Khayyam, Obelisque, Cape Bay and Sherazad (who do a good rosé). The local spirits are bottled to resemble international brands, and include an ouzo called *zibib*, a rum 'Zattos', and a 'Big Ben' gin. Beware of local liqueurs that don labels and names resembling Western brands such as 'Jhony Wakker' and the like, they have been known to contain alcohol so strong that they can cause blindness if drunk to excess.

Festivals in Cairo and the Nile Delta

The Islamic year (*Hejra/Hijra/Hegira*) is based on 12 lunar months that are 29 or 30 days long depending on the sighting of the new moon. The lengths of the months vary therefore from year to year and from country to country depending on its position and the time at sunset. Each year is also 10 or 11 days shorter than the Gregorian calendar. The Islamic holidays are based on this Hejarian calendar and determining their position is possible only to within a few days.

The important festivals that are also public holidays (with many variations in spelling) are *Ras El-Am*, the Islamic New Year; *Eïd Al-Fitr* (also called *Aïd Es Seghir*), the celebration at the end of Ramadan; *Eïd Al-Adha* (also called *Aïd El-Kebir*), the celebration of Abraham's willingness to sacrifice his son and coinciding with the culmination of the *Hajj* in Mecca; *Mouloud* (also called Moulid An-Nabi), the birthday of the Prophet Mohammed.

The day of rest for Muslims is Friday. Observance of Friday as a religious day is general in the public sector, though privately owned shops may open for limited hours. The main exception is tourism where all systems remain operative. Holy days and feast days are taken seriously throughout the country.

Ramadan, the ninth month of the Muslim calendar, is a month of fasting for Muslims. The faithful abstain from eating between dawn and sunset for about one month until an official end is declared to the fast and when *Eïd Al-Fitr*, a three-day celebration, begins. During the fast, especially if the weather is hot or there are political problems affecting the Arab world, people can be depressed or irritable. The pace of activity in official offices slows down markedly, most closing by 1400. You may want to stay out of the area during Ramadan and particularly the *Eïd Al-Fitr*, but for the patient and curious traveller, it can be a fascinating time. As the sun sets during the holy month and everyone rushes homeward to break fast, it offers a rare and delightful occasion to wander through barren Cairo streets. *Iftar* (breaking the fast) in the company of local people is an interesting experience, and anyone is welcome to join a communal meal at one of the mercy tables that encroach on to the street each sunset. The country's poor are looked after by the mosques and the wealthy, who provide set meals every day for whoever is in need; this can involve feeding hundreds of people. Although you shouldn't expect true culinary delights, you might get dates, bird's tongue (a kind of pasta) soup, hearty stews and traditional sweets. For the rushed or impatient traveller, note that travel facilities immediately before and after Ramadan are often very congested since families like to be together especially for the *Eïd Al-Fitr*.

Islamic festivals

These are approximate dates for 2012:

4 Feb Prophet's Birthday.
20 Jul Beginning of Ramadan.
19 Aug End of Ramadan
(Eid El-Fitr).
26 Oct Eid El-Adha.
15 Nov Islamic New Year.

Coptic celebrations

These are approximate dates for 2012:

20 Jan Epiphany.
7 Apr Annunciation.
15 Apr Easter.

Cultural and sporting events

Jan Cairo International Book Fair, Nasr City, Cairo.

Mar Cairo International Fair; Spring Flower Show, Orman Gardens, Giza, Cairo.

Apr Sham El-Nessim (Sniffing of the Breeze, or the first day of spring) is celebrated with family picnics.

Aug Arab Music Festival, Opera House, Cairo; Nile Festival Day (Wafaa El-Nil), Giza, Cairo.

Sep Alexandria Mediterranean Biennale (every 2 years); **International Festival for Vanguard Theatre**, Cairo; **Alexandria Film Festival**, Alexandria; **World Tourism Day**; Nile Festival.

Oct Pharaoh's Rally, 3100-km motor vehicle race across the desert, Cairo.

Nov/Dec International Film Festival, Cairo.

Dec Festival for Arab Theatre, Cairo; Festival for Impressionist Art (every 2 years), Cairo.

Public holidays

1 Jan New Year's Day.

7 Jan Coptic Christmas.

15 Mar El-Fayoum National Day.

25 Apr Liberation of Sinai.

1 May Labour Day.

18 Jun Evacuation Day – the day the British left Egypt in 1954.

23 Jul Anniversary of 1952 Revolution.

26 Jul Alexandria National Day.

6 Oct Armed Forces' Day – parades and military displays.

13 Oct Suez Day.

23 Dec Victory Day.

Shopping in Cairo and the Nile Delta

There are department stores and malls in Cairo but the most interesting shopping is in the bazaars and *souks*. The process can take time and patience, but bargains abound. The main bazaar in Cairo, Khan El-Khalili, has a wide selection of ethnic items. It attracts tourists by the hoards, though wandering far off the main alleys will lead to shops and corridors rarely visited. For a truly off-the-beaten-track shopping experience, visit one of the many fruit and vegetable *souks* scattered throughout the country. You'll find chickens milling about, people singing songs about their wares and dead cows hanging from storefront windows. Prices are clearly marked in Arabic numerals, usually indicating the cost of a kilogram. Bargaining is not appropriate in this context but learn the numerals so that nobody takes advantage of you.

What to buy

Egypt is well known for its **cotton and textiles**. Higher-end stores in luxury hotels and shopping malls around Cairo sell linen and new clothes. For colourful tapestries, scarves and bags, Khan El-Khalili is a good place to start. Also of interest may be the Tent Makers' Bazaar, south of Bab Zuweila in Islamic Cairo, where it's possible to commission the making of a bedcover or a Bedouin tent. Lengths of printed tent fabric cost E£20 per metre, or the appliqué wall-hangings depicting sufi dancers and abstract Arabic motifs cost E£100 and above. If you want a *gallabiyya*, formal or otherwise, wander around the shops surrounding Al-Azhar mosque in Cairo. For handmade rugs, check out the many stores lining Sharia Saqqara, near the Giza Pyramids. Or if you are visiting the oases, wait till then to buy Bedouin designs woven in camel wool either in natural colours or bright with geometric designs.

The art of bargaining

Haggling is a normal business practice in Egypt. Modern economists might feel that bargaining is a way of covering up high-price salesmanship within a commercial system that is designed to exploit the lack of legal protection for the consumer. But even so, haggling over prices is the norm and is run as an art form, with great skills involved. Bargaining can be fun to watch between a clever buyer and an experienced seller but it is less entertaining when a less-than-artful buyer such as a foreign traveller considers what he/she has paid later! There is great potential for the tourist to be heavily ripped off. Most dealers recognize the wealth and gullibility of travellers and start their offers at an exorbitant price. The dealer then appears to drop his price by a fair margin but remains at a final level well above the real local price of the goods.

To protect yourself in this situation be relaxed in your approach. Talk at length to the dealer and take as much time as you can afford to inspect the goods and feeling out the last price the seller will accept. Do not belittle or mock the dealer – take the matter very seriously but do not show commitment to any particular item you are bargaining for by being prepared to walk away empty-handed. Never feel that you are getting the better of the dealer or feel sorry for him. He will not sell without making a profit. Also it is better to try several shops if you are buying an expensive item such as a carpet or jewellery. This will give a sense of the price range. Walking away – regretfully of course – from the dealer normally brings the price down rapidly but not always. Do not change money in the same shop where you make your purchases, since this will be expensive.

Jewellery, in particular, gold, silver and some precious stones, are cheap in Egypt. In the centre of Khan El-Khalili, as well as places scattered about Islamic Cairo, you will find exquisite gold jewellery. Sold by weight, with a bit of money tacked on for craftsmanship, you can have pieces made to order. Particularly popular are cartouches bearing your name or the name of a friend.

Papyrus can be found everywhere. Ensure when you are shopping for papyrus that it is real, not the increasingly common imitation banana leaf. Real papyrus is not chemically treated, a process which causes the picture to disintegrate after three or four years. You can tell chemically treated papyrus by its homogenous surface and pliability. Thick and unmalleable, real papyrus can't be rolled or folded. Authentic papyrus also has variants of colour as the stalks have lighter and darker patches, which you can see in the meshwork when you hold it up to the light. Rest assured that the papyrus sellers you will trip over at every major tourist site are not selling the real thing, though if you just want to pick up some cheap presents then they have their uses. Dr Ragab's Papyrus Institute in Cairo is a bit pricey, but offers good-quality trustworthy papyrus art.

You'll probably smell the **perfume** stalls before you see them. They're all over Khan El-Khalili and most carry an extraordinary variety of smells – ranging from rose to Egyptian musk to replicas of famous scents. Prices range from E£20-50. Ask around at different stalls for the going price before purchasing. Also fragrant and incredibly colourful are the abundance of stalls that sell herbs and spices displayed in large burlap sacks. You will find everything from dried hibiscus to thyme, cumin to saffron, which is priced higher per kilo than gold, but still comparatively cheap. For an alternative spice experience, check out **Harraz Medicinal Plants Co ⓘ** *Sharia Ahmed Marhir St, east of Midan Bab Al-Khalq*, a store in Cairo specializing in ancient remedies and medicinal plants. Upstairs you can consult with the resident herbalist if anything ails you.

Other things of interest you will find in larger *souks* and bazaars: kitsch souvenirs galore, *sheesha* pipes, musical instruments (drums in particular) copper and brass ware, wooden boxes inlaid with intricate designs and backgammon and chess sets.

Bargaining

Haggling is expected in the *souks*. Most shop owners site the start price at two to three times the amount they hope to make. Start lower than you would expect to pay, be polite and good humoured, enjoy the experience and if the final price doesn't suit, walk away. There are plenty more shops. Once you have gained confidence, try it on the taxi drivers and when negotiating a room. The bargaining exchange can be a great way to meet people and practise your Arabic.

Interestingly, a barter exchange system still exists in some rural weekly markets, where goods such as seeds, eggs or beans can be exchanged for a haircut or access to education. This is unlikely to be something you will get involved with as a traveller, however.

Local customs and laws in Cairo and the Nile Delta

Though Egypt is among the more liberal and 'Westernized' of the Arab countries, it is still an Islamic country where religion is deeply embedded in daily life. While Islam is similar to Judaism and Christianity in its philosophical content and the three revealed religions are accepted together as the religions of the book (*Ahl Al-Kitab*), it is wise for travellers to recognize that Islamic practices in this traditional society are a sensitive area. Public observance of religious ritual and taboo are important, just as is the protection of privacy for women and the family. Islam of an extremist kind is on the wane in Egypt but bare-faced arrogance by visitors will engender a very negative response even among normally welcoming Egyptians who generally have no tendencies towards fundamentalist views.

Islam has a specific code of practices and taboos but most will not affect the visitor unless he or she gains entry to local families or organizations at a social level. In any case a few considerations are worthy of note by all non-Muslims when in company with Muslim friends or when visiting particularly conservative areas. (1) Dress modestly. Women in particular should see the dress code, below, for further explanation. (2) If visiting during the holy month of Ramadan where Muslims fast from sunrise to sunset, dress particularly conservatively and avoid eating, drinking and smoking in public places. (3) If offering a gift to a Muslim friend, be aware that pork and alcohol are forbidden. If you choose to offer other meat, ensure it is *hallal*, killed in accordance with Muslim ritual. (4) If dining in a traditional Bedouin setting or context, do not use your left hand for eating since it is ritually unclean. (If knives and forks are provided, then both hands can be used.) Do not accept or ask for alcohol unless your host clearly intends to imbibe. Keep your feet tucked under your body away from food.

Avoiding hassle

Here are some general hints to minimize the pestering that will certainly occur on some level as a woman travelling in Egypt. Try to walk with confidence and at least pretend that you know where you're going. Dress modestly – the less bare flesh the better (especially avoid revealing your shoulders, cleavage and legs). In conservative areas, don't reveal your legs at all and consider tying long hair up. Always carry a thin shawl or scarf to wrap around you in case you suddenly feel over-exposed. When swimming pretty much anywhere outside of the Red Sea resorts, wear leggings and a opaque T-shirt rather than a bathing suit. Ignore rude and suggestive comments and most importantly, avoid looking onlookers in the eye. In general, try not to react in a way that may aggravate a situation – it's best not to react at all.

When riding public transport, if possible sit next to women (on the Cairo subway the first car is reserved for women only) and avoid late-night transport if alone. If seeking advice or directions outside of hotels and other touristy places try to ask a woman or an older businessman-type. If you feel exceptionally uncomfortable, deliberate embarrassment of the man in question can be a powerful weapon – shout *haram* ('it's forbidden'). You may want to don a wedding band to dissuade potential suitors. If you're travelling with a man, you can avoid a lot of interrogations and confusion by saying that you're married. Absolutely avoid going into the desert or solitary places alone with a man you don't know.

Note that men and women in Egypt relate to one another differently from men and women in many Western countries. The Western concept of 'friendship' can be misunderstood. Opt to be conservative in the way you interact and engage with Egyptian men, as a mere smile can be misinterpreted as an expression of more than platonic interest. Most importantly, trust your instincts, be smart and keep a sense of humour. The rewards of travelling alone as a female in Egypt far outweigh any of the hassle. If you cloak yourself in baggy clothes and try to look as androgynous as possible, you'll be able to go wherever you want and be treated as a man would be, with the added bonus of everyone looking out for you just because you are a 'woman on your own'. Remember, the consequences for serious violations against foreigners in Egypt are so dire that the incidence of rape and other forms of extreme harassment and violation is significantly less than in most other countries.

Class discrepancies and the *khawagga* (foreigner)

Compared with other developing countries, there are particularly great discrepancies among Egyptians with regard to their experience, openness, education and worldliness. Some are extremely sophisticated, knowledgeable and well travelled while others (widely known as *fellaheen* – peasants) are markedly conservative and parochial. Class is often a delineating factor, as is education and the urban/rural divide. For the traveller, maintaining awareness of social context is essential for positive and culturally sensitive interchanges with locals.

Another evident discrepancy is the cost of services for Egyptians and foreigners. If you have not yet stumbled upon the word *khawagga* (foreigner), you soon will, as it holds similar implications to the word gringo in many Latin American countries. Taxi fares, entries to many attractions, even the price of luxury accommodation all cost foreigners more. Bear in mind that the average Egyptian makes about US$1500 per head per year; the average foreign tourist lives on approximately US$32,000.

Courtesy

Politeness is always appreciated. You will notice a great deal of hand shaking, kissing, clapping on backs on arrival and departure from a group. There is no need to follow this to the extreme but handshakes, smiles and thank yous go a long way. Shows of affection and physical contact are widely accepted among members of the same sex. Be more conservative in greeting and appreciating people of the opposite sex. Do not show the bottom of your feet or rest them on tables or chairs as this gesture is regarded as extremely rude in Egypt. Be patient and friendly but firm when bargaining for items and avoid displays of anger. However, when it comes to getting onto public transport, forget it all – the description 'like a Cairo bus' needs no explanation.

Dress code

Daily dress for most Egyptians is governed by considerations of climate and weather. Other than labourers in the open, the universal reaction is to cover up against heat or cold. For males other than the lowest of manual workers, full dress is normal. Men breaching this code will either be young and regarded as being of low social status or very rich and Westernized. When visiting mosques, *madresas* or other shrines/tombs/religious libraries, Muslim men wear full and normally magnificently washed and ironed traditional formal wear. In the office, men will be traditionally dressed or in Western suits and shirt sleeves. The higher the grade of office, the more likely the Western suit. At home people relax in a loose *gallabiyya*. Arab males will be less constrained on the beach where swimming trunks are the norm.

For women the dress code is more important and extreme. Quite apart from dress being a tell-tale sign of social status among the ladies of Cairo or Alexandria or of tribal/regional origin, decorum and religious sentiment dictates full covering of body, arms and legs. The veil is increasingly common for women, a reflection of growing Islamic revivalist views. There are still many women who do not don the veil, including those with modern attitudes towards female emancipation, professional women trained abroad and the religious minorities – Copts in particular. Jewellery is another major symbol in women's dress, especially heavy gold necklaces.

The role of dress within Islamic and social codes is clearly a crucial matter. While some latitude in dress is given to foreigners, good guests are expected to conform to the broad lines of the practice of the house. Thus, except on the beach or 'at home' in the hotel (assuming it is a tourist rather than local establishment), modesty in dress pays off. This means jeans or slacks for men rather than shorts together with a shirt or T-shirt. For women, modesty is slightly more demanding. In public wear comfortable clothes that at least cover the greater part of the legs and arms. If the opportunity arises to visit a mosque or *madresa*, then a *gallabiyya* and/or slippers are often available for hire at the door. Most women do not swim in public and if they do, they tend to dive in fully clad. If you choose to swim outside a touristy area, wear shorts and an opaque T-shirt. Offend against the dress code – and most Western tourists in this area do to a greater or lesser extent – and you risk antagonism and alienation from the local people who are increasingly conservative in their Islamic beliefs and observances.

Mosque etiquette
Do not enter mosques during a service and take photographs only after asking or when clearly permissible. Visitors to mosques and other religious buildings will be expected to remove their shoes. Men should never enter the area designated solely for women, but foreign women are tolerated in the main prayer halls of most mosques unless it is actually a time of prayer. If you are wandering somewhere you aren't supposed to be, someone will point it out to you soon enough.

Photography
Photographs of police, soldiers, docks, bridges, military areas, airports, radio stations and other public utilities are prohibited. Photography is also prohibited in tombs where much damage can be done with a flash bulb. Photography is unrestricted in all open, outdoor historic areas but some sites make an extra charge for cameras. Flashes are not permitted for delicate relics. Many museums have now banned photography completely to avoid any accidental use of flash. This includes the Egyptian Museum. Taking photographs of any person without permission is unwise, of women is taboo, and tourist attractions like water sellers, camels/camel drivers, etc, may require *baksheesh* (a tip). Even the goat herder will expect an offering for providing the goats. Always check that use of a video camera is permitted at tourist sites and be prepared to pay a heavy fee (E£100+) for permission.

Essentials A-Z

Accident and emergencies

Ambulance T123. **Fire** T125. **Police** T122 (from any city). **Tourist Police** T126.

Report any incident that involves you or your possessions. An insurance claim of any size will require a police report. If involvement with the police is more serious, for instance as a result of a driving accident, remain calm and contact the nearest consular office without delay. Some embassies advise leaving the scene of an accident immediately and heading straight to your embassy.

Electricity

The current in Egypt is 220V, 50Hz. Sockets are for 2-pin round plugs, so bring an appropriate adapter. If you have US-made appliances that use 110V it's a good idea to bring a converter. Power cuts do not happen that frequently, but in remote hotels be aware that generators are usually switched off at night and for a few hours during the day.

Embassies and consulates

For embassies and consulates of Egypt abroad, see www.embassiesabroad.com.

Health

The local population in Egypt is exposed to a range of health risks not usually encountered in the Western world and, although the risks to travellers are fairly remote, they cannot be ignored. Obviously 5-star travel is going to carry less risk than backpacking on a minimal budget. The health care in the region is varied. It's worth contacting your embassy or consulate on arrival and asking where the recommended clinics are.

Ideally, you should see your GP or travel clinic at least 6 weeks before your departure for general advice on travel risks, malaria and vaccinations. Make sure you have adequate travel insurance.

Vaccinations

Vaccinations are not required unless you are travelling from a country where yellow fever or cholera frequently occurs. You are advised to be up to date with **polio**, **tetanus**, **diphtheria**, **typhoid** and **hepatitis A**. **Rabies** is not generally a risk in Egypt but it has been reported in a few rural areas off the tourist trail.

Health risks

It is a very rare event indeed for travellers, but if you are unlucky (or careless) enough to be bitten by a **venomous snake**, **spider**, **scorpion** or sea creature, try to identify the creature, without putting yourself in further danger. Immobilize the limb with a bandage or a splint and take the victim to a hospital or a doctor without delay. Do not walk in snake territory in bare feet or sandals – wear proper shoes or boots. Spiders and scorpions may be found in the more basic hotels. If stung, rest and take plenty of fluids and call a doctor. The best precaution is to keep beds away from the walls and always look inside your shoes and under the toilet seat. Certain sea fish when trodden upon inject venom into bathers' feet. This can be exceptionally painful. Wear plastic shoes if such creatures are reported. The pain can be relieved by immersing the foot in hot water (as hot as you can bear) for as long as the pain persists or citric acid juices in fruits such as lemon is reported as useful.

Dengue fever is a viral disease spead by mosquitos that tend to bite during the day. The symptoms are fever and often intense joint pains, also some people develop a rash. It should all be over in 7 to 10 unpleasant days. Unfortunately there is no vaccine. Employ all the anti-mosquito measures that you can.

The standard advice to prevent **diarrhoea** or intestinal upset is to be careful with water and ice for drinking. If you have any doubts then boil it or filter and treat it. Food can also transmit disease. Be wary of salads, re-heated foods or food that has been left out in the sun having been cooked earlier in the day. There is a simple adage that says 'wash it, peel it, boil it or forget it'. Also be wary of unpasteurized dairy products. The key treatment with all diarrhoeas is rehydration. Try to keep hydrated by taking the right mixture of salt and water. This is available as Oral Rehydration Salts (ORS) in ready-made sachets or can be made up by adding a teaspoon of sugar and a half teaspoon of salt to a litre of clean water. Drink at least 1 large cup of this drink for each loose stool. You can also use flat carbonated drinks as an alternative.

Pre-travel **hepatitis A** vaccine is advised. There is also a vaccine for **hepatitis B**, which is spread through blood and unprotected sexual intercourse. Unfortunately there is no vaccine for **hepatitis C**, the prevalence of which is unusually high in Egypt.

Malaria is not widespread in Egypt. Minimal risk exists in the El-Fayoum area only. Risk is highest from Jun-Oct. Check with your doctor before you go about which prophylactic (if any) you should take if travelling in this region. Use insect repellent frequently.

Protect yourself adequately against the **sun**. Wear a hat and stay out of the sun, if possible, between late morning and early afternoon. Apply a high-factor sunscreen (greater than SPF15) and also make sure it screens against UVB. A further danger in tropical climates is heat exhaustion or more seriously heatstroke. This can be avoided by good hydration.

Money

Currency ➔ *E£1 = US$0.17, €0.12 or GB£0.10.* You will see prices throughout this guide listed in either **US dollars**, **euro** or **Egyptian pounds** depending on how they're quoted in different parts of the country and for different activities. Due to recent fluctuations in the value of the US dollar, many upmarket hotels and tourist centres in Egypt (such as Hurghada and Sharm El-Sheikh) now quote their prices in euro rather than dollars. However, Egyptian pounds are used for the vast majority of everyday transactions and hotels are generally happy to accept the equivalent value in local currency.

The Egyptian pound is divided into 100 piastres (pt). Notes are in denominations of E£5, E£10, E£20, E£50, E£100, E£200, while the old 25 and 50 piastres notes and E£1 notes are being phased out. Newer E£1 coins are in circulation, and other denominations (which are almost not worth carrying) are 10, 25, and 50 piastres. It's a good idea to always have lots of pound coins to hand so you don't get short changed the odd extra pound or 2 when taking a taxi.

Regulations and money exchange

Visitors can enter and leave Egypt with a maximum of E£10,000. There are no restrictions on the import of foreign currency provided it is declared on an official customs form. Export of foreign currency may not exceed the amount imported. Generally, it's cheaper to exchange foreign currency in Egypt than in your home country. It's always wise to change enough money at home for at least the first 24 hrs of you trip, just in case. The bank counters on arrival at Cairo airport are open 24 hrs. A small amount of foreign cash, preferably US$, although sterling and euro are widely accepted, is useful for an emergency.

Banks

There is at least one of the national banks in every town plus a few foreign banks (such as HSBC and Citibank) in the big cities and Barclays have recently started operating in all major towns. Banking hours are 0830-1400 Sun-Thu (0930-1330 during Ramadan); some banks have evening hours. Changing money in banks can be a bit time-consuming, though commission is not usually charged. **ATMs** are widely available (but not in all the oases) but require a surcharge of between US$3-5, and often have a daily withdrawal limit of around E£2500-4000. They are also known to munch on the occasional card, so beware. Still, using an international credit or debit card is the easiest and quickest way to access your money and means you receive trade exchange rates which are slightly better than rates given by banks. Maestro, MasterCard, Plus/Visa and Cirrus are all widely accepted.

Credit cards

Access/MasterCard, American Express, Diners Club and Visa are accepted in all major hotels, larger restaurants and shops, and tend to offer excellent exchange rates. Outside of the tourist industry, Egypt is still a cash economy.

Traveller's cheques

Traveller's cheques are honoured in most banks and bureaux de change. US$ are the easiest to exchange particularly if they are well-known brands such as Visa, Thomas Cook or American Express. There is always a transaction charge so a balance needs to be struck between using high-value cheques and paying one charge and carrying extra cash or using lower-value cheques and paying more charges. Egypt supposedly has a fixed exchange rate – wherever the transaction is carried out.

Cost of travelling

Depending on the standards of comfort and cleanliness you are prepared to accept for accommodation, food and travel, it is still possible to survive on as little as US$10-15 per person per day. However, prices for everything in Egypt are rising all the time with inflation soaring (basic foods have increased by 50%, gasoline 90%); tourists should be aware that hotel prices and transport costs continue to rise, and that the ticket prices for monuments are put up every Oct/Nov. Accommodation runs from about US$8-15 for a basic double in a liveable hotel to well over US$200 for 5-star luxury comfort. Basic street food can fill you up for less than US$1, or you can opt for a more Western-style meal, still affordable at US$6-10 a plate. Transport varies according to mode, but distances between the major cities can be covered for around US$15-20. The Cairo metro is less than US$0.25 and local buses are around the same. Renting a car is a significantly more expensive option at around US$60 per day.

There are costs often not accounted for in other parts of the world that you will inevitably encounter in Egypt. Most sit-down restaurants include a 12% tax (after the service charge, which is 10%) on the bill and it is common practice to tip an additional 10%. Another kind of tipping, known as *baksheesh*, occurs when you are offered a small service, whether or not you ask for it. If someone washes the windows of your car or looks after your shoes in a mosque, they will expect a modest offering. Carry around a stash of E£1 coins and take it in your stride, it's part of the culture.

Opening hours

Banks Sat-Thu 0830-1400.
Government offices 0900-1400 every day, closed Fri and national holidays.
Museums Daily 0900-1600 but generally close for Fri noon prayers, around 1200-1400.
Shops Normal opening hours are summer 0900-1230 and 1600-2000, winter 0900-1900, often closed on Fri or Sun. Shops in tourist areas seem to stay open much longer.

Tahrir Square

Just to the south of the Egyptian Musuem lies the sprawling Tahrir Square which came to the world's attention in 2011 as the centre of protest against the Egyptian establishment.

Traditionally, it has been the place where the Cairenes come to air their grievances and is well chosen as it is the gateway to the city centre and is overlooked by several key buildings and international hotels. President Nasser renamed it Midan Tahrir, literally Liberation Square. It's huge and large enough to hold thousands. Any protest here quickly brings traffic to a halt for miles around. As a result, the protesters can be virtually guaranteed a voice.

In January 2011, Egypt became one of the key countries in the Arab Spring uprisings. Encouraged by the events in Tunisia, Egyptians gathered in Tahrir Square to voice their dissent against the autocratic Hosni Mubarak, who had been in power for 30 years. Tents and barricades were built to house and protect the protesters, who kept in touch with the outside world by using social media. After 18 days of often bloody clashes, which left 850 dead, Mubarak resigned and Essam Sharaf, the new prime minister, promised to meet the protesters demands for democratic change. There was a huge amount of optimism for the future and spontaneous jubilation broke out. The army cleared the camps from the square on 9 March.

However, since then, there have been further demonstrations (and casualties) as the establishment fails to deliver Essam Sharaf's promises and many believe the new constitution to be an attempt by the military to cling to power.

Safety

The level of petty crime in Egypt is no greater than elsewhere. It is very unlikely that you will be robbed but take sensible precautions. Put your valuables in a hotel deposit box or keep them on your person rather than leave them lying around your room. Avoid carrying excess money or wearing obviously valuable jewellery when sightseeing. External pockets on bags and clothing should never be used for carrying valuables, pickpockets do operate in some crowded tourist spots. It is wise to stick to the main thoroughfares when walking around at night.

Trading in antiquities is illegal and will lead to confiscation and/or imprisonment. Should you need to buy currency on the black market do so only when it is private and safe. Be careful as Egypt, like most countries, has tight laws against currency smuggling and illegal dealing.

Keep clear of all political activities. Particularly in light of the recent events where foreign journalists have been targeted. By all means keep an interest in local politics but do not become embroiled as a partisan. The *mokharbarat* (secret services) are singularly unforgiving and unbridled in their action against political interference.

Following the war on Iraq, there was a fairly widespread anti-American and anti-Anglo sentiment, but for the most part the disillusion is not mis-targeted. Egyptians seem to separate their disdain for foreign governments from individual travellers. Nonetheless, with such a volatile political climate, it's wise to check with your national authorities before departure for Egypt. If coming from the UK, for travel advice, check the Foreign and Commonwealth Office at www.fco.gov.uk; from the US, check the Dept of State at www.travel.state.gov.

9/11, the war on Iraq and the attacks on foreigners in the Sinai in 2004-2006 brought about a new set of challenges for the tourist industry and reinforced the government's attempts at ensuring safety for foreign visitors. Part of the system required most Western tourists travelling in private cars, hired taxis and tourist buses to travel in police-escorted convoys when journeying between towns in certain regions. This still applies in Upper Egypt, where scheduled convoys travel between Aswan and Abu Simbel. In 2010, restrictions were eased in other areas of Upper Egypt and now tourists are permitted on public transport. However, not all drivers are aware of the change in the rules and it can be a headache getting a ride in certain areas. Independent travellers are better off using trains where possible.

Confidence tricksters
The most common 'threat' to tourists is found where people are on the move, at airports, railway and bus stations, offering extremely favourable currency exchange rates, selling tours or 'antiques', and spinning hard-luck stories. Confidence tricksters are, by definition, extremely convincing and persuasive. Be warned – if the offer seems too good to be true, it probably is.

Time
GMT + 2 hrs.

Tipping
Tipping, or *baksheesh*, a word you will fast learn, is a way of life – everyone except high officials expects a reward for services actually rendered or imagined. Many people connected with tourism get no or very low wages and rely on tips to survive. The advice here is to be a frequent but small tipper. The principle of 'little and often' seems to work well. Usually 12% is added to hotel and restaurant bills but an extra tip of about 10% is normal and expected. In hotels and at monuments tips will be expected for the most minimal service. Rather than make a fuss, have some small bills handy. Tips may be the person's only income.

Alms-giving is a personal duty in Muslim countries. It is unlikely that beggars will be too persistent. Have a few small bills ready and offer what you can. You will be unable to help everyone and your donation may be passed on to the syndicate organizer.

Tourist information
Tourist offices in bigger cities tend to be quite well equipped and at least have an English speaker on duty. They're worth a visit if you are nearby. The particularly helpful tourist offices are noted in the relevant chapter sections. When the tourist offices fall short, hotels, pensions and other travellers are often even better resources to access reliable travel information.

Egyptian state tourist offices abroad
Austria, Elisabeth Strasse, 4/Steige 5/1, Opernringhof, 1010 Vienna, T43-1-587 6633, aegyptnet@netway.at.
Belgium, 179 Av Louise 1050, Brussels, T32-2647 3858, touregypt@skynet.be.
Canada, 1253 McGill College Av, Suite 250, Quebec, Montreal, T1-514-861 4420.
France, 90 Champs Elysées, Paris, T33-1-4562 9442/3, Egypt.Ot@Wanadoo.Fr
Germany, 64A Kaiser Strasse, Frankfurt, T49-69-252319.
Italy, 19 Via Bissolati, 00187 Rome, T39-6-482 7985.
Spain, Torre de Madrid, planta 5, Oficina 3, Plaza de España, 28008 Madrid, T34-1-559 2121.
Sweden, Dorottningatan 99, Atan 65, 11136 Stockholm, T46-8-102584, egypt.Ti.Swed@alfa.telenordia.se
Switzerland, 9 rue des Alpes, Geneva, T022-732 9132.
UK, Egyptian House, 170 Piccadilly, London W1V 9DD, T020-7493 5283.

USA, 630 5th Av, Suite 1706, New York 10111, T1-212-332 2570, egyptourst@ad.com.

Egypt on the web

www.bibalex.gov.eg Detailed information and up-to-date news on the new Alexandria Library, and has a calendar of events.

www.touregypt.net A comprehensive site put together by the Ministry of Tourism. Detailed listings include online shopping from Khan El-Khalili, maps of most cities, walking routes of national parks, hotel and tour guide index and general information on life in Egypt.

www.weekly.ahram.org.eg Online version of the weekly English-language sister paper to the national daily *Al-Ahram*, extensive archive with search engine.

Visas and immigration

Passports are required by all and should be valid for at least 6 months beyond the period of your intended stay in Egypt. Visas are required by all except nationals of the following countries: Bahrain, Jordan, Kuwait, Libya, Oman, Saudi Arabia and the UAE. Cost varies between different embassies in different countries but payment must be in cash or by postal order, cheques are not accepted. It can take up to 6 weeks for some embassies to process a postal application, or they can be issued in 1 day if you turn up in person. They are valid for 3 months from date of arrival and for 6 months from date of issue and cannot be post-dated. Visas issued from embassies are either single-entry or multiple entry (which allow you to re-enter Egypt twice). Most Western tourists find it easiest to buy a renewable 30-day tourist visa (US$15 or equivalent in euro or sterling) on arrival at all international airports – but this is not possible when you are entering via an overland border crossing or a port.

Visa extensions can be obtained in 1 day (turn up early) at the Mogamma, Midan Tahrir, in Cairo. You will need your passport, 2 new photographs, cash to pay for renewal (cost varies depending what sort of visa, single- or multiple-entry, you require) and possibly bank receipts to prove you have exchanged or withdrawn enough hard currency to warrant your travels. Overstaying by 15 days does not matter, but after 2 weeks, be prepared for an E£153 fine and some hassle.

Weights and measures

Metric.

Contents

Footprint features

At a glance

✆ **Getting around** Taxis are both inexpensive and plentiful, while the metro is useful for longer journeys. Buses and micros are crowded but cheap.

⟳ **Time required** Allow a minimum of 3 days.

❀ **Weather** Very hot Jun-Sep. Winter days are beautiful, but the nights are surprisingly cold.

✖ **When not to go** It's only the summer heat that makes sightseeing hard work. Avoid Ramadan if eating street food and drinking alcohol are a crucial part of your holiday experience.

Cairo overview

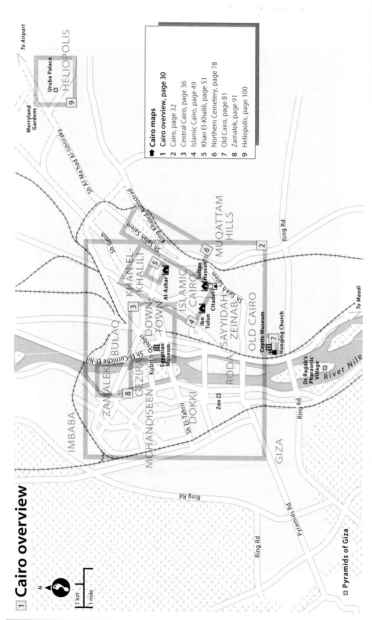

Cairo maps
1 Cairo overview, page 30
2 Cairo, page 32
3 Central Cairo, page 36
4 Islamic Cairo, page 49
5 Khan El-Khalili, page 51
6 Northern Cemetery, page 78
7 Old Cairo, page 81
8 Zamalek, page 91
9 Heliopolis, page 100

Arriving in Cairo → *Population: 17,000,000. Altitude: 75 m.*

Getting there
As one of the world's most crowded and noisy cities, arriving in Cairo can be a daunting experience. Authorities have worked hard to eliminate the once all-pervading hustle on arrival at the airport, taxi drivers are no longer permitted to pick up rides from the curb and other would-be hustlers are left outside if they don't flash the necessary identification. Still, upon reaching the pavement outside the airport, independent travellers may encounter a barrage of unsolicited offers from self-declared tour guides, drivers, hotel vendors, and the like, seeking to take advantage of an unschooled newcomer. Breathe deeply, avoid eye contact, firmly say *la'a shukran* (no, thank you), and stick to your plans. Bear in mind that Cairo is an exceptionally safe city and violent crime is virtually non-existent. The greatest thing to fear is getting severely overcharged for a taxi ride or being lured to a dingy hotel room. With a day or two meandering around the city, you'll figure out how things work soon enough. The easiest way to dodge such happenings from the outset is to work out in advance where you're going and how you intend to get there.

The **airport**, www.cairo-airport.com, is 22 km (about 45 minutes) northeast of Cairo. **Terminal 1** ⓘ *T02-2265 5000/1* caters for all **EgyptAir** flights, and some international airlines. The newer **Terminal 2** ⓘ *T02-2265 2824 (departure information), T02-2265 2077 (arrival information)*, is 3 km away and takes all other international flights. (Terminal 3 is being built, and will handle both domestic and international flights, just to confuse the matter further). In both terminals, there are tourist information booths in the departure hall but they are not overly helpful. Also on site are ATM machines and several banks that remain open through the night as flights arrive. Visas are on sale just before passport control at the bank counter (US$15 or equivalent in euro or sterling).

Taxi drivers will assuage you upon exiting, they ask for E£80-100 to transport you to the centre, locals usually pay E£50. If you can bargain down to around E£60, you've done well. Taxis get cheaper the further you head out of the car park, and if you can pick one up outside the precincts of the airport they are cheaper still. Another good option is the **Shuttle Bus** ⓘ *T02-2265 3937, available from the limousine counter on arrival or leaving every half hour*, who have seven-seater minibuses with set prices to various districts of Cairo.

Despite what any taxi driver at the airport will tell you, it is possible to take public transport into the city. However, it is a big hassle and not really recommended. Buses and minibuses gather by the bus stop, about 300 m in front of Terminal 1, visible as you exit. If you're heading Downtown or to Giza, the most comfortable option is to take one of the air-conditioned buses (E£2). Between 0700-2300, bus No 356 goes from the airport to **Midan Ramses** and on to **Midan Tahrir**. Further public buses, a little cheaper and a bit more uncomfortable, run from Terminal 1 through the night: minibus No 27 (E£1.50) runs from the airport to **Midan Tahrir**; bus No 948 (E£1) runs to **Midan Ataba** (on the outskirts of central Cairo). If you arrive at Terminal 2 and want to take public transport, a free 24-hour shuttle bus connects the two terminals. These line up outside arrivals and, about three minutes after setting off, reach a roundabout by a parking lot where a bus stop has been constructed. Get off here and catch an onward bus to Cairo. There is also a bus direct from the airport to **Alexandria**. ▸▸ *For listings, see pages 102-132.*

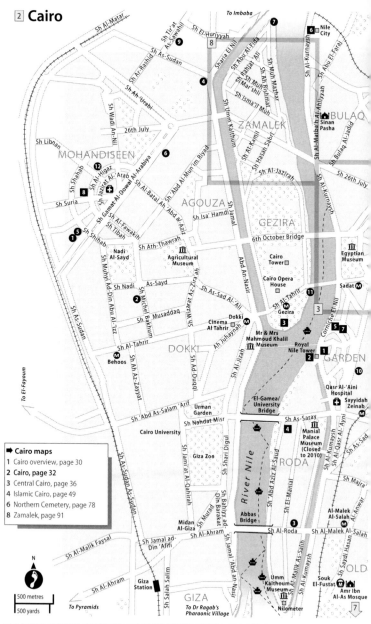

2 Cairo

➡ Cairo maps
1 Cairo overview, page 30
2 Cairo, page 32
3 Central Cairo, page 36
4 Islamic Cairo, page 49
6 Northern Cemetery, page 78
8 Zamalek, page 91

N

500 metres
500 yards

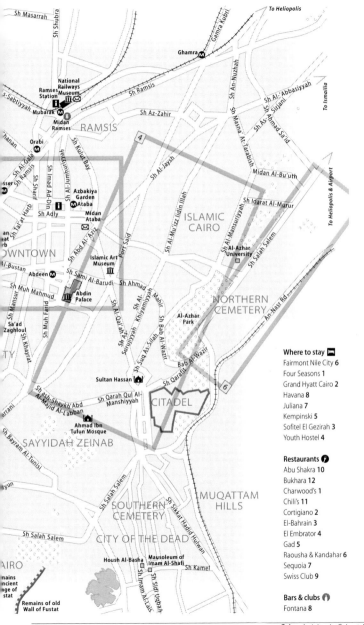

Where to stay 🛏

Fairmont Nile City **6**
Four Seasons **1**
Grand Hyatt Cairo **2**
Havana **8**
Juliana **7**
Kempinski **5**
Sofitel El Gezirah **3**
Youth Hostel **4**

Restaurants 🍴

Abu Shakra **10**
Bukhara **12**
Charwood's **1**
Chili's **11**
Cortigiano **2**
El-Bahrain **3**
El Embrator **4**
Gad **5**
Raousha & Kandahar **6**
Sequoia **7**
Swiss Club **9**

Bars & clubs 🎵

Fontana **8**

24 hours in the city

First stop, the **Egyptian Museum**. Be there when it opens and head straight to the Tutankhamen galleries in an attempt to beat the crowds. After a couple of hours, hop on the metro down to **Old Cairo** and visit the Hanging Church and the Coptic Museum; the Ben Ezra Synagogue (Egypt's oldest) is an optional extra. The Nilometer is easily accessible from here, if you haven't seen one elsewhere.

Take a metro back **Downtown** and head to Felfela's for a filling taste of local food for lunch, before taking a taxi to the Northern Gates and a walk through **Islamic Cairo**. Going south down Sharia Al-Muizz allows you to visit the spectacular Qaloun complex and have a wander around the Khan El-Khalili, Cairo's main *souk* since 1382. Stop for mint tea and *sheesha* at the famed Fishawis coffee shop, before continuing south past the Al-Ghuri's magnificent mosque and mausoleum. Pass through the huge gate of the Bab Zuweila and on through the tentmakers bazaar all the way down to the mosque of Ibn Tulun, where you can climb the spiralled minaret, visit the Gayer-Anderson House and do a bit of souvenir shopping in the Khan Misr Toulun. Take a taxi to Al-Azhar Park to enjoy sunset views over the whole city, before having dinner on a floating restaurant or one of Zamalek's swanky restaurants.

Join the crowds **Downtown** for an evening of window shopping, before having drinks in the rowdy Horiyya coffee shop or (if you've still got the energy) splash out at the Mena House bar with the Pyramid's a mere stone's throw away.

Getting around

Considering its size, getting around Cairo is quite easy. The centre, known as Downtown, is a condensed area and walking is a good way to see the heart of the city. There is a local bus service, metro system, and a profusion of cheap taxis. A few air-conditioned buses that run on the major thoroughfares connect the main *midans* (squares) to Heliopolis and the airport. They are a bit more expensive than the public buses (E£2), but more pleasant to use. For the truly adventurous traveller, the inner-city buses and minibuses (50 pt-1.50 pt) cover every inch of Cairo. They are generally so crowded that people literally hang out of doors, and as they rarely come to complete stops, courageous riders must run and jump to hop on. There are also microbuses that are private van-like vehicles that transport passengers through the maze of Cairo (E£1). There is usually a driver and a navigator that shouts the destination out of a moving van. When it suits you, motion to the van and they'll stop. You can also shout out where you want to go and if it's en route, they will enthusiastically let you on. If you see a large collection of people at what looks like a bus stop, just tell someone where you want to go and they will go out of their way to put you on the right bus/micro or at least point you in the right direction.

The metro is excellent – clean, cheap, and efficient, but with only two lines (and a third in construction), it doesn't cover the entire city. For cheaper and quicker transport, you may want to traverse the city by metro and then take a taxi or microbus for the final leg of your trip. Taxis are so inexpensive, abundant and easy, they really are the most convenient way of getting around. The relatively new white cabs have made life for Cairenes and tourists much easier, as they have working meters which start at E£2.50 and go up in 25 pt increments. The older black and white cabs are everywhere but they don't

Cairo with kids

Divide your time between the Pyramids of Giza and the Egyptian Museum. At the latter, don't expect much in the way of interactive exhibits or even English interpretation. However, what you do get are the dazzling treasures of teenage pharaoh Tutankhamen, including his famous gold funerary mask. Another must-see is the grizzly and engrossing Royal Mummy Room, displaying the remains of 11 Egyptian queens and rulers. Talking above a 'hushed whisper' is forbidden – good luck with that! The last surviving Ancient Wonder of the World, the Pyramids of Giza, is often bemoaned by adult visitors as being 'swamped by Cairo's suburbs' or 'spoilt by touts'. Most children, however, will simply be struck with innocent wonder at the sheer size of these extraordinary monuments. Kids' initial impulse is to climb the things. However, this is a definite 'no-no', so quash any disappointment by exploring the pyramid's long, cramped 'secret' passages that lead to mysterious subterranean chambers.

have working meters so as a newcomer it's best to agree a price before you get in, or when you've got to grips with fares pass the money through the window after getting out of the cab. Less plentiful are **yellow cabs** ① *they can be prebooked by calling T16516 or T19155,* that have air conditioning and working meters; these are cheaper for longer journeys around Cairo but work out more for short dashes. ▸▸ *See Transport, page 126.*

Information

Main tourist office ① *5 Sharia Adly, near Midan Opera, T02-2391 3454, daily 0900-1800 (closed during Fri prayers).* The staff speak English and have a decent map of Cairo plus a few colourful pamphlets, but they have little to offer in the way of useful information. There are tourist offices at the airport, open 24 hours, and at **Ramses Train Station** ① *T02-2579 0767;* **Giza Train Station** ① *T02-3570 2233, 0800-2200;* and by the **Pyramids of Giza** ① *T02-3383 8823, 0800-1700.* Often more helpful than the tourist offices is the information available in hotels.

If you are interested in a more exhaustive explanation than this handbook can offer for the Islamic area of the city, pick up a copy of Caroline Williams' excellent *Islamic Monuments in Cairo* (available in the AUC Bookstore). The Society for the Preservation of the Architectural Resources of Egypt (SPARE) publishes superb and extremely detailed maps of Islamic Cairo with brief accounts of each monument (also available at the AUC Bookstore, Diwan or Lenhert & Landrock, E£13 each).

Opening times In the last few years, the **Historic Cairo Restoration Programme** has exploded in Islamic Cairo resulting in the temporary closure of many monuments, those closed at the time of writing are noted. It also means that sights that have been closed for decades are at last reopening again. Most mosques are open from around 0800 until 2000. All the mosques in Cairo are accessible to the public except those of **Sayyidnah Hussein** and **Sayyidnah Nafisah**. Note that many of the mosques in Islamic Cairo are active places of worship and shouldn't be entered by non-Muslims during times of prayer. The times of prayer vary depending on the season, but are vaguely dawn, midday, mid-afternoon, dusk

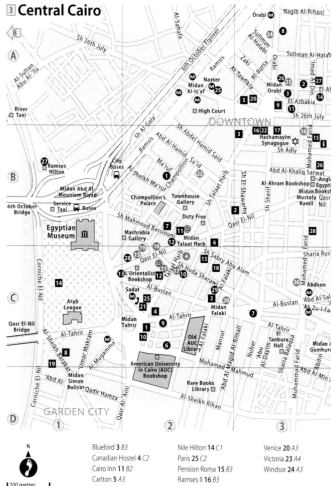

3 Central Cairo

DOWNTOWN

GARDEN CITY

N

200 metres
200 yards

Where to stay 🛏
African Hostel **27** A3
Akram Inn **1** C2
Alexander **28** B3
Amin **2** C2

Bluebird **3** B3
Canadian Hostel **4** C2
Cairo Inn **11** B2
Carlton **5** A3
Cosmopolitan **6** B2
Dahab **7** B2
Dina's Hostel **26** B3
Garden City House **8** C1
Grand **9** A3
Ismailia House **10** C2
Lialy Hostel **11** B2
Lotus **12** C2
Meramees **13** C2

Nile Hilton **14** C1
Paris **25** C2
Pension Roma **15** B3
Ramses II **16** B3
Richmond **17** B3
Safari **20** A3
Sara Inn Hostel **18** C2
Semiramis
    Intercontinental **19** C1
Suisse **7** B2
Sultan **20** A3
Sun **21** C2
Talisman **22** B3

Venice **20** A3
Victoria **23** A4
Windsor **24** A3

Restaurants 🍴
Abu Tarek **1** B2
Akher Sa'a **2** A3
Alfi Bey **3** A3
Arabesque **28** C1
Cilantro's **6** C2
El-Nil Fish **7** C3
El-Tabei **8** A3
Fatatri El-Tahrir **9** C2

and mid-evening. Churches are open Monday-Saturday 0800-1700, and Sundays 1200-1700. The Pyramids of Giza are open 0900-1700, but last entry is at 1600.

Admission charges The Ministry of Tourism, in response to agitated Muslims who did not want to pay admission to pray, have deemed all mosques free to enter. Exceptions are the mosques of Sultan Hassan and Sultan Al-Rifai, which have entry charges. The Citadel, museums and other secular sights have admission charges that vary from E£10-50 and hand out official tickets. For students with ID, there is a 50% discount. Cameras sometimes require an additional fee of E£10-20, videos E£100. There are a few sly touts left lingering about the more touristed mosques who will insist there is an entry fee. There is not. If someone asks you for an admission charge, ask for a ticket, their inability to find one usually facilitates passage. *Baksheesh* is still expected for guides (who may offer to lead you up a minaret), an acceptable amount is E£5 or a bit more for large parties, and it is common courtesy to tip the shoe caretaker E£1.

Background

Since the Arab conquest in AD 641 Egyptians have called both the city and the whole country 'Misr' (pronounced *masr*), the ancient Semitic name for Egypt and also mentioned in the Koran. 'Al-Qahira' ('the Victorious') is the city's official but less commonly used name, derived from Al-Qahir (Mars), because the planet was in ascendance when the Fatimids started the construction of their new city in AD 971. In medieval times, this became corrupted by Europeans to Cairo, the Latin version of the name.

Take a deep breath

According to UN figures lead pollution in the atmosphere in Cairo is equivalent to one tonne per car per year and Cairo now has over 1.5 million cars.

Egypt's Environmental Affairs Agency has reported that lead pollution and other suspended particles in the air over Cairo, which tend to manifest every autumn like a black cloud over the capital reducing visibility down to a few metres and breathing to a desperate struggle, is responsible for between 15,000 and 20,000 additional deaths annually.

USAID has funded a programme, now in its fifth year, that is addressing the problem by moving significant lead smelters out of the city, sponsoring vehicle emissions testing and tune-ups and promoting the use of natural gas (an abundant natural resource in Egypt and a much cleaner burning fuel) in public and private transport. Improvements have already been detected, but lead levels in the air are still well above the World Health Organisation's acceptable levels.

Although Cairo itself is younger than Alexandria, the surrounding region has a very ancient and impressive past. **Memphis**, 15 km south of Cairo across the Nile, was established as the first pharaonic capital in 3100 BC and during this period huge necropoli were developed, starting with **Saqqara** and culminating with the largest of all pyramids at modern-day Giza. During the New Kingdom, another cult centre known as On, or **Heliopolis** to the Greeks, and later Aïn Shams (Spring of the Sun) by the Arabs, was developed further north when a canal was cut between the Nile and the Red Sea. It took the Roman occupation to subdue the influence of Memphis and Om, when Emperor Trajan (AD 98-117) recognized the strategic importance of the east bank fortress town of **Babylon-in-Egypt** and a thriving community soon sprang up around its walls. During the subsequent Christian era Memphis was completely abandoned never to rise again, while Babylon became the seat of the bishopric and the west bank village of **Giza** grew into a large town.

When the Arabs conquered Egypt in AD 641, they were given specific instructions by Khalifa Omar in Damascus to establish their administrative capital in Babylon rather than at the Christian stronghold of Alexandria. The general Amr ibn Al-As built his encampment (or Fustat) in the middle of a deserted triangular plain bounded by Babylon in the south, Aïn Shams (ancient Heliopolis) to the northeast and Al-Maks (the Customs Point), now the site of Ramses Station, to the northwest. The Amr mosque was the first of a number of new and permanent buildings that were erected as the plain was developed and the city rapidly grew in size and importance. It is thought that the name Misr was used in order to distinguish it from the many other towns called Fustat in the Arab world.

By the time the Fatimid heretical Shi'a invaders arrived from North Africa in AD 969, only the south of the plain had been developed. Their military commander, Gohar, therefore chose to build a new walled city (which included the Al-Azhar mosque, palaces, pavilions and gardens for the sole use of the khalifa, his family and retainers), about 1.5 km north of the Fustat complex and called it Al-Qahira. Two centuries later in AD 1168 calamity struck Fustat when, fearing occupation by the invading Crusaders, the vizier Shawar set fire to the city. Over 54 days the fire almost totally destroyed Fustat whose inhabitants fled to Al-Qahira and constructed temporary housing. Three years later the

Flinders Petrie: beginnings of systematic archaeology

Flinders Petrie applied the first systematic excavation techniques to archaeological sites in Egypt. He was born in 1853 in Scotland and arrived in Egypt in 1880 in search of measurements of the pyramids. He excavated many sites, recording in detail each item and layer of his work with consistency and accuracy – in sharp contrast to the acquisitive and unscientific digging of this and earlier periods. It was he who set the chronological framework within which most archaeologists and their colleagues later worked.

Petrie had the reputation, even as a young man, for wanting his own way and there were constant skirmishes between him and his financing committee in London. In 1886 Petrie left his employment with the Egypt Exploration Fund but remained in Egypt for a further 37 years, actively excavating and recording his finds. He eventually left Egypt in 1923 when the law on the division of archaeological finds was changed after the discovery of the tomb of Tutankhamen by Howard Carter. He died in 1942.

last Fatimid khalifa died and his vizier, the Kurdish-born **Salah Al-Din**, assumed control of the country and founded the Sunni Muslim orthodox Ayyubid Dynasty (AD 1171-1249). He expelled the royal family from Al-Qahira, which he then opened up to the populace, and soon it became the commercial and cultural centre.

Salah Al-Din actually only spent one-third of his 24-year reign in Cairo. Much of his time was spent fighting abroad where he recaptured Syria and eventually Jerusalem from the Crusaders in 1187, finally dying in Damascus in 1193. Yet he still found time to expand the walls surrounding the Fatimid city and built the huge **Citadel** on an outcrop of the Muqattam Hills, which became the city's nucleus and remains the focal point of the Islamic city to this day.

Under Mamluk rule (AD 1250-1517) the city grew rapidly to become the largest city in the Arab world. As the east bank of the Nile continued to silt up, the newly elevated areas provided additional space that was developed to house the expanding population.

Under the **Ottomans** (AD 1517-1798) both Cairo and Alexandria were relegated to the position of mere provincial cities with little in the way of public building undertaken in the whole of the 17th and 18th centuries. This changed, however, with the combination of the arrival of the French in 1798 and the coming to power in 1805 of the Albanian-born Ottoman officer Mohammed Ali. As part of his ambitious plan to drag Egypt into the modern world by introducing the best that Europe had to offer, he embarked on a project that included a huge public building programme in Cairo and turned it into a large modern capital city.

The combination of very rapid population growth and extensive rural migration to the city, particularly since the Second World War, has completely overwhelmed Cairo. It has totally outgrown its infrastructure and today a city, intended to house only two million people, is home to perhaps 16 million, with at least a million more commuting in every day. The result is that the transport, power, water and sewage systems are completely inadequate and hundreds of thousands live wherever they can find shelter including the infamous 'Cities of the Dead' cemeteries. What is amazing is that, despite all its problems, this ancient city actually functions as well as it does and that in adversity the Cairenes are so good natured and friendly.

Places in Cairo

There is never enough time to see all the sights that Cairo has to offer, particularly in the two or three days that most visitors have at their disposal. First on the majority of agendas (and what any day-tour of the city will include) are the Pyramids of Giza, the Egyptian Museum and the Khan El-Khalili. With more time, the churches of Old Cairo, the Citadel and Mosque of Mohamed Ali, plus the outlying pyramids and tombs at Saqqara are key destinations. The streets of Islamic Cairo are dense with mosques, mausoleums and Ottoman houses, all (or any) of which are worth exploring, while the Cities of the Dead contain some of the finest Islamic architecture in the city. The modern Egyptian capital has developed on both sides of the river, spreading in all directions, where interesting and eclectic museums can be found. Get a feel for Cairo by cruising down the Nile on a *felucca* at sunset, as the skyline comes alive with city lights, and spend an afternoon or evening in a local *ahwa*. To see Cairo from up high, there are stellar lookout points over the city's labyrinthine sprawl from the Cairo Tower and the top of the Grand Hyatt Hotel.

Central Cairo

Egyptian Museum

ⓘ *The museum takes up the north side of Midan Tahrir (entry is from the sculpture garden fronting the building), T02-2578 2448, www.egyptianmuseum.gov.eg. Daily 0830-1645 (the museum remains open until 1815, last entry at 1645), except on Wed, when the museum closes at 1200 for maintenance. It is hoped that the museum will soon be open in the evenings, daily, until 2200. Ramadan opening hours: 0900-1600. It is strongly recommended to visit the museum either early in the day or last thing in the afternoon, as it is taken over by coach parties most of the time. The Tutankhamen exhibit is particularly in demand and it might even be necessary to queue for entry. Tickets cost E£60, E£30 for students, cameras and video are not permitted, there is an additional fee of E£100 (students E£60), for the Royal Mummy Room. It may be worth buying a detailed guide to the rooms, in which case the AUC Press' Guide to the Egyptian Museum (E£150) is the best and has a picture index to help you find what you are looking for. Tour guides wait around outside the ticket booth, some are more entertaining than others, but most seem to be quite well-informed. The going rate is E£60-80 per hr, it's possible to bargain, a tour lasts about 2 hrs. The museum is overwhelming and you need to allow at least 4 hrs for a full initial viewing of both floors. A shortened tour of about 2 hrs will give you enough time to take in the ground floor followed by a visit to the Tutankhamen Gallery. There is a souvenir shop outside the museum on the right of the entrance and an official sales area on the left inside the main building. Café and restaurant facilities are available on the 1st floor, via the souvenir shop, and there is a new high-class restaurant to the left of the museum, where there is also a courtyard coffeeshop.*

The Egyptian Museum (called in Arabic *El-Mathaf El-Masri* and sometimes, mistakenly, referred to as the Cairo Museum), is one of the wonders of the country. Its most famous exhibits are the spectacular Tutankhamen displays and the world-renowned Mummy Room, but the enormous wealth of other pharaonic materials numbers a staggering 136,000. Unrivalled even by the grand museums of Berlin, London, New York and Paris, for tourists and scholars alike the museum is a must if only for a few hours.

The setting-up of a museum to house the Egyptian national collection was the brainchild of Auguste Ferdinand François Mariette, a distant relation of Champollion, the decipherer of Egyptian hieroglyphics. He himself was a great scholar of Egyptology and, after winning the confidence of the crown prince Sa'id Pasha, was appointed to oversee all excavations in Egypt and to establish a museum in which to protect the treasures that had been uncovered. The museum that he succeeded in establishing in Bulaq in 1858 was, however, flooded 20 years later, and after a soujourn in Giza, the artefacts were rehomed in 1902 in the dusty pink landmark you visit today. It remains well planned for its age, despite the confusing labelling and numbering system, but it's simply not large enough for the sheer volume of treasures it holds, many of which are stored in the basement and never seen by anyone at all. A new purpose-built Grand Museum is being constructed at Giza to overcome these inadequacies, the foundation stone was laid in January 2000 on a site of 600,000 sq m. Costing an estimated US$500 million it will be the world's largest historical gallery, displaying the hundreds of priceless monuments that now lie gathering dust in store rooms. However, progress is slow and the opening date is tentatively set for 2013, though in reality this is unlikely. The statue of Ramses the Great, which stood for decades in the midan that bears his

Egyptian Museum – ground floor

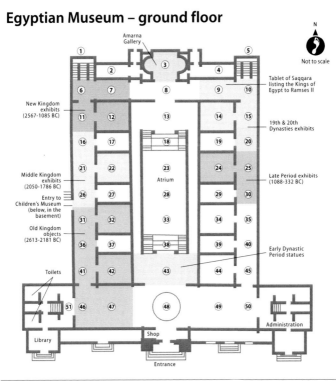

New Kingdom exhibits (2567–1085 BC)

Middle Kingdom exhibits (2050–1786 BC)

Entry to Children's Museum (below, in the basement)

Old Kingdom objects (2613–2181 BC)

Toilets

Library

Amarna Gallery

Atrium

Shop

Entrance

N
Not to scale

Tablet of Saqqara listing the Kings of Egypt to Ramses II

19th & 20th Dynasties exhibits

Late Period exhibits (1088–332 BC)

Early Dynastic Period statues

Administration

name, has already been moved to the site of the Grand Museum of Egypt. After years cloaked in scaffolding, when he finally proceeded at a snail's pace through the main streets of Downtown to his new home, crowds to rival the funeral of Umm Khalsoum waved him off from bridges and buildings. Now he casts a sad and lonely figure dumped on the desert sands near the site of the new museum.

A visit to the museum begins with a look at the **sculpture garden**, where the tomb of Mariette, a number of sphinx-headed statues and a sarcophagus lie under the sun. At the time of writing, the outside area was being renovated into an **Open Air Museum**, and the statues will be better displayed and lit up at night. The museum building has two floors, plus a new little **Childrens' Museum** in the basement. This is entered from the left side of the main building and is uncrowded as well as free. There are some beautiful pieces inside, displayed thematically, interspersed with huge Lego models of the Sphinx, amongst others. Interesting are the blue faiance shabti figures, jewellery and mask (with a stripey turquoise beard) from the Tomb of Hor in Dahshur, two striking copper statues of Pepi I, and children will certainly enjoy the case of bird and animal figurines,

Note In the main museum, rooms are (confusingly) numbered the same on both the ground and upper floor. In the description below, GF = ground floor; UF = upper floor. Rooms and galleries are both described as 'Rooms'.

Egyptian Museum – upper floor

Mummy come home

An elegant tomb (Room **56**) was constructed in the museum in 2006 to provide a final resting place for some of the most famous pharaohs. Dimmed lighting, a vaulted ceiling and individual glass cases equipped with dehumidifiers protect the neatly wrapped desiccated remains. President Sadat banned the public display of mummies as improper shortly after his inauguration, and it was only in 1994 that the dead pharaohs went back on show.

The mummies have suffered many indignities. Take Merneptah, grandson of Seti I. Having survived a spectacular first burial with all the pomp and splendour due to Egyptian royalty, tomb robbers flung his mummy aside and 21st Dynasty priests rewrapped him and placed him with eight other displaced corpses in a side chamber in the Tomb of Amenhotep II. Rediscovery in 1898 was followed by transport to Cairo where he was put on view. Queen Nedjemet, another resident, was slashed by the knives of those who unwrapped her. The great Ramses II, unwrapped in public in 1886 in an unseemly 15-minute strip, has also found a decent home here. Among the 11 who have found, hopefully, a final resting place here beside Ramses II are Merytamum his queen and his father Seti I.

Touring the museum The ground floor arranged chronologically when starting in a clockwise direction in the hallway (Room 48-GF).

In the foyer (**48-GF**, display unnumbered) are recent additions to the museum's collection out of chronological sequence. The chief object to note is the limestone statue of **Zoser**, orchestrator of the Step Pyramid at Saqqara, whose eyes have been gouged out. Room **43-GF** holds a number of Early Dynastic period statues, but most significant is the **Narmer Palette** which, for the first time, shows the unification of Upper and Lower Egypt. Old Kingdom (2613-2181 BC) objects take up **GF Rooms 47, 46, 41, 42, 36, 31** and **32**. In Room **42-GF** there is a notable standing wooden statue of the priest Ka-aper and a beautifully preserved statue of King Chephren, whose pyramid stands in Giza. In Room **32-GF**, display 39 is a painted effigy of **Seneb the dwarf** and his family. He was keeper of the royal wardrobe in the fifth Dynasty. A well-sculpted, painted statue of Ti (display 49), a noble of the same period and other figures such as Prince Ra-hotep and his wife Nofert are also to be found in Room **32** (display 73).

The Middle Kingdom period (2050-1786 BC) is represented in **GF Rooms 26, 21, 22** and **16**. The painted statue of Menutuhotep II in Room **26-GF**, with enormous feet and calves and a sour expression, was found at Deir El-Bahari by Howard Carter. Room **26-GF** also houses a series of sarcophagi including the unmissable **Tomb of Harhotpe** that beautifully illustrates objects in everyday use such as sandals and linen items together with hieroglyphs of magic spells and offerings. King Senusert I is depicted in 10 seated limestone statues in Room **22-GF** though these are outshone for visual impact by his 56-cm wooden statuette (display 88) carrying sceptres in both hands to denote his royal authority. A singular double-headed statue of **Amenemhat III** as the Nile god (display 104), and lion-headed sphinxes of the same provenance are in Room **16-GF** (display 102). The four sphinxes are in grey granite and come from the find by Auguste Mariette at Tanis.

Never smile at a crocodile

In the Ancient Egyptian Agricultural Museum the 5-m-long crocodile complete with wicked grin is fortunately very dead, as are the many other animals on display. A dog lies on its side, prostrate, seemingly sleeping in the sun and a baboon sits back resting on its haunches, huge hands hanging over its knees.

These were the animals worshipped, pampered, hunted and bred by the Ancient Egyptians: fat cats; even fatter Apis bulls; domesticated sheep and horses; birds ranging in size from the falcon and duck to the ostrich and the venerated ibis. The animals depicted in the hunting scenes on the countless reliefs and tomb paintings have not, fortunately, come to life, but their skeletal and mummified remains are on display here.

The New Kingdom ran from 2567-1085 BC. The exhibits in the set of galleries **11**, **12**, **6** and **7** are mainly from the 18th Dynasty, and present more complex garments and headgear than in previous eras. Room **12-GF** is well endowed with notable objects, chiefly the **Shrine to Hathor** from the Temple of Tuthmosis III at Deir Al-Bahri, which contains a life-sized statue of the goddess in the form of a cow. Also of importance are the statues of Senenmut, steward of Queen Hatshepsut and tutor to her daughter, and the mastermind behind the design of the Hatshepsut's Temple at Deir El-Bahri. The figures in Room 12-GF include his block statue with his pupil, Princess Neferure, peering below his chin.

Recently refurbished Room **3-GF** is given over to objects from the **reign of Akhenaten** (Amenhotep IV), who set up his capital at Tell El-Amarna (south of Minya) and altered the mode of public art and architecture in Egypt to one of realism. The ultra-refined, elongated style of the paintings and sculpture of the period is unmistakable from all other pharaonic art, as the objects in this room clearly demonstrate. There are stunning sandstone statues of Akhenaten, and several heads of women are on display, with the quartzite unfinished head of beautiful Nefertiti (display 161) being the most famous. Also on show is the foil and inlay from the KV55 coffin, discovered in 1907 in the Valley of the Kings. It contained a mystery mummy that some archaeologists believe to be that of Akhenaten, in part due to the elongated skull that is clearly apparent on the stone statues displayed around the room. DNA testing is to be carried out to try and determine whose the badly preserved body really is.

The central atrium of the museum (Rooms **13**, **18**, **23**, **28**, **33** and **38-GF**) is used to exhibit mega-statues from a mixture of periods, most eye-catching of which is a 7 m high representaton of Amenhotep III and his wife Queen Tiy (Room **18**).

Objects of the 19th and 20th Dynasties are displayed in Rooms **9**, **10**, **15**, **14** and **20-GF**. Room 9-GF contains the **Tablet of Saqqara** (display 660), which lists the kings of Egypt to Ramses II. The crystalline limestone head of General Nakhtmin (display 195) is in Room 15-GF and shows fine workmanship. The painted bust of **Meryut-Amun**, daughter of Ramses II and queen in succession to Nefertari, is also in Room 15-GF.

Best of the Late Period (1085-332 BC) is concentrated in Rooms **25**, **24** and **30-GF**. Key items include the Psametik group of statues in greenstone of which those of the Psametik, a head jeweller, with Hathor (display 857) and of Isis, wife of Osiris (display 856), are particularly well executed. A statue of Princess Amenartais in alabaster (display 930 in the centre of Room 30-GF) is a beautiful example of 25th Dynasty sculpture.

Not just the Egyptian Museum

There is a lot to be said for visiting small, eclectic museums in Cairo. Not only are they compact enough to only take up an hour of your time, often they are quirky and kitsch, or set in lush and quiet gardens, plus a visit takes you into areas you wouldn't necessarily explore otherwise. Some are full of dusty treasures that in any other country would be highlights of a national collection. Just be prepared for some nonsensical labelling – but then you even get that in the Egyptian museum, and it somehow adds to their charm. Good places to start include:

Agricultural Museum, Dokki – for bizarrely eclectic displays and the princess' art collection, see page 92.

Islamic Ceramics Museum, Zamalek – for exquisite colours and marble interiors, see page 90.

Mahmoud Khalil Museum, Dokki – to have Impressionist masterpieces all to yourself in a grand villa, see page 93.

Manial Palace Museum, Roda – for botanical gardens and glorious royal residence, see page 88.

National Railways Museum, Ramses – for tranquillity amid the chaos of the city's main station, see page 47.

On the Upper Floor, the pride of the museum is contained in the **Tutankhamen collection** in rooms **3**, **4**, **6**, **7**, **8**, **9**, **10**, **15**, **20**, **25**, **30**, **35**, **40** and **45-UF** with 1700 objects on exhibition. The remarkable treasures, found intact by the Englishman Howard Carter in 1922, were saved from grave-robbers by the tomb's position low in the valley hidden under that of Ramses VI and by the construction of workmen's huts across its entrance. Unlike most other archaeological finds before 1922, the Tutankhamen treasure was retained in Egypt and considering that he only reigned for nine years, between the ages of nine and 18, the mind boggles to imagine what Seti I's tomb must have contained. You should look at the entire set of Tutankhamen displays, but if time is short at least look at the following items. The two life-size **Ka statues of Tutankhamen**, which flank the entrance to Room 45, are executed in black bitumen-painted wood and were found in the antechamber guarding his tomb. The king holds a mace in his right hand and a staff in his left, and wears a khat headdress and gilded kilt. **The gold mask of Tutankhamen** (Room 3-UF), garnished with cornelian, coloured glass, lapis lazuli, obsidian, quartz, and turquoise. The 54-cm-high mask wears a ceremonial beard and a headdress knotted at the back of the neck. The blue stripes are in lapis lazuli, and there is a gold ureaus and vulture head above the brow. **The innermost coffin of Tutankhamen** (Room 3-UF) is rendered in gold and semi-precious stones with coloured glass. Some 187.5 cm long and weighing 110.4 kg, the coffin is in the Osiride form of a mummy with crossed arms carrying divine emblems. The body is covered by carved feathers and the representations of Upper and Lower Egypt – the vulture and cobra. The outer two sarcophagi were fashioned from wood, one is on display here while the other lies in situ in his tomb at Thebes. The golden **Canopic chest** (Room 9/10-UF, display 177) was in the antechamber of the king's tomb and is made of wood gilded with gold and with silver, and is ornately decorated with family and hunting scenes. The chest was protected by four statues of Seket, the water goddess, displayed in gilded and painted wood about 90 cm high. The lids of the alabaster **Canopic jars**, containing the remains of the king's entrails, are formed in the king's image and lightly painted. Tutankhamen's **wooden funerary beds** (Room 9/10-UF) are made of stuccoed wood, gilded and painted. The most remarkable is the couch in the image of the goddess Mehetweret with cow's heads and lyre-like horns set about sun disks. The extraordinary **Throne of Tutankhamen** (Room 35-UF, display 179) is 102 x 54 cm, coated with sheets of gold and ornamented with semi-precious stones. In addition to the winged serpent arms of the throne, the seat back carries a scene in which Tutankhamen's wife anoints him with oil. The finely inlaid ebony and ivory **ceremonial chair** (Room 25-UF, display 181) of Tutankhamen is regarded as among the best examples of Egyptian cabinet-making ever found. It is decorated with uraeus snakes and divinities. The tomb of Tutankhamen contained 413 small, approximately 50 cm high, **'shawabti' statues**, some of which are on display here (Room 35-UF). The curious figures would perform tasks the gods set for the pharaoh in the afterlife. Jewellery, cups and amulets were kept in the **Anubis chest** (Room 45-UF, display 185) made in stuccoed wood and ornamented with black resin, gold, silver and varnish. Anubis as a jackal sits on the chest ready to guide Tutankhamen in the afterworld. Adjacent to the Tutankhamen galleries, and well worth looking out for, are the touchingly realistic **Fayoum portraits** in Room **14-UF**. For the most part encaustic (wax) painted on wooden bases by Greek artists in the second century AD to leave a likeness of the deceased for his family (see box, page 144).

In the opposite wing **(Rooms 27 and 32-UF)** is the wonderful 25-piece collection of Meketra's models, found in the tomb of Meketra, a noble of the Middle Kingdom (2000 BC), at a site south of Deir El-Bahari. The miniatures show the form, dress, crops, vessels and crafts of the period. The best known is the offerings bearer (display 74), 123 cm high and made of painted wood, showing a servant, carrying a basket of vases on her head and a duck in her right hand. There are also models of fishermen, cattle, weavers and carpenters in displays 75, 76, 77 and 78 respectively.

Last but not least, if you can afford it, the **Royal Mummy Room** (Room **56-UF**) contains what is left of some of the most famous pharaohs of them all. Eleven mummies are on display, some still shrouded in their wrappings, but most have had at least their faces unwrapped and seem to rest peacefully in the climate-controlled cases. Best preserved are Seti I and Ramses II, whose hair appears to have been tinted, while the mummies of queens Hodjmet and Henttawy are still wearing their wigs.

Downtown

Most independent travellers to Cairo stay in Downtown, the non-stop pulsing heart of the modern city that radiates out from the central Midan Talaat Harb. Laid out in the 1860s when Khedive Ismail sought to replicate the boulevards of Paris, gracious five-and six-level buildings still predominate on the main streets although their street-level windows contain a distracting mass of gaudy signage, spangled displays of shoes and arrays of risqué underwear. Shops and restaurants stay open late into the night, while streams of traffic and consumers pack the streets way into the small hours. It's also the chief hunting-ground (particularly around midans Tahrir and Talaat Harb) of the *kherti*, pesky touts – usually young men – who make it their business to approach foreigners with predictable lines such as 'are you looking for something?' and 'is it me?' Anyone who comes up to you, asking random questions and being overly helpful, is best avoided as there will always be an ulterior motive, even if it's just something as tedious as 'look in my shop' rather than anything sinister.

There are many characterful and ethereal turn-of-the-century buildings dotted around Downtown that are worth looking out for as you traverse between museums, Islamic Cairo and the other sights. Especially atmospheric and decrepit is the former palace of Prince Said Halim, usually (and wrongly) referred to as **Champollion's Palace**. Dating from 1896, it is a pink-marble mix of Baroque and Belle Époque themes, adorned with the Ottoman logo, the prince's initials and numerous stone angels. Now in a state of complete disrepair and infested by bats, the gates are locked and the awaited restoration project shows no sign of materializing. The palace is on Sharia Mimaar Hussein Pasha off Sharia Champollion (a tree-lined street nice for walking) and adjacent to the Townhouse Gallery and a couple of locally famed outdoor *ahwas* that are worth stopping into.

On Sharia Adly, is the stern and imposing **Hashamayim Synagogue** ① *open 0800-1700 (except Sun), entrance US$5/E£30 (no student discount), no photo/video allowed, bring your passport*, which, though it appears to be art deco judging from the wonderful exterior adorned with palm trees, is actually significantly earlier, dating from 1905. The grey edifice would be better placed in Gotham City, an aura that is compounded by the heavy police presence outside. Inside, the enormous dome and stained glass windows are most impressive.

Abdin Presidential Palace Museum ① *Just east of Midan El-Gumhurriya, entered from the rear of the palace, T02-2391 0130. Sat-Thu 0900-1500. E£10, students E£2, cameras E£10.*
This imposing building, completed in 1872, became the official royal residence when Khedive Ismail relocated the seat of state here as part of his schemes to modernize Cairo. For the previous 700 years the rulers had occupied the Citadel, but Abdin was not to know such longevity and King Farouk was deposed when the Egyptian republic was born in 1952. The rooms of the actual palace are not for viewing, being still used on official state occasions, but 21 halls contain exhibits. The first section, President Mubarak's Hall, contains a selection of the gifts he has received – a varied collection of medals, portraits, clocks and plaques. Crossing the courtyard, where there is a shrine to Sidi Badran, brings you to the Military Museum, which takes up 13 of the halls. Here are displayed a host of weaponry and suits of armour, as well as unusual items such as Rommel's dagger and two guns belonging to Napoleon Bonaparte. The final section is of silverware, porcelain and crystal owned by the descendants of Mohammed Ali Pasha, indicating a very luxurious lifestyle. Who lifted the 125-kg silver tray when it was laden?

National Railways Museum ① *north of Downtown, next to Ramses station, T02-2576 3793, daily 0800-1400 E£10, Fri E£20.*
A silent haven away from the madness of Ramses. A couple of gleaming steam locomotives are the highlights unless you are a signalling enthusiast, but the old Egypt tourist posters fading on the walls, amber lighting and industrial architecture make it a gratifying half hour or so. It's recommended to pop in if you have time to kill when waiting for a train.

Midan Ataba, Midan Opera and Ezbakiya Gardens
The old heart of colonial Cairo (the original Shepheard's Hotel stood on Ezbakiya Gardens), this area is now full of crowded markets among the European-style buildings. The **Post Office Museum** ① *on Midan Ataba, T02-2391 0001, Sat-Thu 1000-1400, E£10, students E£5*, is a quaint diversion in an attractive building. Also worthy of a visit is the **Sednaoui** department store,

which has a glorious atrium with art nouveau glasswork, creaking wooden staircases up three storeys and gigantic chandeliers – but practically no goods for sale. It was owned by Nazarenes from Syria until 1961, when nationalization meant that Parisian hats and foreign cosmetics came to an end. Another classic piece of architecture is the **Tiring Building**, designed by Oscar Horowitz, which opened as a department store in 1912. Look up to see its landmark cupola upon which four figures of Atlas support the globe.

Bulaq

The cacophony of car horns, lines of fruit carts, and endless rails of clothes spilling off the pavement make a walk down Sharia 26th July in Bulaq something of a mission. A separate suburb in the 19th century, Bulaq used to be the commercial port of Cairo when Sharia 26th July was an avenue lined with flowering trees leading tourists to Shepheard's Hotel. It was also visited by soldiers from the canal zone who frequented the prostitutes in the 'seven houses' of Bulaq, as they were the cheapest in the city and easily linked to the barracks by train. The women had to have regular medical check-ups and would first visit the hammams, singing songs on the way from the brothels as they rode along in carts. At one time the Egyptian Antiquities Museum was situated in Bulaq, and the locale is still worth a visit for a taste of *baladi* Cairo, a couple of interesting mosques, and some of the cities last-remaining functioning hammams. Public baths were generally found near market areas serving workers who couldn't get home to bathe, with the water heated by burning rubbish.

Mosque of Sinan Pasha   The Albanian-born Sinan Pasha was recruited for service as a boy at the Sublime Porte in Istanbul and rose to become Sulayman the Magnificent's chief cupbearer. He was governor of Cairo between 1571-1572 and is best remembered for his building activities rather than political events. He erected buildings in Alexandria and re-excavated the canal between the Nile and Alexandria, but the major buildings he initiated in Egypt were at Bulaq and included this mosque, essential as the focal point of the community, a *sabil*, a *maktab*, commercial buildings, a hammam, residential houses, shops, a mill and a bakery. The small, square Ottoman mosque stands in a scruffy garden, with entrances from three sides into the large central domed chamber with two tiers of stained glass windows. While most of the Sinan Pasha complex has long since disappeared, the adjacent public bath (men only) is still in operation. It is a beautifully peaceful place.

Islamic Cairo

As noted in the history of Cairo (see page 37), the city initially developed as a series of extensions and walled mini-cities that radiated in a northeast direction from the original encampment of Fustat outside the walls of the Babylon-in-Egypt fortress. Built with defence purposes in mind, the streets of the Islamic city are narrow and, in addition to looming Mamluke mausoleums and age-old mosques on every corner, the feeling of having stepped back in time is deepened by the ceaseless trading, shouting and everyday life all around. Congested with hissing men pushing hand-carts and shuffling shoppers laden with bags, scented with spices and criss-crossed by cats, getting lost in the ancient alleyways is what this city is all about. It's a pity that the ambiance on some of the main streets (notably near the Khan on Sharia Muski and Sharia Al-Muizz) is being eradicated by the concerted restoration efforts that are in effect. The streets of Gamaliya are being repaved with slippery cobbles and

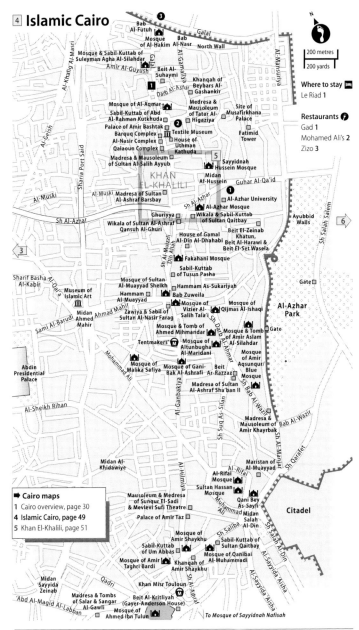

4 Islamic Cairo

Bab Al-Futuh
Mosque of Al-Hakim
Bab Al-Nasr
Galal
North Wall
Al-Mansuriya

Mosque & Sabil-Kuttab of Suleyman Agha Al-Silahdar
Amir Al-Guyush
Beit Al-Suhaymi
Khanqah of Beybars Al-Gashankir

Mosque of Al-Aqmar
Medresa & Mausoleum of Tatar Al-Higaziya
Site of Musafirkhana Palace

Sabil-Kuttab of Abd Al-Rahman Kutkhuda
Palace of Amir Bashtak
Textile Museum
Fatimid Tower

Barquq Complex
House of Uthman Kathuda

Al-Nasir Complex
Qalaoun Complex

Madresa & Mausoleum of Sultan Al-Salih Ayyub
Sayyidnah Hussein Mosque
Midan Al-Hussein

KHAN EL-KHALILI

Al-Muski
Madresa of Sultan Al-Ashraf Barsbay
Guhar Al-Qa'id
Al-Azhar University

Al-Muski
Al-Azhar Mosque

Sh Al-Azhar
Ghuriyya
Wikala & Sabil-Kuttab of Sultan Qaitbay
Ayubbid Walls

Wikala of Sultan Al-Ashraf Qansuh Al-Ghuri
House of Gamal Al-Din Al-Dhahabi
Beit El-Zeinab Khatun, Beit Al-Harawi & Beit El-Set Wasela

Fakahani Mosque
Gate

Sabil-Kuttab of Tusun Pasha

Museum of Islamic Art
Mosque of Sultan Al-Muayyad Sheikh
Hammam As-Sukariyah

Hammam Al-Muayyad
Bab Zuweila
Mosque of Qijmas Al-Ishaqi
Al-Azhar Park

Zawiya & Sabil of Sultan Al-Nasir Farag
Mosque of Vizier Al-Salih Tala'i
Gate

Midan Ahmed Mahir
Mosque & Tomb of Ahmed Mihmandar
Mosque & Tomb of Amir Aslam Al-Silahdar

Tentmakers
Mosque of Altunbugha Al-Maridani
Mosque of Amir Aqsunqur/ Blue Mosque

Mosque of Malika Safiya
Mosque of Gani-Bak Al-Ashrafi
Beit Ar-Razzaz

Abdin Presidential Palace
Madresa of Sultan Al-Ashraf Sha'ban II

Al-Sheikh Rihan
Madresa & Mausoleum of Amir Khayrbak

Maristan of Al-Muayyad

Midan Al-Khidawiye
Al-Rifai Mosque
Al-Rifai

Mausoleum & Medresa of Sunqur El-Sadi & Mevlevi Sufi Theatre
Sultan Hassan Mosque
Qani Bey As-Sayfi

Palace of Amir Taz
Midan Salah Al-Din
Citadel

Mosque of Amir Shaykhu
Sabil-Kuttab of Sultan Qaitbay

Sabil-Kuttab of Um Abbas
Mosque of Qanibai Al-Muhammadi

Mosque of Amir Taghri Bardi
Khanqah of Amir Shaykhu

Midan Sayyida Zeinab
Khan Misr Touloun

Madresa & Tombs of Salar & Sangar Al-Gawli
Beit Al-Kritliyah (Gayer-Anderson House)

Mosque of Ahmed Ibn Tulun
To Mosque of Sayyidnah Nafisah

➡ Cairo maps
1 Cairo overview, page 30
4 Islamic Cairo, page 49
5 Khan El-Khalili, page 51

200 metres
200 yards

pavements have taken the place of onion and garlic stalls, resulting a more artificial air that long-time visitors to Cairo will find upsetting. Designated a pedestrian zone between 0600-2400, shopkeepers can now only receive deliveries in the depths of night and the chaos that defined Islamic Cairo might be dimmed as palm trees are planted and faux-Arabesque street lighting takes the place of swinging single light-bulbs. Fortunately, these changes haven't encroached too far into the mayhem as yet, and south of Al-Azhar the streets are still an absorbingly dirty labyrinth filled with the rickety tables of vendors and hoardes of people browsing in the shadows of Mamluke mosques.

There are literally hundreds of mosques in Cairo – the city of 1000 minarets – and it is difficult for any visitors to know where to begin. Broadly speaking, the most important sights to visit in Islamic Cairo lie in a wide belt to the east of the main Sharia Port Said. Take as much small change with you as you can gather as, although entry to almost all mosques is free, a bit of *baksheesh* is expected if you climb minarets. People might demand E£10 or even E£20, but E£3 is acceptable (E£5 if you have taken a particularly long time). It can also enable you to wheedle your way into sights that are not yet officially open to the public.

Arriving in Islamic Cairo

The easiest way to get to Islamic Cairo is by taxi or microbus. Taxis from the centre should cost around E£5. Public bus services around Al-Azhar have essentially ceased with the government's attempt to lessen congestion in the area. Walking from Downtown is interesting and easy. From **Midan Ataba**, there are two routes. You can either stroll along **Sharia Al-Azhar** (under the flyover) or wander down the fascinating, jam-packed and narrow **Sharia Muski**, which eventually winds up in the **Khan El-Khalili** (both routes take 15-20 minutes).

Etiquette

Islamic Cairo is a particularly conservative area so it's wise to dress especially modestly. Women should wear clothes that cover their legs and arms and should bring along a headscarf for use in mosques. Men should avoid shorts and sleeveless T-shirts. Shoes must be removed for entry into mosques.

Khan El-Khalili

ⓘ *Most shops are shut on Sun, and some shut on Fri.*

Although it also refers to a specific street, Khan El-Khalili is the general name given to the vast maze of individual *souks* that are an essential ingredient of any visit to Cairo. The ultimate market experience, it is a labyrinthine criss-crossing of hundreds of covered alleys and tiny stalls, manned by sharp-witted merchants adept at spotting what catches your eye. The Arab/Islamic system of urban planning traditionally divided the *souks* by professions or guilds and while the system is less rigid than formerly there is still a concentration of one particular trade in a particular area. Khan El-Khalili includes streets that almost exclusively sell gold, silver, copper, perfume, spices, cloth or any one of a number of particular products. Many of the products are manufactured within the *souk*, often in small workshops behind or on top of the shops. If you're lucky or courageous enough to enquire, someone may welcome you in for a look around to see how things are made.

Known to locals simply as 'the Khan', this has been the main *souk* in Cairo since 1382 when it was first created around a caravanserai by Amir Jarkas Al-Khalil, the Master of Horse to the first of the Burji Mamluk Sultans, Al-Zahir Barquq (1382-1389). The caravanserai attracted many foreign and local traders and expanded rapidly to become a base for the city's subversive groups and was consequently frequently raided. Much of the area was rebuilt by Sultan Al-Ashraf Qansuh Al-Ghuri (1501-1517) but it still maintained its role as Cairo's main area for traders and craftsmen. It is essential to bargain because the traders will always start at about double the price they actually expect. It is traditional to respond by offering them about

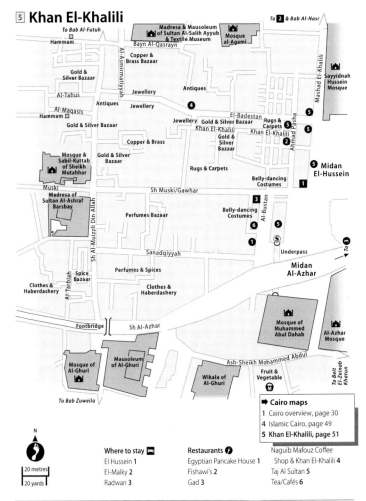

⑤ Khan El-Khalili

To ② & Bab Al-Nasr
To Bab Al-Futuh

Hammam

Madresa & Mausoleum of Sultan Al-Salih Ayyub & Textile Museum

Mosque al-Agami

Bayn Al-Qasrayn

Al-Asmirmaliyyah

Copper & Brass Bazaar

Mashad El-Khalili

Gold & Silver Bazaar

Jewellery

Antiques

Sayyidnah Hussein Mosque

Al-Tahus

Antiques

Jewellery

Al-Maqasis

Hammam

Gold & Silver Bazaar

Jewellery Gold & Silver Bazaar

El-Badestan

Rugs & Carpets ⑤

④

Khan El-Khalili

Ahmad Pasha

⑤

⑤

Copper & Brass

Khan El-Khalili

Gold & Silver Bazaar

②

Mosque & Sabil-Kuttab of Sheikh Mutahhar

Gold & Silver Bazaar

⑤ Midan El-Hussein

Muski

Rugs & Carpets

Belly-dancing Costumes

①

Madresa of Sultan Al-Ashraf Barsbay

Sh Muski/Gawhar

③

Belly-dancing Costumes

Al-Bustan

Sh Al-Muizzi Din Allah

Perfumes Bazaar

⑥ ⑤

To ③

①

$

Underpass

Sanadqiyyah

Midan Al-Azhar

Al-Tarbiah

Spice Bazaar

Perfumes & Spices

Clothes & Haberdashery

Clothes & Haberdashery

Footbridge

Sh Al-Azhar

Mosque of Muhammed Abul Dahab

Al-Azhar Mosque

Ash-Sheikh Mohammed Abdul

Mosque of Al-Ghuri

Mausoleum of Al-Ghuri

Wikala of Al-Ghuri

Fruit & Vegetable

To Beit El-Zeinab Khatun

To Bab Zuweila

➡ **Cairo maps**
1 Cairo overview, page 30
4 Islamic Cairo, page 49
5 Khan El-Khalili, page 51

N

20 metres
20 yards

Where to stay 🛏
El Hussein 1
El-Malky 2
Radwan 3

Restaurants 🍴
Egyptian Pancake House 1
Fishawi's 2
Gad 3

Naguib Mafouz Coffee Shop & Khan El-Khalili 4
Taj Al Sultan 5
Tea/Cafés 6

one third of what they originally quoted. This is not so for precious metals, which are sold by weight, prices for gold and silver being given daily in the paper. On a bracelet for example a small percentage is added for workmanship, and this is the only thing that is negotiable. Antique jewellery is of course more expensive. Today the main area of the *souk* is occupied by tourist shops but a few of the streets to the west are more authentic and much more interesting. For a more baladi (local) feeling there's the Muski: leading west away from the Khan, Sharia Muski gets increasingly crowded to the point where pedestrian traffic has to shuffle along in lanes, cramming sideways to let hand-carts towering with bundles trundle past, while the wares on offer range from pyramids to plastic goods.

Mosque of Al-Azhar ① *See plan, page 52, Sat-Thu 0900-1500, Fri 0900-1100 and 1300-1500. Tip any guides. No bare legs allowed, shawls provided for women.*
On the southwest of Midan El-Hussein, an underpass below busy Sharia Al-Azhar leads to the famous and very influential **Al-Azhar Mosque and University** whose leader, known as the Sheikh Al-Azhar, is appointed for life and is Egypt's supreme theological authority.

The mosque was built in AD 970 and established as a university in AD 988 which, despite a counter-claim by Fes' Qarawiyin Mosque in Morocco, may make it the world's oldest university. With the exception of the main east *liwan*, however, little remains of the original building because additions and modifications were made by successive rulers, including modern buildings to the north, designed to house the university's administration block. The latest addition is an unsightly fence around the outside that seems to serve no purpose at all.

During the Shi'a Fatimid era (AD 969-1171), the university was used as a means to propagate the Shi'a faith in a predominantly Sunni city, but it fell into disrepair under Salah Al-Din and his successor Ayyubids (Sunni Muslim rulers), before being reopened by the Bahri Mamluks (1250-1382) and eventually becoming a bastion of Sunni orthodoxy.

Mosque of Al-Azhar

Not to scale

1 Entrance
2 Gawhar Medersa
3 Aqbugha Medersa
4 Taybars Medersa
5 Sahn
6 Bab Qaitbai (Barber's Gate)
7 Bab al-Muzayyinin
8 Bab al-Abbas
9 Bab al-Maghariba
10 Bab al-Shawam
11 Bab al-Saayidal
12 Bab al-Haramayn
13 Bab al-Shurbah
14 Bab and minaret of Qaitbai
15 Tomb of Sitt Nafisa
16 Tomb of Abdel al-Rahman Karkhuda
17 Toilets
18 Minaret of Qahnsuh al-Ghawri
19 Riwaq of Abbas II
20 Riwaq Al-Hanafiyyah
21 Qibla
22 Mihrab

Islamic Cairo: suggested routes

North from Al-Azhar via the concentration of buildings in the **Qalaoun/Al-Nasir/Barquq complex**, to the **Al-Hakim Mosque** at the north gates of the old city. See page 53.

South from Al-Azhar to the **Al-Muayyad Mosque** that stands at the **Bab Zuweila** gate at the south edge of the old city and the buildings on Sharia Darb Al-Ahmar to the **Sultan Hassan Mosque** and the modern **Al-Rifai Mosque**. See page 61.

West from the Citadel, continuing to the mosques and museums in the imposing fortress and the huge ancient **Ahmed Ibn Tulun Mosque**. See page 74.

To the mosques and tombs in the **City of the Dead**, which lies in the 'Northern Cemetery' to the east of Islamic Cairo. See page 77.

The ancient **Al-Azhar Mosque** and the nearby *souqs* in the **Khan El-Khalili** district are at the centre of modern-day Islamic Cairo.

Later, during the rise in Arab nationalism in the late 19th and early 20th centuries, Al-Azhar became a stronghold for independent thinkers and it was from here that in 1956 President Nasser made his speech against the Suez invasion.

The entrance to the mosque is through the **Barber's Gate** (where students traditionally had their hair shaved), which was built in the second half of the 15th century by Qaitbay. This opens out on to the 10th-century Fatimid *sahn* (courtyard) overlooked by three minarets. With the exception of the Mamluk *madresa* (theological schools) surrounding the *sahn*, most of the buildings date back to the Fatimid period. Take the opportunity to climb one of the five minarets for an excellent view over the surrounding area.

North of Al-Azhar

On the north side of Midan El-Hussein, opposite the Al-Azhar complex, is the **Sayyidnah Hussein Mosque**, Cairo's official mosque where some 10,000 people pray daily and where dignitaries worship on important occasions. This is closed to non-Muslims. This mosque is named after, and contains the head of, the Prophet Mohammed's grandson Hussein. The rest of his body is perhaps in Iraq. He was killed at Karbala in AD 680 at the climax of the struggle that led to the early schism in the Muslim world between the orthodox Sunni (followers of the way) and the Shi'a (party) followers of Ali. Hussein, son of Mohammed's daughter Fatima, was the father of the Prophet's only direct descendants, who revere Hussein as a martyr and a popular saint like his sister Zeinab. His mosque is the focus of his annual *moulid*, one of Cairo's most important, chaotic and intense festivals that is held over a fortnight during the month of Rabi El-Tani, attracting thousands who camp in the streets.

Midan Hussein to Bayn Al-Qasrayn From Midan Hussein, walking 200 m west along Sharia Muski brings you to the intersection with Sharia Al-Muizzli Din Allah. On the southwest corner of the crossroads is the **Madresa of Sultan Al-Ashraf Barsbay** (1422-1437). This liberal and enlightened Mamluk Sultan, originally from the Caucasus, financed his capture of Cyprus in 1426 by turning the spice trade (which is based just to the south of his *madresa*) into a state monopoly. The *madresa* is cruciform in plan with the *sabil-kuttab* near the entrance, marked by a splendid onion-shaped dome. An offset corridor leads into the courtyard containing two marble tombs, those of the wife and the son of the sultan who is himself buried in the Northern Cemetery. Though not remarkable architecturally, the exterior is splendidly striped and the interior a peaceful haven, heady with the scent of spices – still intoxicating from the top of the minaret.

At the northwest corner is the **Mosque and Sabil-Kuttab of Sheikh Mutahhar**, erected in 1744. Turn right at the crossroads and head north along Sharia Al-Muizz passing some of the many goldsmiths and coppersmith shops. These are concentrated in the alleys to the right, including the actual Sharia Khan El-Khalili. If you have time and want to get away from other tourists, strike off into the warren of goldsmiths' stalls on the left of the street where you will happen upon ash-coloured mosques and monumental houses that are not yet part of the restoration programme. If you get lost, just ask anyone to point you back in the direction of Muski or the Khan.

On the right-hand side of the Sharia Al-Muizz, on the site of the former slave market, is the **Madresa and Mausoleum of Sultan Al-Salih Ayyub** (1240-1249) who was the last of the Ayyubid Sultans and the first to introduce the foreign Mamluk slave-soldiers. Look for the minaret set back behind the shops, which at first glance looks as though the top has fallen off but is in fact the only remaining example of an Ayyubid 'pepperpot' or 'incense-burner' crown left in Cairo. The **Sabil-Kuttab of Khesruw Basha** protudes from the restored outer wall, and is free to enter. Further on is Ayyub's mausoleum, a serene final resting place for his wooden cenotaph, with walls enhanced by two beautifully painted and embossed Koranic borders. The domed ceiling contains stained-glass windows and is hung with lamps, and the columns and *mihrab* are of striped black, white and ruby-coloured marble. The *madresa* is special because it was the first to include all four of Egypt's schools of law, while the tomb was the first of any sultans to be placed next to the *madresa* of its founder. Previously, all tombs were built inside the necropolis so this marks the beginning of what was to become the standard Mamluk mosque-*madresa*-mausoleum formula, initiated by Ayyub's wife Shagarat Al-Durr (Tree of Pearls).

Housed in the restored *sabil-kuttab* of Mohamed Ali is the **Textile Museum** ① *daily 0900-1930 (winter), 0900-2200 (summer), entrance E£20, students E£10, no photos*, which illuminates the 7000-year history of weaving in Egypt. The museum is uncrowded and crammed with beautiful and colourful pieces, ranging from pharaonic times to the last days of the royal family. The ground floor starts by displaying linens from ancient Egypt, including gloves from a mummy, a baby's nappy found at Deir Al-Medina in Luxor, and shrouds bearing the image of Osiris. One of the earliest-known textiles is a fragment of linen from Fayoum, dating to 4400 BC, two millennia older than the Giza Pyramids. The ancient weavers also embroidered and decorated the cloths with faience beads, gold and pieces of coloured glass. In the second room, look up to see the restored ceiling. The rich tradition of Coptic weaving is well-represented, with bold colours depicting human figures and stylized leaves and flowers. Look out for the 18th century priest's vestements, decorated with images of the apostles and the virgin and child. The Coptic displays continue on the upper level, and it is clear to see how their traditions were incorporated by the Umayyad weavers, though Christian symbols were replaced by Islamic motifs and scripts. The sultans brought weaving under government control, and commissioned lavish clothing, while Byzantine emperors, Roman popes and the European courts all dressed in Egyptian-made fabrics. Impressive are the pieces of the *qiswa*, the cloth which covers the *ka'aba* in Mecca and was produced in Egypt until the 20th century. These black curtains of embroidered silk could weigh up to half a tonne.

Opposite, with a wonderful unbroken 185-m-long façade, stands an amazing complex of *madresas* founded by three of the most influential medieval sultans, Qalaoun, Al-Nasir and Barquq. This section of the street is known as **Bayn Al-Qasrayn** (Between Two Palaces) because in the Fatimid period the magnificent great Western Palace and Eastern Palace stood on either side. Nothing is left of these now except the name, which also inspired the title of Naguib Mahfouz's first book in his *Cairo Trilogy*, usually translated as 'Palace Walk'. The three buildings have recently opened to the public after a successful restoration process, and are open from 0900-2100 daily (entrance free).

Qalaoun Complex ① *A bit of baksheesh gets you up the minaret*. The earliest and most impressive *maristan-madresa-mausoleum* was built by Sultan Al-Mansur Qalaoun Al-Alfi (1280-1290). Like so many other Mamluk ('possessed') slave-soldiers he was a Kipchak Turk who used the name Al-Alfi because he was originally bought for the high price of 1000 (or *alf*) dinars. He subsequently diluted the influence of his own Kipchaks amongst the Mamluks by importing Circassians whom he billeted in the Citadel. These Burgis Mamluks (*burg* meaning 'tower') were rivals to the Bahri Mamluks (1250-1382) stationed on Roda Island and eventually created their own dynasty (1382-1517). Qalaoun was a constant headache to the Crusaders and eventually died of a fever in 1290 aged 79, on an expedition to recapture Acre.

The complex, built on the site of the Fatimid's Western Palace, only took just 13 months to complete in 1284-1285. It includes a *madresa* and mausoleum to the left and right, respectively, of a 10-m-high corridor that led to the *maristan*. Visit the mosque/*madresa* first, which has Syrian-style glass mosaics on the hood of the *mihrab* and is a beautifully proportioned and impressive space. But save yourself for the beauty of the mausoleum as it's like stepping inside a jewellery box. The restored ceilings are brilliantly coloured and gilded, tinted glass casts subtle light, ancient granite pillars and marble inlays all ornament the interior, while the dome soars 30 m above. The tomb of Qalaoun and his son Al-Nasir Mohammed is in the middle of the room surrounded by a beautifully carved *mashrabiya* screen.

Al-Nasir Complex To the north is the Sultan Al-Nasir Mohammed complex that was started by Sultan Kitbugha in 1295 and finished by Al-Nasir during his second reign in 1304, an era commemorated by over 30 mosques and other public buildings throughout the city. The nine-year-old Mohamed was elected Sultan when Qalaoun's eldest son Khalil was assassinated in 1294, only to be deposed a year later by the Mongol regent Kitbugha. Lajin (1297-1299) forced Kitbugha into exile, but he didn't last long either and was assassinated while playing chess. Following this chapter of 'accidents', Mohammed was restored to the throne, but was kept in terrible conditions by his regent until he escaped to Jordan 10 years later. He eventually returned with a large army the following year, executed his enemies, and ruled unchallenged for another 30 years until his death in 1341.

The complex consists of a mosque, *madresa* and tomb. It is worth going in to see the *qibla* wall, which still has its original decoration and Kufic inscriptions. The fabulous Gothic doorway was filched from one of the Crusader churches at Acre by Al-Nasir's elder brother, Khalil.

Sugar and spice and all things nice

A visit to the spice market (Souk Al-Attarin) is highly recommended both for the visual impact and the tremendous aromas. Anything that could possibly be wanted in the way of herbs, spices, henna, dried and crushed flowers and incense are on display, piled high on the ancient pavements in massive burlap bags or secreted away in tin boxes in various drawers inside. Ask if what you want does not appear to be in stock but do not be fobbed off with old merchandise, fresh spices are always available. Prices are extremely low by Western standards and shopkeepers are prepared to sell small amounts, weighing out the purchase into a little paper cornet. Saffron is the best buy, far cheaper than at home, but sometimes only the local rather than higher-quality Iranian saffron is available. The main street of the spice market runs parallel to Sharia Al-Muizzli Din Allah beginning at the Ghuriyya. Here, many of the shops have been in the same family for over 200 years. Some of the owners are also herbalists (etara), practising traditional medicine and offering cures for everything from bad breath to rheumatism. Cairo's most famous herbalist, however, is Abdul Latif Mahmoud Harraz, 39 Sharia Ahmed Maher, near Bab El-Khalq. Founded in 1885, the shop attracts a devoted following throughout the Middle East.

The Arabic names for the more common herbs and spices are:

Allspice	kebab es-seeny
Arabic gum	mystica
Bay leaf	warra randa
Basil	rihan
Cardamon	habbahan
Cayenne	shatta
Celery salt	boudra caraffs
Chervil leaves	kozbarra
Chilli	filfil ahmar
Cinnamon	erfa
Cloves	orumfil
Coriander	kosbara
Cumin	kamoon
Fennel	shamar
Ginger	ginzabeel
Horseradish	figl baladi
Mace	bisbassa
Marjoram	bardakosh
Mint	naanaa
Oregano	zaatar
Paprika	filfil ahmar roumi
Peppercorns	filfil eswed
Rosemary	hassa liban
Saffron	zaa'faran
Sage	maryameya
Savory	stoorya
Sesame	semsem
Tarragon	tarkhoun
Turmeric	korkom

Barquq Complex This is followed to the north by the *madresa* and tomb that make up the Sultan Barquq complex, built in 1384-1386. The marble entrance and the silver-encrusted bronze-plated door are very impressive and lead through an offset corridor to the *sahn*, which has four *liwans* arranged in a cruciform shape. The *qibla liwan*, to the east, is divided into three aisles by four massive pharaonic columns that support beautifully carved ceilings painted blue and gold. Upstairs there are cells for the Sufi monks who once inhabited the building. From the *madresa* a door leads to the marble-walled mausoleum where Sultan Barquq was originally buried before being transferred to the mausoleum specially built by his son Al-Nasir Farag in the city's Northern Cemetery (see below).

Sultan Al-Zahir Barquq (1382-1389 and 1390-1399), whose name means 'plum', reigned twice and was the founder of the dynasty of Circassian slave-soldiers who became the Burgis Mamluk rulers of Egypt. He was reportedly an enlightened ruler, who admired piety and intelligence and surrounded himself with learned scholars, before dying of pneumonia aged 60 in 1399.

Palaces and madrasas Besides the Qalaoun/Al-Nasir/Barquq complex, there are a number of other interesting, if less important, buildings on and near the east side of the street on the route north to the Al-Hakim mosque. This area, which is the heart of Islamic Cairo, is definitely worth exploring if you have a full day.

Directly opposite the Qalaoun complex is Sharia Beit Al-Qadi. About 40 m down on the left-hand side stands the modern-looking house, No 19, marked with a green plaque. Visitors should knock to be shown around in return for a little *baksheesh*, someone will find the key if it is not open. This is the remains of a palace built in 1350 but better known as the **House of Uthman Kathuda** who restored it during the 18th century.

Further north opposite Barquq's complex are the remains of the **Palace of Amir Bashtak** (Al-Nasir's son-in-law) built in 1334-1339 and a fine example of the domestic architecture of the time. The original five-storey structure has been reduced to two and the windows in the rather plain façade are covered with *mashrabiyya*. Access is via an offset courtyard to the left of the complex. After you have had a peek at the courtyard, continue down the alley through the door at the end, where Mohamed Ali's *fuul* cart lies waiting in case you need some sustenance (see Restaurants, page 112).

Sabil-Kuttab of Abd Al-Rahman Kutkhuda ① *Daily 0830-1730, tickets E£10, students E£5.* There used to be many of the these Ottoman-influenced *sabil-kuttab* throughout Cairo, which combine a water supply for the public at street level and a Koranic school in the building above. A fair few remain but this is a particularly elegant example, built in 1744 by a powerful *amir* seeking absolution for his former sins. Standing on a triangular piece of land where the road forks in two, the building is tall and slim. A beautifully carved timber screen on the upper storey protects the *kuttab* on its three open sides and the balcony (now unfortunately glassed in) permits a good view. Below, the double arches are supported by delicate columns. The *sabil* is entirely faced with gorgeous aquamarine and turquoise Syrian tiles, including a depiction of the *Kaba'a* at Mecca. The circular well from which the water supply was drawn is tucked away in the little room to the back of the sabil. If you don't feel like paying, you can squint through the glass from the street to get an idea, but then you'll miss out on the exquisitely painted ceilings in the *kuttab* above.

Mosque of Al-Aqmar About 75 m further north on the right up the main road is the Mosque of Al-Aqmar that was built in 1121-1125 by the Fatimid Vizier of Khalifa Al-Amir (1101-1131). It was originally at the northeast corner of the great eastern Fatimid palace. It is particularly important for three reasons: it was the first Cairo mosque with a façade following the alignment of the street, rather than the *qibla* wall, so that its ground plan was adjusted to fit into an existing urban environment; it was the first to have a decorated stone façade, the colour giving it its name, which means moonlight; and it introduced the shell motif and the stalactite, which subsequently became favourites in Cairo, into architectural styles.

The mosque has been restored over the centuries. Amir Yalbugha Al-Salami restored the *minbar*, *mihrab* and ablution area in 1393 and added the minaret in 1397. The minaret was apparently removed in 1412 because it had started leaning, but the current structure includes the original first storey, which is made of brick covered with unusual carved stucco decorated with chevron patterns. Because the street level has risen since the mosque was built there are steps down to the entrance, which is offset from the main part of the mosque. Despite its importance and unique features, the original interior of the mosque is unspectacular. Around the base of the almost square *sahn* the arches bear Koranic verses in the early angular and unpointed Kufic script on an arabesque background.

Beit Al-Suhaymi ① *Daily 0900-1700 or until 1500 during Ramadan, E£30, students E£15, entrance includes 2 other buildings: the Beit Kharazati next door and the Beit El-Gaafar nearby.* Take the next right-hand turn for a detour to Darb Al-Asfar, a highly renovated street that presumably gives an idea of what the whole of Gamaliya will look like once the restorers have finished their job. Here is the Beit Al-Suhaymi, built in 1648 and 1796 and inhabited until 1961, one of the finest examples of a luxurious Mamluk mansion in the whole of the city. Beautifully restored, it has a lovely courtyard and a *haramlik* (harem) for the women with superb tiling and a domed bathroom. It is the wonderfully atmospheric venue for weekly folk music and songs, plus occasional special events and performances particularly during Ramadan.

Returning to the main street and continuing north, one reaches the **Mosque and Sabil-Kuttab of Suleyman Agha Al-Silahdar** ① *0900-1700, during Ramadan 0800-1500*, built in 1837-1839 by one of Mohammed Ali's ministers who also built many other *sabils* throughout the city. The style of the building is very much influenced by the contemporary style in Istanbul including the minaret with an Ottoman-style cylindrical shaft and pointed conical top. It is now being restored.

Mosque of Al-Hakim ① *Entrance free, but aggressive demands for* baksheesh *to climb the minarets. Almost as good views can be had from the top of the Northern Walls.* At the north end of Sharia Muizz is the giant Mosque of Al-Hakim, named after the third Fatimid caliph, abutting the **North Wall** of the old city of Fustat and commemorating its most notorious ruler. It was begun in AD 990 by the Shi'a Muslim Fatimid Khalifa Al-Aziz and was eventually finished some 23 years later by his son who took the name **Al-Hakim bi-Amr Allah** (Ruler by God's Command) and ruled between AD 996-1021.

Possibly having a Christian wife was the reason why his reportedly tolerant and humane father Al-Aziz had been more forbearing towards Christians and Jews than towards the indigenous Sunni Muslim population. In contrast his son was intolerant of everyone (see box, page 59). With such a colourful history, the enormous mosque itself is actually rather plain. It is organized around a large central *sahn* and built of bricks with a large porch in the traditional Fatimid style. It has been restored many times throughout the centuries, notably after the major earthquake in 1302 and by Sultan Al-Hassan in 1359. Originally the two minarets stood separate from the walls; the huge salients, added in 1010 to strengthen them, are in fact hollow shells. After the 14th century it was converted to house Crusader prisoners-of-war, then was used as a stable by Salah Al-Din, during the French occupation it was a fortified warehouse, and in the mid-19th century it stored items destined for the Museum of Islamic Art. Since 1980 the mosque has been

Al-Hakim – the vanishing despot

In AD 996 at the age of 11 Al-Hakim succeeded his father as the second Egyptian Fatimid Khalifa and began a despotic reign. At the age of 15 he had his tutor assassinated and started his extremely cruel and relentless persecution of Christians, Jews, Sunni Muslims, women and dogs. He prohibited any Christian celebrations and had the Church of the Holy Sepulchre in Jerusalem demolished. He also prohibited Sunni ceremonies and tried to established Shi'a Islam as the only form of Islam. Women were forbidden to leave their homes and, in order to enforce this, cobblers were not permitted to make or sell women's shoes. At one time all of Cairo's dogs were exterminated because their barking annoyed him. Merchants who were found to have cheated their customers were summarily sodomized by his favourite Nubian slave while Al-Hakim stood on their head. Wine, singing, dancing and chess were also prohibited and the punishments for disobeying these laws were very severe and usually resulted in a gruesome death.

His erratic rule, with laws often changing overnight, led to tensions within Fustat/Cairo, particularly between the various religious communities. In 1020, the news that Al-Hakim was about to proclaim that he was a manifestation of Allah provoked serious riots to which

he responded by sending in his Sudanese troops to burn down the city where they clashed not only with the civilians, but also the Turkish and Berber soldiers. An alternative story is that one particular quarter of Fustat was torched because he thought that was where his favourite sister Sitt Al-Mulk (Lady of Power) took her lovers, but when she was proved to be a virgin by the midwives he examined the ruins and asked: "Who ordered this?" Whatever the truth, he then sent his chief theologian Al-Darazi to Syria for safety where he is believed to have originated the theology of the Druze who consider Al-Hakim to be divine.

Despite his ruthless public acts Al-Hakim's personal life was very abstemious and he was a very generous alms-giver. He took to riding around the city and surrounding countryside on a donkey with only a couple of servants but disappeared in February 1021. Following the discovery of his knife-slashed robe, it is believed he was murdered, possibly on the instructions of Sitt Al-Mulk with whom he apparently argued because of her refusal to begin an incestuous marriage with him. The fact that his body was never discovered led the Druze to believe that he had retreated from the world to return at a later date, while the Copts believe that he had a vision of Jesus, repented and became a monk.

---

practically rebuilt in white marble by the Indian-based Bohra sect of Ismaili Muslims, who claim direct spiritual descent from the Fatimid imams whom they worship.

The Northern Walls ⓘ *Keys and a 'guide' can be found if you enquire by Bab Al-Nasr, at the wooden shack just south of the gate. E£5 baksheesh should cover things.* The northern walls and gates of the Fatimid city are a masterpiece of military architecture (although they were were never actually put to the test by a siege) and are monumentally impressive when viewed from the main street beyond. At present, access is through the square-towered **Bab Al-Nasr** (Gate of

Victory), where French troops that were garrisoned here during Napoleon's occupation renamed the towers – 'Tour Juien', 'Courbin' and 'Pascal' are neatly engraved above the doorways. From the towers there are views out to the Bab Al-Nasr cemetery opposite, an organic mixture of tombs and ramshackle houses. Walking the dark 200-m-long stretch of wall between Bab Al-Nasr to Bab Al-Futuh you appreciate how soldiers could move between the two towers under cover, stealthily firing arrows through slits in the walls. Towards the end of the tunnel, a block of masonry on the right is carved with pharaonic inscriptions and there are more on the stairs showing processions of oxen and a hippopotamus, pieces of Memphis being reused. The round towers of **Bab Al-Futuh** (Open Gate) are a mirror of Bab Zuweila at the southern boundary of the Fatimid City, just discernable in the distance from the top of the gate. Walk back to Bab Al-Nasr along the top of the wall, noting holes in the floor through which boiling oil could be poured on enemies, and to get a good look at Al-Hakim's mosque and minarets.

Sharia Al-Gamaliya Taking you south back to Midan Al-Hussein, Sharia Al-Gamaliya has several fine old buildings but many of them are works in progress and will be open to the public in the near future. The **Khanqah of Beybars Al-Gashankir**, on the left side, is the oldest sufi monastery in Cairo dating from 1310. Beybars was sultan for only a year, and when Al-Nasir Mohammed came back to power he had him flogged and strangled, and obliterated his name from the façade of the khanqah. If you can get inside, the marbling is particularly beautiful, otherwise look for the bulbous dome of the exterior and the rare turquoise tiles on top of the minaret.

The **Madresa-Mausoleum of Tatar Al-Higaziya** is in a small street that connects Sharia Al-Gamalia with Midan Beit Al-Qadi. Tatar was the daughter of Sultan Al-Nasir Mohammed, the sister of Sultan Hassan and the wife of the Amir Baktimur Al-Higazi. Little else is known about her except that she died of the plague in 1360, yet her tomb is still visited by women seeking her blessing. Built in two phases, the mausoleum for her murdered husband dates from 1347 and the palace itself was converted into a *madresa* in 1360, which explains the irregular shape.

Entrance to the building leads via a porch with a lovely ceiling into the *sahn*. The octagonal minaret to the southwest of the *sahn* has been missing its top for over a century. Access to the minaret, the ablution area and storage areas are all via doors off the *liwans*. The ribbed stone dome over the mausoleum, one of the earliest in Cairo, is on the corner of two streets and passers-by can solicit a blessing or invoke a prayer via the open windows. The restoration work carried out in the 1980s was done with care and consideration.

At the next crossroads are a couple of towering *wikalas*, and standing beneath them gives a sense that this alley was indeed once the second-most major thoroughfare of the medieval city. On the west side, the **Wikala Al-Bazara** ① *daily 0900-1700, E£20, students E£10*, though largely rebuilt, is a good example of the layout of the caravanserai. Downstairs, the animals were stabled and goods stored, while the merchants slept on the upper floors. Further east is the void where once stood the Ottoman **Musafirkhana Palace** (House of Guests). What used to be a rather fine rambling building, constructed between 1779 and 1788 by the merchant Mohammed Muharram, burnt to a crisp in 1998. There is talk of rebuilding it, but it probably won't happen for at least another decade.

The hammam

A visit to the hammam or Turkish bath is still part of life for many Egyptians. Some Egyptian families have no bathing facilities at home and rely on the public hammam. A ritual purification of the body is essential before Muslims can perform prayers, and even for the well-off classes in the days before bathrooms, the 'major ablutions' were generally done at the hammam. Segregation of the sexes is of course the rule at the hammam: some establishments are open only for women, others only for men, while others have a shift system (mornings and evenings for the men, all afternoon for women). In the old days, the hammam, along with the local *zaouia* or saint's shrine, was an important place for women to gather and socialize, and even pick out a potential wife for a son.

In the older parts of the cities, the hammam is easily recognizable by the characteristic colours of its door. A passage leads into a large changing room-cum-post-bath rest area, equipped with masonry benches for lounging on and (sometimes) small wooden lockers. Here one undresses under a towel.

This is the procedure. First into the hot room: 5-10 minutes with your feet in a bucket of hot water will see you sweating nicely, and you can then move back to the raised area where the masseurs are at work. After the expert removal of large quantities of dead skin, you go into one of the small cabins or *mathara* to finish washing. (Before doing this, catch the person bringing in dry towels, so that they can bring yours to you when you're in the *mathara*.) For women, in addition to a scrub and a wash, there may be the pleasures of an epilation with *sokar*, an interesting mix of caramelized sugar and lemon. Men can undergo a *taksira*, which involves much pulling and stretching of the limbs. And remember, allow plenty of time to cool down, while reclining in the changing area.

In Cairo, you can visit the 18th-century **Hammam El-Malatili**, 40 Sharia Amir El-Gyushi (0700-1900) or the back alley **Hammam El-Tabbali**, 1 km east of Ramses on Bayn El-Haret. There are also a few hammams around the Bab Zuweila. Women can visit the **Hammam Beshtak**, a cleaner public bath, at Sharia El-Silah (1000-1700; men 1800-0800).

South of Al-Azhar

The lanes south from Al-Azhar mosque have a number of very interesting buildings including the **Mosque of Sultan Al-Muayyad Sheikh** at the medieval **Bab Zuweila**. Further to the south of Fustat is the **Sultan Hassan Mosque** and the much more modern **Al-Rifai Mosque**, which stand side by side below the mighty **Citadel** (see page 70). One can then head west to the huge and very old **Mosque of Ahmed Ibn Tulun** and the nearby **Gayer-Anderson House**. Allow a minimum of half a day to take in all the sights on a tour of the southern part of Islamic Cairo.

Butneya Immediately to the south of Al-Azhar is an area known as **Butneya**, once notorious as the base for Cairo's underworld where drugs were openly traded by powerful and locally popular gangsters. After a major crackdown in 1988 most of them left, but the area is still home to minor local gangs who tend to prey on shops, restaurants and middle-class Egyptians rather than on tourists. Directly behind Al-Azhar mosque is the

Wikala and Sabil-Kuttab of Sultan Qaitbay, the first of two hostels founded by this sultan, found along the alley that terminates in a little square where three houses are open to the public. The most rewarding is first on the left, the **Beit El-Zeinab Khatoun** ① *daily 0900-1700, E£20, students E£10*, which dates from 1468, was rebuilt in 1713, and restored in 1996. It is worth visiting for its excellent views over Al-Azhar and to appreciate the function of *mashrabiya* windows, designed to let the breezes cool water in earthenware pots placed in the screens. Opposite, across the square, is the **Beit Al-Harawi** ① *daily 0900-1700, E£20, students E£10*, with a grand ground-floor reception room, handsomely decorated and adorned with Koranic inscriptions. Concerts are frequently held here, check www.weekly-ahram.org.eg. The adjoining **Beit El-Set Wasela** has recently opened to the public after being largely rebuilt. It is now a cultural venue used for performances of Arabic poetry; it is free to wander around the warren-like structure, and although most rooms are empty there is a beautiful painting on the interior walls. Also on the square is a very chic homeware and interiors shop, while back on the alley behind Al-Azhar are the most famous book-binders in the city, both worth having a browse through on the way past (see Shopping, page 121).

The Wikala, Mosque-Madresa and Mausoleum of Al-Ghuri ① *Wikala 0900-1800, E£15 students E£8; Mosque-Madresa 0900-2000, entrance free although* baksheesh *very much expected; Mausoleum and Sabil-Kuttab, 0900-1700, E£20 students E£10*. Immediately to the south of the Al-Azhar complex are a few of the 20 remaining *wikalas* (hostels for merchants that were usually above a bonded warehouse for their goods), which numbered over 200 in the 1830s. The restored **Wikala of Sultan Al-Ashraf Qansuh Al-Ghuri**, originally built in 1504, is down the backstreet off the southwest corner of Al-Azhar. Four floors high, the façade has an impressive array of windows and the rooms upstairs where traders from around the world would have slept, have now been converted into workshops for artisans; a selection of handicrafts made by artisans in for sale in the building next door. It is best to come on a Monday, Wednesday or Saturday night when it's the venue for a free Sufi concert.

Back on Sharia Al-Azhar, next to the footbridge, is the Ghuriyya, the magnificent complex of Sultan Al-Ashraf Qansuh Al-Ghuri (1501-1517), which is bisected by a continuation of Sharia Al-Muizzli Din Allah. The complex is made up of the **mausoleum and sabil-kuttab** to the east of the street and the **mosque-madresa** to the west. Built in 1504-1505, this was the last great Mamluk public building before the Ottoman conquest. Al-Ghuri died of a stroke, aged about 76, during a battle near Aleppo against the Turks, who then immediately invaded and captured Egypt to begin their lengthy rule from 1517 to 1805. Because Al-Ghuri's body was never found he could not be buried in his magnificent and hugely expensive tomb and his successor, Tumanbey, who was hanged to death from the Bab Zuweila, occupied it in his place. The mausoleum's interior of black and white marble appears almost art deco, the floor is a patchwork of patterns, and the walls are carved in an arabesque design. Open the wooden doors in the walls to reveal the rich green and red paintwork on the insides. The dome up above was the crux of the restoration process. Having already collapsed three times since it was first built, the current project opted for a flat drum-topped solution that can be seen from the roof but not from below. The adjacent room, now also used for concerts, has an impressive wooden *khankah* dome where stained-glass windows allow light onto the astonishing cedar wood ceilings. From the *sabil-kuttab* you can climb up to the roof to look at the

Adhan – the call to prayer

Listening to the first call to prayer just before the sun begins to rise is an unforgettable experience. This is known as the *adhan* and is performed by the *muezzin*, originally by the strength of his own voice from near the top of the minaret but today is probably a recording timed to operate at a particular hour.

There is no fixed tune, but in Egypt there is one particular rhythm used all over the country for the *adhan*. The traditional Sunni *adhan* consists of seven phrases, with two additional ones for the morning prayer. There are some variations that the well-tuned ear will pick up.

1 Allahu Akbar (Allah is most great) is intoned four times. This phrase is called *al takbir*.

2 Ashhadu anna la ilah ill'-Allah (I testify that there is no god besides Allah) is intoned twice.

3 Ashhadu anna Muhammadan rasul Allah (I testify that Mohammed is the apostle of Allah) is intoned twice. This and the preceeding phrase are called the *shihada*, a confession of faith.

4 Hayya 'ala 'l-salah (come to prayer) is intoned twice.

5 Hayya 'ala'l-falah (come to salvation) is intoned twice. This and the preceeding phrase are called *tathwib*.

6 Allahu Akbar is intoned twice.

7 La ilah ill'Allah (there is no god besides Allah) is intoned once.

The two additions to the morning prayer are: **Al-salatu khayr min Al-nawm** (Prayer is better than sleep), which is intoned twice between the fifth and sixth phrases, and **Al-salatu wa'l-salam 'alayka ya rasul Allah** (Benediction and peace upon you, Oh Apostle of Allah) intoned after the seventh phrase.

---

clothes market below and admire the mosque opposite, which gives a real sense of passing back through the centuries.

After restoration, the stripy exterior of the mosque-*madresa* is stunning and once again looks like David Roberts' iconic painting from 1839. Inside the mosque (women have to cover their heads), the original stained-glass windows and exquisite marbles are a feast for the eyes. It's possible to watch prayer-time from the balcony above the women's section at the rear, and from the minaret (*baksheesh* will be expected to unlock the door) the views over Al-Azhar and all the way to the Citadel are fantastic.

Between Ghuriyya and Bab El-Zuweila The stretch of **Sharia Al-Muizz li-Din Allah** between the massive monuments of Al-Ghuri has been re-roofed in accordance with its original appearance when it was the site of the exotic silk market. Today mainly household goods and women's clothes are sold in the shops and stalls, throngs of ladies peruse underwear and crockery while motorbikes weave in between. Each section of this thoroughfare, Islamic Cairo's main street, was named after the merchandise sold in that particular stretch. For example the fruit-sellers had their own mosque, the **Fakahani Mosque** (rebuilt in 1735), about 200 m down the street on the left-hand side. Make a detour by walking left from its northwest corner and then left again where, 70 m to the east at No 6, is the **House of Gamal Al-Din Al-Dhahabi** ① *daily 0900-1700, E£10, students E£5,* Cairo's richest gold merchant in 1637 when this beautiful house was built. After restoration, you can now visit the peaceful courtyard with a central fountain and see the finely painted wooden ceilings and magnificent inlaid marble dadoes of the interior rooms. Back to the south of the mosque, is the ornate **Sabil-Kuttab of Tusun Pasha** ① *daily 0900-1700, E£10, students E£5*, built in his name by his father Mohammed Ali Pasha in 1820. From here the south gates of the ancient city are just ahead. Before going through the gates turn left at the *sabil-kuttab*. About 75 m along the side street is an old 18th-century men's bath-house known as **Hammam As-Sukariyah,** which was originally owned by a rich woman who also owned the nearby *wikala* and *sabil* of Nafisah Bayda. Although, like the other remaining bath-houses in the city, it is no longer a den of vice, it is still an interesting place to visit and relax. Today it helps the local community by allowing its fire for heating the water to be used to cook *fuul mudammas* (beans) for the locals' breakfast.

Bab Zuweila ① *Daily 0830-1700, E£15, students E£8.* The Bab Zuweila, built by Badr Al-Gamali in 1092 when Fatimid fortifications were being reinforced, was one of the three main gates in the city walls. At 20 m high, with a 4.8-m-wide multi-storey arch between two solid stone towers topped by twin minarets, it presents a beautiful and impressive sight particularly from the south. It is named after mercenaries from the Al-Zuweila tribe of Berbers who were stationed in the nearby barracks. The gate was soon inside the city following the successive expansions and Salah Al-Din's construction of larger walls further out from the centre. Cairo was in effect divided into two with the inner walls still in existence and both sets of gates locked at night.

Bab Zuweila also has a more popular history linked to the annual caravans departing both to Mecca and the south, which the caliph used to watch depart from his window. It was not only the location of street performers including snake-charmers, storytellers and dancers, but after the 15th century it also became the site of grisly public executions. Common criminals were beheaded, garrotted or impaled, while cheating merchants were hanged from hooks or rope. Defeated Mamluk Sultans, including the last one in 1517, were hanged and sometimes nailed to the doors. Well into the 20th century, sick people came to Bab Zuweila to be cured by miraculous healings worked by the spirit of a saint. They would tie bits of clothing or an offending tooth to the knobs of the gate and rub their foreheads and chests against it, while praying to the saint, Zuweila. From the top of the minarets there is an excellent view over the surrounding area and the adjacent mosque.

Mosque of Sultan Al-Muayyad Sheikh Immediately to the west of the gate is the Mosque of Sultan Al-Muayyad Sheikh (1412-1421) built on the site of the old Kazanat Al-Shamaii prison. Al-Muayyad had been incarcerated here on a number of occasions because of his love of alcohol when he was a Mamluk slave-soldier. On being released after one particularly long and unpleasant stretch, he vowed to replace the prison with a mosque, which he began in 1415 after becoming Sultan.

The mosque, now repaired and restored, is sometimes known as the Red Mosque because of the colour of its external walls. It was one of the last to be built in the ancient large enclosure style before the Turkish style was adopted as the norm. The superb bronze-plated wooden entrance doors leading to the mosque were originally intended for the Sultan Hassan Mosque but were purchased by Al-Muayyad and installed here. The entrance leads into a vestibule with an ornate stalactite ceiling. From the vestibule, the door on the left leads to Al-Muayyad's mausoleum and marble tomb with Kufic inscription, while nearby is the tomb of his son, Ibrahim, who died in 1420.

Down a little alley behind the mosque is a large and elegant building that looks like a small palace but is in fact the **Hammam Al-Muayyad** bath-house, built in 1420. This has fallen into disrepair and is now often flooded. The area between the two is known as Bab El-Khalq after a medieval gate that has long since vanished, and in the weeks before the start of Ramadan the shops here display row upon row of shiny lanterns in every possible size, shape and colour. The iconic *fanous* (lantern) is an Egyptian tradition that goes back to the time of the Fatimids and, while a large proportion are now imported from China and play absurd tunes and 'dance', traditional metal and glass designs are still hand-fashioned from old tin cans in tiny workshops.

From here a 20-minute walk or a five-minute taxi west of Bab Zuweila along Sharia Ahmed Maher brings you to the Museum of Islamic Art.

The Museum of Islamic Art ① *Junction of Sharia Port Said and Sharia Qala'a equidistant between Midan Ataba and the Bab Zuweila, Daily 0800-1700, entrance E£50, students E£25, T02-2364 7822, T02-3390 9390. No photography; bags must be left at the entrance.*
This museum underwent lengthy renovations (various upsets delayed the restoration, from electrical fires to the collapse of its foundations when an ill-conceived extra floor was built) and reopened in October 2010. It contains the rarest and most extensive collection of Islamic works of art in the world. It was originally established in the courtyard of the Mosque of Al-Hakim (see page 58) in 1880 but it was moved to the present building in 1903.

The recently re-opened Islamic Art Museum is a triumph. Carefully chosen exhibits from the museum's extensive store are displayed in a tasteful, uncluttered environment. The walls are a muted grey with white accents and pierced metal lamps resembling bird cages are hung in profusion. There has been great attention to detail in the refit, even the modern blinds echo traditional Islamic design.

From the ticket barrier, steps lead up to a small display area where a beautiful eighth-century Quran in Kufic script is on show. Around the walls are well-written information panels putting the periods in Egypt's history that are represented in the museum into context. The right side of the museum showcases items in chronological order, in rooms which encircle a 15th-century sunken fountain and an intricately decorated wooden ceiling panel. Passing a display case of enamelled glass mosque lamps leads you into a room of Umayyad and Abbasid items. Look out for the deeply carved stucco and wood friezes showing birds and a ninth-century coffin fragment inlaid with bone and ebony. Three rooms of Fatimid artefacts follow, with intricately decorated wood panels. In the final Fatimid room are two wonderfully carved 12th-century *mihrabs* (niches which show the direction of Mecca) and on the end wall is the original stucco *mihrab* from Ibn Tulun mosque. From here, you can exit to the courtyard, passing between a pair of elaborate door panels, to view the superb collection of *mashrabiyya* attached to the side of the building and perhaps visit the courtyard café.

Re-enter to rejoin galleries dedicated to the art of the Mamluks. Here, glass cases gather together colourful potsherds, brass ewers and small items of furniture. Most striking is a 14th-century Quran box/table inlaid with ivory and ebony. On the walls are framed panels of vivid, blue tiles decorated with plants, flowers and geometric shapes. The next Mamluk room contains fragments of ceramic bowls and tiles with designs including a bird and a deer. The two curved steel swords with gilt inlay and intricate calligraphy on the blades belonging to Al-Ghouri and Tumanbey are a highlight of this room. The final room on this side of the museum showcases carved wooden pieces, including an elaborate 14th-century *minbar* (pulpit) inlaid with ivory and bone. Leave here, passing a marble door which was a gift from the King of Afghanistan and more exquisitely coloured tile panels, to return to the central gallery.

The second half of the museum is arranged thematically. After the collection of Ottoman ceramics and gold coins, turn left to follow the rooms in a clockwise direction. The first room is dedicated to science and medicine; beautiful pages from illuminated Arab manuscripts on herbs are displayed, among other medical paraphernalia. Look out for the Iranian paper-thin cotton shirt covered with Quranic talismans, and a rich blood-red agate bowl. The next room is also science-related and showcases three complicated 18th-century Ottoman sundials, intricate astrolabes, compasses and hour glasses. Some stained-glass windows are backlit to reveal their true complexity, while an enormous stucco facade in the shape of a *mihrab* hangs over the sunken fountain. In the next room look for sections from a fountain decorated with highly realistic catfish. A glass case of metal flasks leads to a room exhibiting a profusion of ewers, mosque lamps and *mashrabiyya*. Wood and marble panels show examples of both Kufic and Cursive script, including deeds of ownership, carved on panels over 2 m long. Two rooms of delicate and exquisite textiles from Iran, Turkey, Yemen, Iraq and Egypt follow. Wool, cotton, silk, linen and silver thread are all used in the collection of carpets and tapestries. A large 17th-century Persian carpet made of wool lies under a finely carved ceiling panel. In the room to the left carved tombstones show extraordinarily skilled calligraphy. The majority of the stones are made of marble, but two striking basalt blocks from the 12th-century stand out. A giant wooden cenotaph from the Mosque of Al-Hussein is also on show. Complete Mamluk and Ottoman tombs are surrounded by cases of beautifully gilded manuscripts. Also notable are the 17th-century ceramic panels showing the Haram Al-Sharif in Mecca. Vibrant panels of rich blue-green, 14th-century Iranian tiles are on the wall. Exit this gallery and walk past a huge, ornate carved wooden panel with a built-in Quran niche to your right. This is from Rashid (Rosetta) and dates from the 17th century. On your left four exquisite, 18th-century jewellery boxes from India inlaid with ivory can be seen. They have many tiny drawers and compartments and show such a high level of craftsmanship that in any other museum they might be the highlight. Finally, walk through the long gallery (leading back to the entrance), which is dedicated to works of art from Iran. Highlights include exquisitely inlaid 17th-century door panels, metal lamps, coffee pots and mirrors, alongside bird-shaped incense burners. Particularly fetching are the bowls decorated with animals, depicting lifelike camels and delicately painted human figures. A large 13th-century, hammered and inlaid copper alloy candlestick is decorated with a line of ducks around its top and lions round the base.

Bab Zuweila to the Tentmakers From the south of Bab Zuweila there are two routes you can take to reach the **Sultan Hassan** and **Al-Rifai mosques** that stand north of the Citadel. One is to continue straight along what is officially known as Sharia Al-Muizzli Din Allah but which, like so many other long roads, changes its name in different sections and at this point is also known as Sharia Al-Khiyamiyya, or the Tentmakers' Bazaar because of its colourful fabrics market. After about 1 km you reach a major crossroads where you should turn left (southeast) along Sharia Al-Qala'a, which leads to the rear of the two mosques. A much more interesting route includes a few nearby sites on Sharia Al-Khiyamiyya before heading east along Sharia Darb Al-Ahmar, after which the whole area is named, towards the Citadel.

Immediately south of the gates are two buildings that are bisected by Sharia Al-Khiyamiyya. To the west is the *zawiya* (Sufi monastery) and *sabil* (public fountain) of **Sultan Al-Nasir Farag** (1405-1412) who was Barquq's son and successor (now open to the public). To the east is the much more magnificent **Mosque of Vizier Al-Salih Tala'i**, which was both the last Fatimid mosque and, when it was built in 1160, was the country's first suspended mosque resting on top of a series of small vaulted shops which, with the rise in the street level, are now in the basement. Tala'i reportedly died regretting the construction of the mosque because, being directly outside the walls of the city, it could be used as a fortress by an enemy.

The great earthquake of 1303 destroyed the minaret, which was restored together with the rest of the mosque by Amir Baktimur Al-Gukandar (Polo-Master) and subsequently in 1440, 1477 and lastly and very badly in the 1920s after the minaret had collapsed yet again.

The entrance porch, with its large portico and an arcade of keel-arches raised on ancient columns with Corinthian capitals, is unique in Cairo. The decoration around the entrance is, however, similar in style to the earlier Al-Aqmar mosque. The porch's *mashrabiyya* dates from the first restoration and the bronze facings on the exterior door are also from 1303 while the carvings on the inside of the door are a copy of the original that is now in the Islamic Museum.

The highlight of the interior is the exquisite *minbar*, the fourth oldest in Egypt and a very fine example of Mamluk wood carving, above which is the first appearance in a Cairo mosque of a wind vent (*malqaf*), which was an ingenious early Islamic form of air conditioning. In the northeast *qibla liwan* the tie-beams, which are inscribed with Koranic inscriptions in floriated Kufic script, are original although the ceiling is modern.

Tentmakers' Bazaar to Safiya Mosque Further south down the street is what is probably the city's best preserved example of a **roofed market** which, because of the multitude of coloured printed fabrics sold here, is known as the **Tentmakers' Bazaar**. Slightly further along the street is the **Madresa-Mosque of Amir Gani-Bak Al-Ashrafi**, which was built in 1426 and is named after a favourite of Sultan Al-Ashraf Barsbay. Gani-Bak's meteoric rise to *amir* in 1422 naturally created many enemies, who poisoned him at the age of 25. He was such a favourite that the Sultan had his body transferred to a tomb in his own Eastern Cemetery complex. Although the mosque has similarities to a number of other Mamluk mosques of the same period and despite the loss of both a coloured marble lintel over the portal door and the windows, its decoration even now is more ornate than other examples. Nearby is what little remains of the **Souk Al-Surugiyyah** (saddle-makers' market).

The Turkish-style **Mosque of Malika Safiya**, built in 1610, lies to the west in a small street off Sharia Mohammed Ali. It is one of the few mosques in Cairo to bear a woman's name although Queen Safiya acquired it deviously rather than constructing it herself. Safiya, who was from the noble Venetian family of Baffo, was captured by pirates along with a large party of other women in 1575 while on their way to Corfu. Because of her beauty she was presented to the Sublime Porte where she became chief consort of Sultan Murad III. He made her his *Sultana Khasski* (favourite) which gave her considerable power and influence, increased further when she produced Murad's first-born son. At her son's death Safiya was exiled to a harem where she lived in obscurity until she died in 1618.

Darb Al-Ahmar Returning to Bab Zuweila and turning right (east) into Sharia Darb Al-Ahmar (Red Road) there is an fascinating and unspoilt 1.25-km walk to the Citadel. The street gets its name from the incident in May 1805 when the Mamluks were tricked into going to discuss their grievances with Mohammed Ali Pasha. He had them slaughtered as they travelled 'Between the Two Palaces' and their heads sent to Istanbul as a demonstration of his power and independence. In March 1811, they fell for a similar trick on the same street when 470 Mamluks and their retainers were persuaded into going to a banquet at the Citadel and were slaughtered on their return near Bab Zuweila.

About 150 m after the Bab Zuweila, on a corner of the fork in the road is the beautiful late-Mamluk era **Mosque of Qijmas Al-Ishaqi** who was Sultan Qaitbay's Viceroy of Damascus. Although the mosque was built in 1480-1481, it is now known locally as the **Mosque of Abu Hurayba** after the 19th-century sheikh who occupies the tomb.

At this point you can make a detour off the main road east up Sharia Abu Hurayba where the left-hand fork leads 250 m to the **Mosque and Tomb of Amir Aslam Al-Silahdar** built in 1344-1345 and then follow the road around southwest and back to the main Sharia Darb Al-Ahmar.

Alternatively, forget about the detour and just continue south from the Mosque of Qijmas Al-Ishaqi along Sharia Darb Al-Ahmar. About 50 m on the right is the **Mosque and Tomb of Ahmed Al-Mihmandar**, built in 1324 but restored in 1732, but much more interesting is the beautiful, relaxing and very peaceful **Mosque of Altunbugha Al-Maridani** (1339-1340), which is 100 m further along the street. This is one of the most impressive 14th-century buildings in Cairo. Altunbugha (Golden Bull), originally from the Turkish town of Mardin, rose through the ranks to become *amir* and then married one of Sultan Al-Nasir Mohammed's daughters and became his cupbearer. After the sultan died in 1340 his successors imprisoned Altunbugha until 1342, when he was made governor of Aleppo only to die the following year at the age of 25.

Altunbugha's courtyard mosque, which was extensively restored in 1895-1903, is one of the oldest remaining buildings in this area. The minaret, to the right of the entrance, was the first in Cairo with an entirely octagonal shaft. It was built by Mu'allim Al-Suyufi, the chief royal architect, who also built the minaret of Aqbugha at Al-Azhar. The shafts of both are decorated by two-coloured inlaid stonework. Fortunately the restoration work followed the original plans so that the bulb-crowned canopy supported on stone pillars, the earliest existing example, was retained. The courtyard is particularly beautiful, with trees growing and cats aplenty.

Another 200 m further south past a small Turkish mosque, by which time the road is now called Sharia Bab Al-Wazir, is the large **Madresa of Sultan Al-Ashraf Sha'ban II**. It was built in 1368 when he was only 10, for his mother who was one of Al-Nasir Mohammed's concubines, which is why it is known locally as *Umm Sultan Sha'ban* (mother of Sultan Sha'ban). However, she outlived him as the Sultan was murdered in 1378 and ended up being buried here himself. The *madresa* and prayer area have recently reopened after being restored. Next door to the mosque is the large and well-restored **Beit Ar-Razzaz**, a palace complex which contains at least 180 rooms, dating from between the 15th to 18th centuries. Some remarkable examples of Islamic decoration, such as *mashrabiyya*, exist here and it is worthy of a visit.

On the road south is the **Mosque of Amir Aqsunqur** who was the son-in-law of Al-Nasir Mohammed and later became Viceroy of Egypt. It is sometimes known as the **Mosque of**

Ibrahim Agha by locals and the **Blue Mosque** by Europeans because of both the exterior's blue-grey marble and the beautiful indigo and turquoise tiling of the *qibla* wall. In the 1650s Ibrahim Agha usurped the mosque, started in 1346, and it was he who decorated it with imported tiles.

The **Madresa-Mausoleum of Amir Khayrbak** was built in stages with the earliest, the mausoleum, being erected in 1502. Khayrbak, the Mamluk governor of Aleppo, betrayed his master Sultan Al-Ghuri at the Battle of Marj Dabiq in 1516 where the Turks routed the Mamluks. He was rewarded for his treachery by being appointed the first Ottoman governor of Egypt, and became renowned for his cruelty and greed. Squeezed between existing buildings the complex is best viewed from the Citadel end from where one can see the minaret (which has just had its missing upper storey replaced) and the intricately carved dome of the tomb raised above arched windows. To the left of the entrance corridor is the *sabil-kuttab* and to the right the portal entrance to the mosque, which one enters by stepping over a piece of pharaonic stone. From the windows of the tomb it's possible to get a good view of the ruined Alin Aq palace and Salah Al-Din's city walls.

Mosque of Sultan Hassan

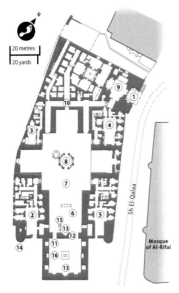

20 metres
20 yards

Sh. El-Qalaa

Sh El-Qalaa

Mosque
of Al-Rifai

1 Entrance
2 Hanifi medersa
3 Hanabali medersa
4 Malaki medersa
5 Shafi'i medersa
6 Sanctuary/liwan
7 Sahn
8 Water for ablutions
9 Antechamber (domed)
10 Corridor
11 Bronze-faced door with gold and silver inlay
12 Qibla
13 Mihrab
14 Base of minaret
15 Minbar
16 Tomb chamber/mausoleum

The *madresa* became a Friday mosque in 1531 when the *minbar* was added. Documents show that the staff included one imam, six *muezzins*, 23 *qari* (Koran readers) – nine of whom recite the Koran at the windows – and a *sufi sheikh*.

The mosques of Sultan Hassan and Rafai ⓘ *Entrance to each E£25, students E£15, open Sat-Thu 0800-1630, Fri 0800-1100 and 1500-1630, during Ramadan until 1430.* Directly below the Citadel on Midan Salah Al-Din, these two adjacent mosques present themselves best at dusk when the atmosphere becomes charged with the call to prayer and the very air seems to shimmer around their colossal forms. The Sultan Hassan Mosque was started in 1356 by Sultan Al-Nasir Hassan and finished seven years later, but not before his assassination in 1361. It is one of the largest mosques in the world and was at times used as a fortress, being conveniently placed for hurling roof-top missiles at enemies in the Citadel.

The building is a masterpiece of Islamic art and is of incomparable simplicity and beauty;

it is said that the Sultan ordered the hand of the architect to be cut off, in order that the building would remain unique. The main entrance is through a large, impressive doorway decorated with stalactites and finely sculpted ornaments. This leads into an antechamber connected to the magnificent cruciform courtyard where an ablutions fountain is covered by a large dome, originally painted blue. Each of the vaulted *liwans* served as a place for the teachings of one of the four doctrines of Sunni Islam. The *liwan* containing the *mihrab* has richly decorated marble-lined walls and a Koranic frieze in Kufic writing carved in the plaster work. The marble *minbar* here is one of the finest in Cairo, its height accentuated by hanging lamp-chains. The original glass lamps from these chains can be found in the Museum of Islamic Art in Cairo and in the Victoria and Albert Museum in London. A bronze door with gold and silver motifs leads to the mausoleum of Sultan Hassan, again a room of grand proportions, dominated by a 21-m-diameter dome that was actually built later, during the Turkish period. As Sultan Hassan was murdered and his body never recovered, two of his sons are buried here in his place.

The three-section 86-m minaret by the mausoleum is the highest in Cairo, with each new section decorated at its base with stalactites. Another smaller 55-m minaret on the east side of the mosque was built in 1659 to replace the existing one that was decaying.

Despite its appearance, the Al-Rifai Mosque, directly to the east of Sultan Hassan Mosque, was only started in the late 19th century and finished in 1912. However, the mosque, which is named after Sheikh Ali Al-Rifai who was the founder of the Sufi order of *tariqa* bearing his name, blends remarkably well into the surroundings. It was begun by the Dowager Princess Khushyar, the mother of Khedive Ismail who died in 1885 before it was finished, and was intended to contain the tombs of her descendants. Besides Al-Rifai and herself it contains the tombs of Khedive Ismail (1863-1879), his sons Sultan Hussein Kamil and King Ahmed Fouad I, and King Farouk who died in exile and was initially buried in the Southern cemetery. It is also the last resting place of the last Shah of Iran (Mohammed Reza Pahlavi), who died in exile in 1980 and, on President Sadat's instructions, was buried with great ceremony in a tomb made of green marble imported from Pakistan.

The Citadel ① *T02-2512 1735, daily 0800-1600 winter, 0800-1430 summer, E£50, students E£25, tips might be necessary for guides in the museums and shoe attendants in the mosques, entrance into the museums ends 1 hr before closing time, enter via Bab Al-Gebel. The Citadel can be reached direct from Midan Abdel Mounim Riyad (near Midan Tahrir) by taking bus No 72 or minibus No 154; a taxi from the centre costs about E£10. Tell the taxi driver to take you to 'Al-Qala'a', with a guttural 'q'.*

The **Citadel** (also known as *Al-Qala'a Al-Gebel* – Citadel of the Mountain – or *Al-Burg*) perches on the steep slopes of the Muqattam Hills, its multiple minarets piercing the skyline and the silver (tin) dome of the Mosque of Mohamed Ali glinting in the sun. It was begun by **Salah Al-Din** in 1176 as part of an ambitious general fortification plan that included enclosing the whole city with a new wall that could be controlled from the main fort. The original fortress and remaining fortifications were strongly influenced by the architecture of castles built in Palestine and Syria by the Crusaders, and incorporate pieces of demolished Fatimid mosques and tombs as well as blocks of casing stone from the Pyramids of Giza. It was built in two walled enclosures, linked by their shortest walls, with the military area to the northeast and the residential quarters in the southwest. Every 100 m or so along the walls there is a tower connected to its neighbours by upper ramparts and by internal corridors that run the full circuit of the walls. The whole complex is still under military control and there are large areas that are closed to the public.

Later the Citadel was abandoned until the Mamluks' arrival, when it became the Sultan's residence and the base of the *Burgi Mamluks* (1382-1517). In the 14th century Sultan Al-Nasir Mohammed (1310-1340) added a number of buildings including a mosque and later, because of the development of warfare and the use of canons, the Turks undertook major reinforcements. The most recent modification to the Citadel was by Mohammed Ali Pasha (1805-1840) who built an impressive mosque on the site of the original palaces. Today the most interesting features of the Citadel are the **Mosque of Mohammed Ali Pasha**, which provides an amazing view west over Cairo and the restored **Sultan Al-Nasir Mohammed Mosque**.

Walls, towers and gates The Ayyubid walls and towers (1176-1183) around part of the northern enclosure are from the time of Salah Al-Din. The dressed stone walls are 10 m high, 3 m thick and 2100 m in circumference interspersed with half-round towers. The **Bab**

The Citadel

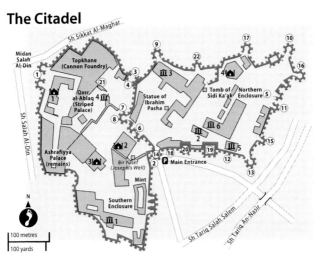

Gates & Towers ◯

Bab Al-Azab **1**	Burg Al-Imam (Imam's Tower) **11**	Burg At-Turfa	National Police Museum **4**
Bab Al-Gabal **2**	Burg Al-Matar (Flight Tower) **12**	(Masterpiece Tower) **19**	Seized Museum **5**
Bab Al-Gadid **3**	Burg Al-Muballat	Burg Kirkilyan	Archaeological
Bab Al-Mudarrag **4**	(Paved Tower) **13**	(Tower of the 40 Serpents) **20**	Garden Museum **6**
Bab Al-Qarafah **5**	Burg Al-Muqattam **14**	Lion's Tower **21**	
Bab Al-Qullah **6**	Burg Al-Muqusar	Tower of Muh 'Ali **22**	**Mosques**
Bab Al-Wustani **7**	(Concave Tower) **15**		Ahmed Katkhuda Al-Azab **1**
Burg Al-Wustani (Middle Tower) **8**	Burg Ar-Ramia (Sand Tower) **16**	**Museums** 🏛	Sultan Al-Nasir
Burg Al-Ahmar (Red Tower) **9**	Burg As-Sahra (Desert Tower) **17**	Qasr Al-Gawhara **1**	Mohammed **2**
Burg Al-Haddad	Burg As-Suffa	Carriage Museum **2**	Mohammed Ali Pasha **3**
(Blacksmith's Tower) **10**	(Alignment Tower) **18**	Harim Palace Military Museum **3**	Suleyman Pasha **4**

Al-Azab, enclosed by a pair of round-headed towers, stands on the west side of the Citadel. It was the original entrance to the Southern enclosure and has brass-bound wooden doors dating from 1754. **Bab Al-Qullah** (16th century) connects the two separate parts of the Citadel. The original Mamluk gate was replaced after the Ottoman conquest and was widened in 1826 to allow Mohammed Ali's carriage to pass through. **Bab Al-Gadid** (New Gate) was built in 1828 and is in reality a large tunnel with a vaulted ceiling, with guard rooms on either side. Built in 1207 by the Mamluk Sultan Baybars, the **Burg As-Siba** (Lions' Tower) is so called because it is decorated with a frieze of stone lions, the sultans' heraldic symbol. **Burg Al-Muqattam** (16th-century) is the largest tower in the citadel, over 25 m high and 24 m in diameter, with 7-m-thick walls built to withstand artillery attack.

Mosque of Mohammed Ali Pasha   The Mosque of Mohammed Ali Pasha, was started in 1824 but only finished eight years after his death in 1857. The architecture was strongly influenced by the Ottoman mosques of Istanbul with the characteristic high, slender, octagonal minarets and an imposing dome that had to be rebuilt in the 1930s. The marble-floored courtyard is very finely proportioned, with a beautiful central ablutions fountain. To the northwest is a small square tower for a clock that was a gift from King Louis-Philippe of France in 1846 in exchange for the obelisk now in the Place de la Concorde in Paris, but the clock has never worked. The mosque is covered by a large dome with four half-domes on each side. Once inside, it takes some time to become accustomed to the dim lighting. The white marbled tomb of Mohammed Ali is to the right after the entrance, behind a bronze grille. This mosque is unusual, having two *minbars*. The large wooden construction, carved, painted and gilded, was installed by Mohammed Ali. It was too large to erect in the conventional space by the *mihrab* and was placed under the central dome making the weekly sermon inaudible to most of the congregation. In 1939 King Farouk installed a smaller alabaster *minbar* carved with a geometric pattern – to the right of the *mihrab*.

Sultan Al-Nasir Mohammed Mosque   The Sultan Al-Nasir Mohammed Mosque was built between 1318 and 1335. It is certainly the best preserved Mamluk building in the Citadel and is claimed to be one of the finest arcade-style mosques in Cairo, the arches being supported by pharaonic and classical columns plundered from elsewhere. The two distinctive minarets, one above each entrance, are covered in the upper part with green, blue and white ceramic tiles attributed to craftsmen from Persia as are the onion-shaped bulbs on the tops of the minarets. The magnificent marble that covered the floors and lined the walls was unfortunately removed on instructions of the Ottoman ruler Selim I, although the *mihrab* remains in good condition.

The little-visited **Mosque of Suleyman Pasha** (1528), in the northern enclosure of the Citadel, was the first domed mosque to be built in Cairo during the Ottoman period. Its stalactite portal leads not directly into the paved courtyard like most Ottoman mosques but into the prayer hall on its southwest side. This is due to its cramped position by the Citadel's walls. The minaret is typical of the style common in Istanbul, a tall slender cylinder with a conical top, but like the Mamluk minarets it has two galleries. The minaret's pointed cap is covered with green tiles, as are the surrounding mosque and prayer hall, similar to a number found in Cairo's mosques of the period.

The mosque interior comprises a richly painted domed central area flanked on three sides by three supported semi-domes. The frescoes on the walls were restored in the

19th century and it is uncertain how faithful they are to the original Ottoman decoration. There was insufficient space adjacent to the *mihrab* for the *minbar*, which had to be placed under the central dome. The conical top of the marble *minbar* is decorated with a Mamluk-inspired geometric pattern based on the stars and polygon forms, similar to the Ottoman minarets.

Citadel museums The **Carriage Museum** was housed in the dining hall used by British officers stationed in the Citadel. At the time of research it was closed to the public, and is supposed to reopen in a restored building in Bulaq, when it will display eight carriages once used by the Egyptian royal family and some painted wooden horses.

The **Prison Museum** contains the cells where prisoners were detained, which you can view through the bars, the most famous convict being Anwar Sadat who was held here by the British for his revolutionary activities.

The **Military Museum** is in the **Harim Palace** built in 1827 as the private residence of Mohammed Ali. There are three extensive wings with many halls and side rooms, all decorated in lavish style. It is a splendid spectacle, well worth a visit. King Farouk ordered its conversion into a museum, which traces the history of the Egyptian army from pharaonic times to the present day. There are military uniforms, rifles and cannons on display, while the tanks captured in the October 1973 conflict are in the courtyard and make a popular photo spot.

The **National Police Museum** has some strange and interesting exhibits of policing problems ranging from assassination attempts to the protection of Egyptian antiquities. Note the sensational crimes of the serial killer sisters from Alexandria who murdered 30 women prior to being captured in 1921. It is constructed on top of Burg as-Siba and the view from the terrace takes in the Pyramids on the left through to the minaret of the Mosque Al-Fath in Midan Ramses to the right. It's absolutely breathtaking – on a clear day. The adjacent terrace café is an excellent place to relax, with equally amazing views and amazingly high prices to match.

The **Seized Museum** is unfortunately closed, with no indication of when it might reopen. Inside two small rooms exhibits items confiscated from dealers in the antiquities black market, spanning the history of Egypt. The first room is set aside for pharaonic items including a painted wooden sarcophagus and funerary beads in excellent condition. The second room is cramped with an assortment of treasures, including a collection of Byzantine, Islamic and European gold coins, a small group of beautiful books in the Arabic script, seven stunning Coptic icons and a set of official seals from the reign of the Mohammed Ali.

The **Qasr Al-Gawhara** (Palace of Jewels) stands on the site of the palace of the Circassian Mamluk sultans. It was built in 1814 as the first of two palaces with French-style salons that Mohammed Ali erected in the Citadel, and contains an impressive audience hall and guest rooms. Having been the residence of Egypt's rulers since the 12th century he predicted that his descendants would rule Egypt as long as they lived in the Citadel: sure enough, Ismail's move to the Abdin Palace foreshadowed the decline in their fortunes. At the time of writing the museum was closed for restoration, but should reopen with displays of portraits, costumes, furniture and ornaments that belonged to King Farouk.

The **Archaeological Garden**, in the Northern Enclosure, contains a small collection of bits and pieces – pieces of columns and monuments – as well as welcome benches. It is a very quiet and attractive place to take a rest.

Just south of the Mosque of Sultan Al-Nasir Mohammed, covered by a tower and locked at the time of writing, stands **Joseph's Well**. Also known as the Well of the Snail, an enclosed spiral staircase leads down some 87 m through solid rock to the water level of the Nile. Two platforms with pumps operated by oxen raised the water, which was then carried to the surface by donkeys. It was built between 1876 and 1182 by Crusader prisoners and provided a secure supply of drinking water for all of the Citadel.

Qasr Al-Ablaq (Striped Palace) was built in 1315 by Al-Nasr Mohammed for official receptions. Mohammed Ali Pasha had the building torn down but a remaining portion of outer wall shows its alternating bands of black and yellow marble.

West from the Citadel

From Midan Salah Al-Din it's a 15- to 20-minute walk west along Sharia Saliba to the Mosque of Ibn Tulun. On the left you'll soon see the second decorated **Sabil-Kuttab of Sultan Qaitbay** (1477), which is now gorgeously restored and home to a library. Continue west past the small **Mosque of Qanibai Al-Muhammadi** to the imposing architectural buildings with matching minarets that face each other across the street. On the right is the **Mosque of Amir Shaykhu** (1349) and on the left his **Khanqah** (1355). Amir Shaykhu was the Commander-in-Chief of the Mamluk army during the reign of Sultan Hassan. The *khanqah* had small cells for up to 70 sufis around the inner courtyard and in the northeast corner of the arcaded prayer hall is Amir Shaykhu's tomb.

There is an option to turn right here, up Sharia Suyufiya, for a worthy detour to the hugely impressive **Palace of Amir Taz** ① *T02-2514 2581, free*. One of the last great Mamluk palaces, and the most intact, it was built in 1352 by Amir Taz to celebrate his marriage to the daughter of Sultan Al-Nasir Mohamed. He never really got the chance to enjoy his magnificent abode as conspiracies and intrigues against him pursuaded him to flee Cairo, despite the fact he was described as being tall and courageous. A mainstay of the Historic Cairo Programme, the restoration of the palace is regarded as a great success, with positive effects on the local area in the provision of a community centre, a space for art exhibitions, and as the venue for music events (check the listings on www.weekly-ahram.org.eg). Enclosed by high stone walls, the central courtyard and gardens are a peaceful and austere space, while inside the decoration becomes more flamboyant. The main *qa'ah* has traces of the original paint and gilding, in the Bahri Mamluk style, and the stunning vaulted ceilings in the ground-floor bathrooms are pierced with coloured glass. The *maqad* looks onto the courtyard through four soaring arches, resting on marble columns topped with Corinthian capitals. Wooden waterwheels, cisterns and aquaducts were revealed during the restoration process, these and the *haramlik* fountain have now been excavated. A small museum traces the history of the Mamluks and displays choice artefacts and alabaster ornaments.

Just over the crossroads, on the right, is the **Mevlavi Sufi Theatre** ① *T02-2510 7806, open 0900-1800*, also known as the Cairo Tikiyya, lovingly and painstakingly restored over many years by a joint Italian-Egyptian team. Part of the Rumi sect, the 'whirling dervishes' who lived and practised here came to Egypt just after the Ottoman conquest, and were the last of the sect to be dissolved in 1945. The polished circular wooden floor (scuffed by the feet of devotees) of the main *sama-khana*, or Hall of Listening, is overlooked by two galleries supported on slender pillars. The *minrab* serves as an anchor point of a horizontal axis that symbolically divides the space into the known and unknown worlds. The interior is decorated with botanic designs, while the flying birds on the dome represent the liberation of the soul from a materialist life. It's the perfect place to reenergize, as is the peaceful Turkish garden outside. A small museum displays uniforms and belongings of the Sufis, as well as pottery and porcelain. The adjacent **mausoleum-madresa of Sunqur El-Sadi** has some of most sensational carved stucco in Cairo on its dome, with beautiful arabesque designs and inscriptions relating to death from a popular medieval text. Look for the unusually shaped crescent upon atop its minaret.

Retrace your steps and and turn right onto Sharia Saliba at the cross roads, with the **Sabil-Kuttab of Um Abbas** on the corner, passing the small but impressive **Mosque of Amir Taghri Bardi** (1440) with a carved stone dome. While the structure of this building follows the east-west line of Sharia Saliba, the interior is aligned southeast to Mecca.

Mosque of Ibn Tulun ⓘ *Daily 0800-1700. Bus No 72 or minibus No 154 go from Midan Abdel Mounim Riad to to the Citadel, via the Saiyyida Zeinab area and then past the mosque. A taxi from Downtown costs E£5-10.* The largest mosque in Cairo and the oldest to retain its original features is the Mosque of Ahmed Ibn Tulun, built between AD 876-879. The cosmic proportions and austere interior make it stand out among a million other mosques in Cairo, while the captivating Gayer-Anderson house next door and tasteful souvenirs in the shop opposite make it an excellent place to start a day's wanderings. Ahmed Ibn Tulun, the son of a Turkish slave, was made governor of Egypt but then proceeded to declare independence from the Baghdad-based Abbasid Khalifas. He thereby became the first of the Tulunids (AD 868-905) at the new town of Al-Qata'i (the Concessions or the Wards), northeast of Fustat and near the foothills of Muqattam. When the Abbasids regained power in Egypt in AD 905 they destroyed much of the town except for the mosque, which fell into decay until it was restored in 1296 by Sultan Lagin. He had hidden there after being implicated in an assassination attempt against his predecessor (at which time the mosque was believed to be haunted) and vowed he would restore the place.

The mosque was originally designed by a Syrian Jacobite Christian architect, which probably explains the presence of many designs and motifs inspired by Coptic art. Legend says that the sycamore beams were brought from Mount Ararat and were part of Noah's ark. External measurements are 140 x 122 m making it the largest place of worship in Cairo. The central courtyard is 92 sq m yet despite its huge size, the overall impression is of harmony, simplicity and sobriety. The walls have been plastered but the ornamentation is sculpted rather than moulded. Kufic inscriptions, almost 2 km long, circle the mosque several times below the roof and relay about 20% of the Koran. The marble-plated *mihrab*, added in the 13th century, is surrounded by a glass mosaic frieze. Directly above is a small wooden dome. The *minbar*, presented by Sultan Lagin in 1296, is a fine work of art. The minaret has an unusual outside spiral staircase, which appears to be a copy of the one at Samarra in Iraq; the view from the top over the surrounding area is excellent and worth the climb. You'll have to tip E£1 for shoe-covers to wear inside the mosque, but it's fine to keep footwear on for climbing the minaret.

Gayer-Anderson House ⓘ *T02-2364 7822, daily 0900-1600, E£35, E£20 for students, E£20 video cameras.* The **Gayer-Anderson House** should be given priority over other restored houses if you have limited time in Cairo, as it is exquisitely detailed and full of Orientalist period pieces. Also known as the **Beit Al-Kritliyah** (House of the Cretan Woman), it's actually two adjoining houses that abut the southeast corner of Ibn Tulun's mosque. Originally one house was for men's accommodation (*salamlik*) and the other for women (*haramlik*). The roof area was solely for the women who crossed from one building to the other by a small bridge on the second floor. A *mashrabiyah*-screened balcony overlooks the large two-storey sitting room (*qa'ah*) with its marble floor and ornately tiled fountain, permitting the women to see the male visitors and the entertainments without being seen themselves.

In 1934, the government allowed Major Robert Gayer-Anderson (1881-1945), a retired British doctor and member of the Egyptian Civil Service, to restore and refurnish the houses with Ottoman-era furniture and fittings. A passionate collector, the major filled the rooms with curios gathered from around the region, resulting in differently themed rooms including the Damascus room, Persian room, Turkish room and Byzantine room. Gorgeous carpets cover the floors, you can wander amongst the furniture while light comes in through fine *mashrabiyah* windows, ceilings have been faithfully restored and are bright with colour, and the rooftop provides awesome views over Ibn Tulun. Other rooms include a library containing historical books, a writing room and a display room for the Major's collection of pharaonic antiquities. Guides will take you on a tour, if you wish, and they'll expect tips afterwards.

Sayyidah Zeinab The area to the west of the Ibn Tulun Mosque is known as Sayyidah Zeinab after the Prophet Mohammed's granddaughter Zeinab (AD 628-680) who settled in Fustat in AD 679 with her five children and the son of her brother Hussein who was murdered at Karbala in the Sunni-Shi'a conflict. Because of her position as closest kinswoman to the martyred Ali and Hussein the area has become a site of pilgrimage for foreign Shi'a Muslims. This is focused on the mosque built, and continuously rebuilt, over her tomb, located off Sharia Bur Said but closed to non-Muslims. Her *moulid* (saint's day) between 13-27 Ragab attracts up to half a million revellers who come to watch the wild Sufi parades and evening festivities.

The **Madresa and Tombs of Amirs Salar and Sangar Al-Gawli** was once a much larger set of buildings than what you see today, but even so the remaining tombs and the *madresa* indicate some of the original grandeur. The domes over the tombs are of varying sizes, that to the east being the largest. The slender minaret stands about 45 m high, with a square first storey, octagonal second storey and a cylindrical third that culminates in a cornice of stalactites capped with a ribbed dome. Passing through the stalactite arch, steps lead you up to the vaulted corridor and to the tombs. The most ornate is the Tomb of Amir Salar, 7 m sq, encircled by a wooden frieze and with a fine marble *mihrab*. Note the design of the windows in the dome. Turning east from the stairs leads to the mosque. The larger courtyard had small rooms for students (the grills over the doors need some explanation) and a smaller courtyard off which is the *mihrab*.

Cities of the Dead

① *The easiest way to the Southern Cemetery from Sultan Hassan Mosque, is to head south towards Sharia Imam Al-Shafi for about 1.5 km, more pleasant by taxi than on foot, E£3-4. The easiest way to the Northern Cemetery is either by taking a taxi direct to Qarafat Al-Sharqiyyah, or by walking east along Sharia Al-Azhar from the Al-Azhar mosque for about 15 mins until you reach the roundabout junction with the north-south dual carriageway of Sharia Salah Salem and then north for 250 m. Then cut into the cemetery and head for the dome and minaret, which are clearly visible.*

The Cities of the Dead is the name given by Europeans to Cairo's two main cemeteries that spread north and south from the Citadel. Half a million people are thought to live among the mausoleums and tombs of the sprawling necropoli, and the communities here have shops, electricity and even schools. In Egypt there has long been a tradition of living close to the dead but the very large numbers are a relatively recent trend caused by an acute scarcity of housing. Consequently the people who live in the cemeteries tend to be comparatively poor and, although certainly not dangerous, it is obviously advisable not to flaunt your wealth, to dress modestly and remember that these are people's homes. The Cities of the Dead are one of few intimidating places in Cairo (lone women will certainly feel conspicuous, either sex will feel more comfortable with company) and somewhere you can get very lost after dark. The vast majority of people are as welcoming as all other Egyptians, but if anyone in Cairo is likely to throw stones at you, it will be the children here.

The **Southern Cemetery** (*Al-Qarafa Al-Kubra*) is older and spreads to the southeast but there are relatively few monuments to see. The **Mausoleum of Imam Al-Shafi** is the focus of a visit here, with splendid marbling and a quite astounding dome, gilded and painted red and blue, and topped by a metal boat. Remember this is an active shrine and be very respectful when visiting (see box, page 79, for more about the sights in the Southern Cemetery). The **Northern Cemetery**, which is known locally as Al-Qarafa Al-Sharqiyyah (the Eastern Cemetery) because it was east of the old city, is more interesting and has been the burial place of the sultans since the 14th century. It contains a number of the most beautiful mausoleums in the city, including those of Barquq and Qaitbay.

Mausoleums in the Northern Cemetery In the Northern Cemetery the **Mausoleum of Sultan Al-Zahir Barquq** ① *daily 0900-2000,* was built over a 12-year period in 1398-1411 by his son Al-Nasir Farag. It was the first royal tomb to be built in the necropolis after Barquq had expressed a wish to be interred alongside a number of pious Sufi sheikhs already buried there. Therefore his body was moved from his *madresa* on Sharia Al-Muizzli Din Allah once the 75-sq-m complex had been completed. It is square with two minarets symmetrically placed on the façade. The entrance in the southwest corner leads along a corridor to the *sahn*, which has an octagonal fountain in the centre and is surrounded by four *liwans*. The east *liwan* has three very simple *mihrabs* and an extraordinarily finely sculpted stone *minbar*. Doors lead from either side of the *liwan* into mausoleums. The north mausoleum contains Barquq's own marble cenotaph, which is richly decorated with Koranic inscriptions, together with the tombs of an unknown person and another intended for Farag whose body was left in Damascus after he had been assassinated on a military campaign in Syria. The mausoleum to the south holds the tombs of Barquq's wife and two granddaughters.

A little to the south is the **Madresa and Mausoleum of Sultan Al-Qaitbay** ① *daily 0900-1700*, built in 1472-1474, which is a magnificent example of 15th-century Arab art and one of Egypt's most beautiful monuments from the Arab era. From the outside, the building's proportions are pleasingly harmonious, with boldly striped masonry, and a dome finely decorated with polygonal motifs. The minaret is also remarkable for its square base, octagonal middle section and cylindrical top tier, all finely inscribed. Seventeen steps climb to the cruciform *madresa* with narrow side *liwans* and a covered *sahn* with an exquisite octagonal lantern ceiling. The sheer volume and complexities of the marble decoration that seems to coat every surface is breathtaking. The east *liwan*, where the ceiling is modern, still has a very well preserved and finely encrusted *minbar*. A door in the south corner of the *qibla liwan* leads to the mausoleum, which is decorated with an equal wealth of marbling, however its high dome is simply decorated in contrast with the highly ornate walls. Sultan Qaitbay's tomb is enclosed behind an elaborate wooden *mashrabiyya* while the other tomb is that of one of his sisters.

Al-Azhar Park ① *Sharia Salah Salem, T02-2510 3868, www.alazhhzarpark.com, daily 0900-2300 (0900-2200 on Wed), E£5, the entrance gate is on Salah Salem, a taxi from Downtown costs about E£10.* Called in Arabic *Hadiyka Al-Azhar* (which will help taxi drivers), the Al-Azhar Park is an emerald-green success story built on top of the immense mound of the Islamic city's rubbish dump. For centuries, waste matter was thrown over the historic wall east of Darb Al-Ahmar, eventually submerging the wall and piling into a veritable mountain. An impressive 1300-m stretch of the **Ayubbid wall** has been excavated, and the Darb Al-Ahmar buildings flanking it have been spruced up to give a much-needed boost to a poor and deprived neighbour-

6 **Northern Cemetery**

➡ Cairo maps
1 Cairo overview, page 30
6 Northern Cemetery, page 78

Midan Barquq

Tomb of Qansuh Abu Sai'id

Tomb of Princess Shawikar

Tomb of Qurqumas & Khangah (sufi hostel)

Sharia Ahmed Ibn Inal

Sh Salah Salem

1967 War Cemetery

Mausoleum of Sultan Al-Zahir Barquq

Tomb/Mosque of Barsbai

Sharia Sultan Ahmed

Sharia Qaitbai

Mosque/Mausoleum of Sultan Al-Qaitbay

Tomb of Khedive Tawfiq

Tomb of Tughai

Tomb of Kuzal

Sharia Qarafat Bab al-Wazir

Tomb of Tulbai

Sh al-Afifi

Tomb of Tankizbugha

Sh Qarafat Bab al-Wazir

N
Not to scale

Tomb of Yussef Al-Dawadar

Muslim cemeteries

One of the lasting monuments in Islam is the *qarafah* or graveyard. All are different, ranging from undefined rocky areas near villages, where unnamed head and foot stones are barely distinguishable from the deserts surrounding them, to the elaborate necropoli of Cairo, where cities for the dead are established. In all cemeteries bodies are interred with head towards the *qibla* – Mecca.

In Egypt, graveyards often contain a series of simple whitewashed mud brick tombs of holy men (*marabouts*), around which his disciples and their descendants are laid. More grandly, in Cairo at the City of the Dead is the Eastern Cemetery, known as the Tombs of the Mamluks, a set of Muslim graveyards, developed particularly from the 15th century. It contains large numbers of notable tombs, most importantly that of Tomb of Sultan Al-Zahir Barquq. A second and even more elaborate cemetery is Cairo's Southern Cemetery. This ancient graveyard includes a number of the earliest examples of Muslim funerary architecture in Egypt and is home to the Tomb of the Imam Shafa'i, the most significant mausoleum in Cairo. The Imam Shafa'i was born in Palestine in AD 767 and was the originator of the Shafi'ite School of Islamic jurisprudence, one of the four great Sunni Schools of Law. He spent his last years (until his death in AD 820) in Fustat in Cairo. Salah Al-Din set up the Shafa'i Mosque in 1180, which included the Imam's new tomb. Although subject to numerous subsequent reconstructions, the last under the Khedive Tawfiq in 1891, the tomb is in an adequate state of repair to justify a visit. The large Shafa'i complex takes in a mosque, a ceremonial gateway and the mausoleum itself. The tomb is simple but decorated at various times with silver and paintings. The mausoleum has some fine beams and a wooden cupola together with much of the inscriptions and ornamentation undertaken by Salah Al-Din's builders. Shafa'i's tomb lies to the north of the building. Its religious focus is a delicate 20th-century sandalwood screen or *maqsurah* and a marble stela. These are kissed by visiting Muslims as a sign of faith. Also entombed at the site are Mohammed abd Al-Hakim and Princess Adiliyyah, mother of Sultan Al-Kamel, while the Sultan himself (interred elsewhere) is commemorated by an uninscribed tomb in the south of the chamber. A walk along Sharia Sidi Uqbah and Sharia Imam Shafa'i takes you past a wide variety of funerary constructions, many in a sad state of decay. Also worth a visit is the Al-Basha *Housh* (house) which backs onto the Shafa'i tomb on a parallel road (Shariyah Imam Al-Lais) to the west. This is the 19th-century mausoleum of the family of Mohammed Ali Pasha.

Death and funerals are times for noisy outbreaks of wailing and crying. In traditional families, the approach of a person's death is signalled by wailing, increased on actual death by the addition of the mourning neighbours and relatives. Occasionally in villages the body is laid in a large room where funeral dances are performed by mourning women, singing the praises of the deceased. Corpses are washed and wrapped in a simple shroud for interment. Mourners follow the cortege to the cemetery often in large crowds since every person who walks 40 paces in the procession has one sin remitted. At the grave side a *shedda* or declaration of Islamic faith is recited.

hood. The epic project to transform this into a pleasure garden took over a decade and was funded by the Aga Khan Trust for Culture, who have negotiated an agreement with the government that will allow them to manage the park for at least 20 years. The next phase is underway to create an 'urban plaza' with extra car parking, a café, a small retail area and a new museum. This **Museum of Islamic Cairo** will prepare visitors for the experience to come in the lanes of the old city and has opened up a western exit into Darb Al-Ahmar. The remains of the original mud-brick Fatimid wall that were uncovered during the park's construction will also be displayed in the future, near the museum.

The park is amazingly lush, with shrubs, trees and flowers in abundance, and full of Cairene families enjoying the palm-lined walkways and children's play area. Come to the park for sunset and you will get sweeping views across the city as monuments are lit up and the green neon lights of minarets glow. The high vantage point provides one of Cairo's best views over the mausoleums of the Cities of the Dead, past the skyscrapers of Downtown and over the Nile to the pyramids in Giza. The fabulous **Citadel View Restaurant** (see Restaurants, page 112) on the northern hill is worth splashing out on, or the outside café is a delightful place to sit with a cool drink (although there's a minimum charge and painfully slow service).

Old Cairo and Roda Island

This settlement was constructed by the Persians in about 500 BC to guard the junction of the Nile and the canal linking it to the Red Sea. During the Christian period the fortified settlement of Babylon-in-Egypt grew into a large town. It was perhaps named by the fort's homesick building workers from modern-day Iraq or from the name for Gate of Heliopolis (Bab-il-On). Later the Arabs called it Qasr Al-Sham'ah (Fortress of the Beacon). Whatever its origins, it is now commonly known as Old Cairo (Masr Al-Kadima) or identified, not entirely correctly, by some as Coptic Cairo.

Old Cairo is located on the east bank of the Nile, opposite the southern tip of Roda Island to which it was connected by a pontoon bridge. Leaving Mar Girgis station, you are confronted by two circular Roman towers some 33 m in diameter which comprised the west gate of the fortress. Built on what was at that time the east bank of the Nile, now 400 m further west, the towers sit on foundations now smothered beneath 10 m of Nile silt and rubble. Between them is the Coptic Museum, while the Hanging Church is entered to their right and the modern Church of St George to their left. The other main churches and synagogue of Ben Ezra are accessed via the little flight of sunken steps to the left of the metro exit.

Arriving in Old Cairo and Rosa Island

The easiest and cheapest way to get to Old Cairo is via the metro, E£1, which drops you right in front of the Coptic quarter. Get off at **Mar Girgis** (St George), four stops from **Sadat** in the Helwan direction. For more of an adventure, river-taxis leave Maspero Dock between 0700-0800, E£1, and call at Mar Gigis five stops later. Alternatively, a taxi from Downtown costs E£10. The churches do not charge admission, but most have donation boxes. To get a taste of Coptic culture and see heaps of Coptic Cairenes milling about from holy sight to holy sight, come on Sunday; if you are in search of a peaceful stroll through Old Cairo, it is best to avoid it on Wednesday, Friday and Sunday.

The Coptic Museum

ⓘ *T02-2362 8766, www.copticmuseum.gov.eg and www.coptic-cairo.com, daily 0900-1700 (last entrance at 1600), during Ramadan supposedly until 1500 though it might shut earlier, E£50, students E£25, cameras are not permitted and must be deposited by the turnstiles.*

Recently restored and reorganized, the Coptic Museum is among Egypt's principal displays of antiquities and houses an outstanding collection of Coptic treasures. It was founded in 1908, with the support of the royal court, as a means of preserving Coptic artefacts and Egypt's Christian heritage against the acquisitive activities of local and foreign collectors. There was an expansion programme in 1947 that enabled the collection to include a number of small but very valuable objects and items from Coptic churches and monasteries throughout Egypt.

The museum gives an interesting insight into the evolution of Christian (and to some extent secular) art and architecture in Egypt in the period AD 300-1800. As well as demonstrating the interchange of ideas with the larger Islamic community, earlier pieces show how the transition from paganism to Christianity was a gradual process with many Graeco-Roman myths incorporated in proto-Coptic art and sculpture. The displays are arranged thematically across two floors in the New and Old Wings; reckon on about three hours for a thorough viewing or an hour to just whip round. It's a good idea to go over

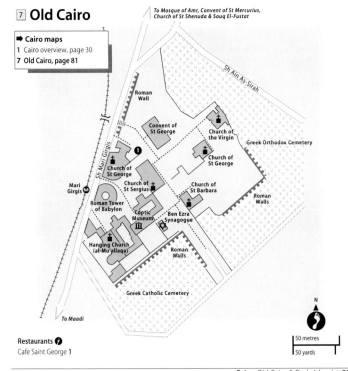

7 Old Cairo

➡ **Cairo maps**
1 Cairo overview, page 30
7 Old Cairo, page 81

To Mosque of Amr, Convent of St Mercurius, Church of St Shenuda & Souq El-Fustat

Sh Ain As-Sirah

Roman Wall

Convent of St George

Church of the Virgin

Greek Orthodox Cemetery

Church of St George

Sh Mari Girgis

Church of St George

Mari Girgis Ⓜ

Church of St Sergius

Church of St Barbara

Roman Tower of Babylon

Coptic Museum 🏛

Ben Ezra Synagogue

Roman Walls

Hanging Church (al-Mu'allaqa)

Roman Walls

Greek Catholic Cemetery

To Maadi

N

Restaurants 🔴
Cafe Saint George 1

50 metres
50 yards

lunchtime, when the museum is virtually empty. The enclosed garden is neatly laid out with benches and large pieces of old stonework. There is also a gift shop, library and a small café, though the nearby Café Saint George (next to the church of the same name; see map, page 81) is a nicer place to relax.

Beginning on the ground floor of the New Wing, go in an anticlockwise direction through the museum. Among the chunky Ahnas sculptures in **Room 3** look out for the pediment on the right-hand wall showing the nymph Daphne in the laurel leaves, with

Coptic Museum

New wing - ground floor

Stairs to upper floor

2 Masterpieces
3 Sculpture from Ahnas
4 Ankhs
5, 6 & Courtyard Objects from the Monastery of St Jeremiah at Saqqara
7-9 Pieces from the Monastery of Apollo at Bawit

New wing - upper floor

10 Coptic culture
11 Religious themes
12 Liturgical vestments
13 & 14 Textiles
15 Nag Hammadi Codices
16 Writing
17 Psalter
Tube Kellia Monasteries

Old wing - upper floor

18 Nilotic scenes
19 Daily life & saints
20-22 Icons
23 Metalwork
24 & 25 Ceramics & glass

N
Not to scale

pudding-bowl haircut and classic almond-shaped eyes, and further along a frieze containing the faun Pan, both from the third or fourth century. **Room 4** is devoted to early Christian reliefs, which give weight to the suggestion that the Christian cross developed from the pharaonic *ankh*. **Room 5** contains stylized friezes of uniform acanthus and vine leaves from the fifth-century monastery of St Jeremiah in Saqqara (see page 138), barely eroded either by the desert or by time. In the courtyard is a splendid array of column capitals individually carved into lotus leaves, vines, palm fronds and acanthus (a couple still have traces of paint) and a six-step limestone pulpit (the earliest recorded). Treasures from St Jeremiah continue in **Room 6** where a perfectly preserved and fresh-painted niche depicting Christ floating above a seated Virgin Mary steals the show. Pieces from the Monastery of St Apollo in Bawit, probably the richest hoard of church sculpture ever discovered in Egypt, are in **Rooms 7, 8** and **9**. The lintels, door jambs, panels and dados from Bawit are all exquisite but the highlight is an unusually bright oratory apse showing Christ enthroned by the mythological creatures of the Apocalypse; below, on either side of the virgin and child, the apostles are personalized by their differing facial hair and expressions. Note also the magnificent remains of an arch in **Room 9**, supported by columns carved with modernistic geometrical designs.

Upstairs in **Room 10-11** religious and thematic elements, portrayed through various media, are grouped together. Look in the first case for the weaving of a centaur surrounded by medallions containing baskets of fruit and animals – it is hard to believe that it's over 1500 years old. The Old and New Testaments are of equal importance in the Coptic faith, and both sets of Biblical stories are represented in the rest of Room 11. At the end of the left wall, particularly impressive is the 11th-century Fayoumi painting showing Adam and Eve among the fruit and foliage of the Garden of Eden, before and after their fall from grace. **Room 12** contains liturgical vestments, and then a display of the famed skill of Coptic weavers starts in earnest in **Room 13**. Remarkably, nothing in the room is newer than the eighth century and some remnants are as old as third century. Floral designs, agricultural scenes, human figures, animals and birds are prominent subjects, giving Coptic textiles a personal feel as well as divulging detailed information about the society that created them. **Room 15** displays the Nag Hammadi Codices. Only two pages are on show, plus some leather book-bindings, but this is the primary source for study of Gnosticism and early Christian mysticism. The theme of writing continues in **Room 16** with some marvellous illuminated manuscripts, a variety of writing accoutrements and some messages on ostracon (pot-shards) that deal with grain sales, health enquiries and other matters of daily life. **Room 17** is devoted to the 1600-year-old Psalter found near Beni Suef, then it's a quick dash through the tube linking the New Wing to the Old, via a small display about the hermitages found at Kellia. It's worth looking at the diagram of a reconstructed hermitage, which is very far removed from any previous notions you might have had of a hermit's cell.

In the Old Wing, the building itself is as rewarding as the artefacts. The ceiling carvings throughout this section are from Coptic houses in Old Cairo and have been incorporated into the building along with panels and tiles. Coptic woodwork was very varied and ornate, heavy work being executed in acacia and palm and finer work in imported cedar, pine and walnut. Ebony too was very popular. A frieze in **Room 18** depicts a large crocodile and further on in **Room 19** look for the pull-along wooden toys, fashioned into horses, an elephant and birds, which are presumed to come from children's graves. **Rooms 20-22** require you to have saved some energy and are a true highpoint of the museum. They contain the icons, spanning a huge range of iconographic styles – Byzantine, Greek, Cretan, Syrian and more. Seek out the icon of St Barbara, from the nearby church dedicated to her, leaning on a Rapunzel-esque tower and dressed in the Western medieval style. **Room 23** has some unimaginably heavy and ornate keys from the monastery doors of Middle Egypt, plus jewellery, intriguing lamps fashioned into animal shapes, and a wealth of incense censers – so important in the Coptic liturgy – swinging on chains. The pottery in **Room 24** is arranged according to decoration and size. There are red clay jugs, small pots for make-up, and beautifully painted urns and bowls. You might feel by now that the collection of ceramics and glass in **Room 25** is mercifully small, but it's worth lingering over the two-handled miniature flasks that pilgrims used to take holy water back from Abu Menas, depicting the martyred saint between two camels, and marvel at the unbelievably fiddly designs on the base of water jugs used to filter out impurities. After exiting down the stairs, it's possible to see the old Roman Water Gate that is down some steps in the courtyard.

Church of Al-Mu'allaqah (The Hanging Church)

10 metres
10 yards

1 Entrance from Sharia Mari Girgis
2 Passage
3 Covered courtyard
4 Narthex
5 Nave (wagon-vaulted)
6 Aisle
7 Marble pulpit
8 Altar screen
9 Sanctuary of St George
10 Sanctuary of Virgin Mary
11 Sanctuary of St John the Baptist
12 Shrine of Takla Hamanout
13 Baptistry with basin

The Hanging Church

ⓘ *Daily 0800-1700. Coptic Masses held on Fri 0800-1100 and Sun 0700-1000, photography permitted. There are often volunteers about who will give a free guided tour – enquire with staff by the church door to see if anyone is available.*

Beside the Coptic Museum, the other main attraction in Old Cairo is the Hanging Church (*Al-Mu'allaqah* or 'The Suspended One'). It is so called because it perches on top of the three stone piers of the semi-flooded Roman Water Gate from where the Melkite bishop Cyrus, the last Byzantine viceroy, fled by boat as the Muslim army arrived. The original church, built in the fourth century, was demolished in AD 840 by Ali Ibn Yahya who was the Armenian Governor. It was rebuilt in AD 977 and modified several times, most recently in 1775. The church is approached through a narrow courtyard from which steep steps lead, via a 19th-century vestibule, to the church's entrance. The painting of the Virgin on the right-hand wall on entering is known as the Coptic Mona Lisa, as her eyes and face follow you when you move from side to side. Against the left-hand wall are relics of saints contained in cylindrical vessels wrapped in red cloth: it is to these you should appeal for blessings. The church is divided into a wide nave and two narrow side aisles by two rows of eight columns with Corinthian capitals. Look out for the odd-one-out black basalt capital. The vaulted roof is of timber, and echoes the hull of the upturned ark. There are three supporting columns in the centre of the nave and an 11th-century marble pulpit supported by 15 delicate columns. On examination each pair of columns is identical but no two pairs are the same. One of the columns is black, representing Judas, and another is grey, representing either Doubting Thomas or Peter, who denied Christ. The 13th-century *iconostasis*, which separates the congregation from the three *haikals* (altar areas), is an incredible feat of fine woodwork and appears virtually transparent. To the right of the altar is a room that is built over the eastern tower of the southern gateway of the old fortress – there is a cordoned-off hole in the floor, through which you can see 13 m down to appreciate the fact there are no foundations – just date palm trunks holding the church up. The screen dividing this room from the main church is of very delicate woodwork – the mother of pearl inlay is enhanced by holding a candle or torch behind. To its left and right, two secret passageways lead down to the foundations. These recent discoveries are thought to be escape routes used by the Christians during times of persecution.

The Convent of St George
① *Access down the sunken steps in front of the exit of Mar Girgis metro, 1000-1600.* St George was a Roman soldier and one of the many Christians who fell foul of Diocletian. His body was brought to Egypt in the 12th century. Although you cannot enter the actual convent you can descend into the soaring main hall, a remarkable feature of which are the 8-m-high wooden doors studded with nails. Within are some beautiful icons while the windows are *mashrabiya*, as this was once a Fatimid house. In the small room at the left hangs a chain which, it is claimed, was used to secure early martyrs.

The Church of St Sergius
① *Turn left out of the convent, then turn right at the end of the lane, open 0800-1600.* The fifth-century Church of St Sergius is dedicated to two soldiers, St Sergius and St Bacchus, who were martyred in Syria in AD 303. The earliest pieces of the building date from the fifth century. It lies some 3 m below street level and was rebuilt in the Fatimid period after having been virtually destroyed by fire in the eighth century. The architecture of the church, which contains many antiques recovered from ancient monuments, follows the style of a traditional basilica with the nave divided from the side aisles by two rows of six marble pillars. Eleven of these monolithic columns are marble and one is of red granite. The remains of illustrations on these pillars represent the apostles or saints. Some of the series of icons found here are 17th century and show scenes from the lives of Christ, the Virgin Mary and some of the saints. The partially flooded crypt, to the left of the sanctuary, the only remaining vestige of the original church, is intriguing because it is claimed that the Holy Family sought refuge here during their flight to Egypt and the places where they sat are still visible. It has always been a popular place of pilgrimage and a special Mass is held annually on the 24th day of the Coptic month of Bechens (1 June) to commemorate the flight.

No peace for the holy either

In the grim, barren desolation of the Moqattam hills to the south of Cairo were a number of abandoned windmills. These had been used by the British army during the First World War to produce flour supplies and were no longer required.

In 1936 a monk called Mina obtained one to use as a place of retreat and prayer. With the door replaced and the roof made safe he constructed a small living area downstairs and an even smaller chapel above. His intention to devote himself to peaceful contemplation proved impossible. The monk in the windmill was good news to those needing a release from their mental and physical problems. The number of visitors increased and set times were allocated for services each day.

The area was declared unsafe during the Second World War and Mina moved, with some reluctance, to the neighbouring churches of Archangel Michael and St Mary in Old Cairo, just 3 km away.

After the hostilities Mina purchased the land adjacent to the former windmill site and built a church dedicated to St Mina the martyr. To this was added a large monastic complex complete with accommodation where he stayed until he was elected patriach in 1971 and became Pope Shenuda III.

Whereas the monasteries in Egypt had suffered from serious decline, the influence of a Pope who had spent so many years in retreat caused a revival of interest in monasticism among the Coptic community. Buildings have been restored, visitors welcomed and the number of monks has increased.

The Church of St Barbara

ⓘ *0800-1600.* Just behind the church of St Sergius is the very similar 11th-century Church of St Barbara standing on the site of an older church dedicated to St Cyrus and St John in AD 684 that was destroyed during an Arab assault. It is said that when some Christians from Damanhur, including Cyrus and John, confessed to their faith they were shot with arrows, burned in a furnace, tied to a horse's tail and dragged through the streets and survived – to be beheaded. The remains of these two martyrs are in the side chapel approached from the left of the altar. The third-century relics of St Barbara were brought to the church and are now contained in a lovely little chapel to the left of the altar. St Barbara was an attractive young woman from Nicomedia in Asia Minor. In one version of her history she tried to convert her father to Christianity and he killed her. In the second version she was denounced by her family when she decided to become a nun – then tortured and finally put to death by the Romans along with her faithful attendant St Juliana.

The Ben Ezra Synagogue

ⓘ *0900-1600, photography strictly forbidden.* South of the Church of St Barbara is the Ben Ezra Synagogue in the former sixth-century Church of St Michael the Archangel, which itself had been built on the site of a synagogue destroyed by the Romans. This is the oldest surviving synagogue in Egypt. In the 12th century it was sold back to the Jews by the Copts in order to pay taxes being raised to finance the Ibn Tulun mosque. The synagogue is built in the basilica style with three naves and an altar hidden by doors, which are wonderfully worked and encrusted with ivory. When the synagogue was extensively repaired in the 19th century, medieval Hebrew manuscripts, known collectively as the **Geniza documents** and providing details of the history of the 11th-16th centuries, were discovered. These are now kept in libraries around Western Europe.

Church of St George
① *Via the first door on the left of the main entrance to the museum, 0800-1600.* The Church of St George is a modern construction from 1904 and the only circular church in Egypt, so shaped because it is actually built on top of the north tower of the old fortress. Part of the Monastery of St George, which is the seat of the Greek Orthodox Patriarchate of Alexandria, the church is nevertheless the scene of one of the largest Coptic *moulids* in Egypt on 23 April (St George's Day). It is worth a quick look for the brightly stained glass, enormous chandelier, heady scent of incense and a few nice icons. The adjacent Café Saint George is a bit expensive but the best place to re-group after seeing so many churches, with alfresco wicker seating, whispering trees, good lemon juice (*asir lamoon*) and passable coffee.

If you are going to walk from the main Coptic sights to the mosque and monasteries to the north, you will pass by the **Souk Al-Fustat**, about 400 m north of the metro station, on the right-hand side of Sharia Saydi Hassan Al-Anwar, before the Mosque of Amr. You can't miss the freshly constructing building, which provides workspaces for local artisans (metal workers, leather workers, glass blowers, etc) in an attempt to keep traditional crafts alive. Well-priced high-quality goods are on sale in the chic shops on the ground floor (see Shopping, page 124).

Other sacred sights
Mosque of Amr Ibn Al-As The original Mosque of Amr Ibn Al-As (Gama Amr), 500 m north of Mari Girgis metro station, was built in AD 642 by the commander of the Arab army that captured Egypt in that year. Built near to both Babylon-in-Egypt and the Arabs' encampment (Fustat), it is the oldest mosque in Egypt and one of the oldest in the entire Islamic world. Because of the continual enlargements, which began in AD 673 only 10 years after Amr's death aged 93, and included major restoration work in the 15th and 18th centuries and the most recent one in the 1970s, nothing of the original mud-brick thatched-roof mosque still exists. Recently repainted and cleaned, its aspect today is virtually modern. As is often the case in the older mosques the interior includes many pillars taken from ancient Egyptian monuments. As a result the whole mosque is a hybrid with parts of the fabric dating from before the conquest of Egypt until the 19th-century alterations. In the north corner under the dome and surrounded by a bronze screen, on the site of Amr's house in Fustat, is the tomb of his son Abdullah who was born when Amr was only 13, became a Muslim before him and was a close companion of the Prophet.

Convent of St Mercurius ① *10-min walk north of the central Coptic area, past the Mosque of Amr Ibn Al-As and on the left, 0700-2000.* This walled complex of churches is worth visiting to escape the presence of the soldiers, tourists and shops that infiltrate the main sights of Coptic Cairo. After a vision in which St Mercurius was presented with a luminous sword (hence his Arabic name *Abu Seifein* – Mr Two Swords) in order to fight for the cause of Christianity, he was persecuted and killed for his faith. Relics are said to be here in the convent and also in the adjacent church. The convent has its origins in the sixth century but has gone through many stages of rebuilding especially in the 10th century. The **Church of St Mercurius**, the largest church here, is actually a church and four large chapels, the chapel on the ground floor dedicated to St Jacob (containing the font used for adult baptism) (at the time of writing this chapel was closed for restoration) and those upstairs (only reliably open on Fridays) dedicated to St George, John the Baptist and the children killed by Herod.

In the church itself steps lead down to a damp cellar room which is the cell of the Great Hermit Saint Barsoun. You need to take your shoes off if you want to enter this cell. In the courtyard behind the church is a small, very basic café and some toilets. In the same complex is the **Church of St Shenuda**. This church, noted for its 18th-century icons, is adjacent to the church of St Mercurius. There are seven icons in the ebony and cedarwood screen, the central one shows the Virgin and the others each have pictures of two apostles. Shenuda is associated with the Red and White monasteries. Nearby, the **Church of the Virgin** is thick with icons and hanging lanterns which, as shafts of sunlight pierce the gloom, create an intensely spiritual atmosphere.

If you have ventured this far, you can avoid backtracking by exiting the convent by the door next to the blue bridge over the Metro tracks. Turn right out of the convent, keep the tracks to your left and walk along the road for 300 m to pick up the Metro at Malek El-Salah station. On your right as you walk away from the convent are four vast cemeteries. Apart from the Commonwealth War Graves Commission cemetary (open 0800-1430) there are no set opening times, but there is often a man with a key who is happy to let you wander around for a small amount of *baksheesh*.

Coptic Orthodox Cathedral

There are more than 100 Coptic Orthodox churches in Cairo but the special pride is the **Coptic Orthodox Cathedral** (1965) dedicated to St Mark. This is just off Sharia Ramses. It can seat 5000 worshippers, houses the patriarchal library and accommodates the patriarch Pope Shenuda III.

Roda Island

An island south of Zamalek, accessible by bridge from Garden City at the northern end and from Old Cairo at the bottom, Roda has a couple of interesting sights, the eccentric Manial Palace being chief among them. Strolling the 2 km between the palace in the north and the Nilometer to the south along mainly post-1950s streets is something few tourists find time to do, but offers plenty of scope for a relaxing *sheesha* and *ahwa* in shady streets that are more peaceful than most.

The Manial Palace ① *Daily 0900-1630, E£20, E£10 for students. Currently closed for restoration and scheduled to reopen soon.* An oasis of tranquillity in noisy Cairo and well worth visiting, the palace was built in 1903 and is now a museum. It was the home of King Farouk's uncle Prince Mohammed Ali and comprises a number of buildings in various styles including Moorish, Ottoman, Persian, Rococo and Syrian. The first is the **Reception Palace** at the gate, beautifully decorated with polychrome tiles and stained glass. Upstairs are a number of luxurious rooms, of which the **Syrian Room** is the finest, and a mother-of-pearl scale model of Sultan Qaitbay's mausoleum. To the right is a mosque with a tall mock Moroccan minaret and then a macabre yet curious **Trophies Museum** with tatty and poorly stuffed animals including a hermaphrodite goat and a table made of elephant's ears. The **Royal Residence** in the middle of the garden is a mixture of Turkish, Moroccan, Egyptian

Umm Khalsoum, Egypt's Mother Diva

The taxi driver has put his favourite cassette on. Who does that forceful voice, rising above the slithering quarter tones of the violins, belong to? It could well be that of Umm Khalsoum, the best known Egyptian of this century after Gamal Abd Al-Nasser and still the most popular Arab singer. There was nothing in her background to suggest that Umm Khalsoum was to become the greatest diva produced by the Arab world.

Born in 1904 in a small village in the Nile Delta region, Umm Khalsoum became interested in music through listening to her father teach her brother Khalid to sing religious chants for village weddings. One day, when Khalid was ill, Umm Khalsoum accompanied her father and performed instead of her brother. The guests were astonished at her voice. After this, she accompanied her father to sing at all the weddings. In 1920, the family headed for Cairo. Once in the capital, Umm Khalsoum's star rose fast. She met the poet Ahmad Ramzi and made her first commercial recordings. In 1935, she sang in her first film. She subsequently starred in numerous Hollywood-on-the-Nile productions.

In 1946, personal and health problems made Umm Khalsoum abandon her career, temporarily as it turned out. Due to her illness, she met her future husband, the doctor Hassan El-Hafnawi, whom she married in 1954. She then resumed her career. Songs such as *Al awal fil gharam wal hubb* ('The first thing in desire and love'), *Al hubbi kullu* ('Love is all') and *Alf layla wa layla* ('A Thousand and One Nights') made her name across the Arab lands. In the 1960s, her Thursday-evening concert on the Cairo-based Radio Sawt Al-Arab ('Voice of the Arabs') became an Arab-wide institution. During the Yemeni civil war, the Monarchist troops knew that Thursday evening was the best time to attack the Egyptian troops supporting the Republicans as they would all be clustered round their radio sets listening to their national diva. So massive was her fame that she was dubbed the 'Fourth Pyramid'.

Umm Khalsoum's deep, vibrant voice was exceptional, of that there is no doubt. Nevertheless, the music may be difficult for Western ears. Though the lyrics are often insufferably syrupy, the diva's songs continue to enjoy wide popularity and her films, subtitled in English or French are often shown on Egyptian satellite channel Nile TV. If there is one piece of modern Arab music you should try to discover, it has to be the Umm Khalsoum classic love song, *Al Atlal* ('The remains of the camp fire'). The theme, a lament sung over the ashes of the camp fire for the departed lover, goes way back to the origins of Arab poetry.

Umm Khalsoum died in 1975, and her funeral cortège filled the streets of Cairo with hundreds of thousands of mourners. Her voice lives on, played in cafés and cars, workshops and homes all over the Arab world.

and Syrian architectures and contains a number of rooms, nearly all of which are decorated with blue earthenware tiles. The **Throne Hall** behind the residence contains impressive royal portraiture and the **Private Museum** includes a varied collection of Korans, manuscripts, carpets, plates and glassware, and is fascinating. The palace gardens are 5500 sq m and contain a rare collection of trees brought back to Egypt by Mohammed Ali.

The Nilometer and Umm Khalsoum Museum On the southern tip of Roda island stands a small kiosk containing the **Nilometer** ① *daily 0900-1600, E£15, students E£8*, originally built in the ninth century BC. There has probably been a nilometer here since ancient times but this one was constructed in AD 861 and is considered the second oldest Islamic structure in Cairo, after the Amr Ibn Al-Aas Mosque. The original measuring gauge remains today and there is exquisite Kufic calligraphy on the interior walls and an elaborately painted dome.

The **Umm Khalsoum Museum** ① *Sharia Al-Malek Al-Salah, Roda, daily 1000-1600, E£2*, contains memorabilia from the life of Egypt's ultimate diva (see box, page 89). It's a small and well-curated museum set in pleasant grounds next to the Manasterli Palace (an impressive Rococco structure where concerts are infrequently held). In the museum are Umm Khalsoum's famous sunglasses and ubiquitous pink scarf, alongside photos, press cuttings and audiovisuals – most poignant of which shows her funeral procession that brought the streets of Cairo to a standstill in 1975. You can listen to her songs and if they appeal to you there is an enterprising stall outside selling her CDs. There is also an impressive display of aged audio equipment that was no doubt once state-of-the-art.

Zamalek and Gezira

This island in the Nile was unoccupied until the middle of the 19th century when Khedive Ismail built a magnificent palace and landscaped its surrounds into sprawling royal gardens populated by exotic animals. These days, the palace is part of the Marriott hotel and **Zamalek**, the northern part of the island, is a leafy, upmarket residential area popular with expats and the Egyptian elite. There are many decent restaurants (some of them floating), welcoming places for a drink, excellent shopping (books, art and souvenirs) and the delightful Islamic Ceramics Museum. **Gezira** occupies the southern half, mostly taken up by the grounds of the Gezira Club and the Opera House complex, plus there are some attractive gardens along the river and the landmark Cairo Tower.

Islamic Ceramics Museum
① *1 Sharia Sheikh Al-Marsafy, next to the Marriott, Zamalek, Sat-Thu 1000-1400 and 1700-2100, entrance E£25, students E£12.50. Photos permitted upon application.*
The palace of Prince Amr Ibrahim is a cool, marbled haven and provides a beautiful home for exquisite ceramics dating from the seventh century to the modern day. The soft tints, hues and glazes bring out the designs on vessels and dishes collected from countries stretching from Morocco to Persia. The garden contains some pieces of sculpture, while in the basement there's an art gallery (free) that has interesting displays by contemporary Egyptian artists.

Cairo Tower
① *Sharia Hadayek Al-Zuhrey, Gezira, T02-2736 5112, daily 0900-0100 (-2400 in winter), E£70.*
The 187-m tower with a lotus-shaped top is a prominent icon of the Cairo skyline, especially at night when it is lit with waves of neon lights that constantly change colour. It was built with Soviet help in 1957-1962 and has recently undergone a revamp. Although the Sky Garden revolving restaurant at the top and cafeteria are very decent, it is the viewing platform that is most impressive. Providing the pollution is not too bad, you can

look east across the modern city centre to the minarets and mosques of Islamic Cairo and the Muqattam Hills beyond; to the west the Pyramids and desert sprawl out on the horizon. It's a great view of the city at night.

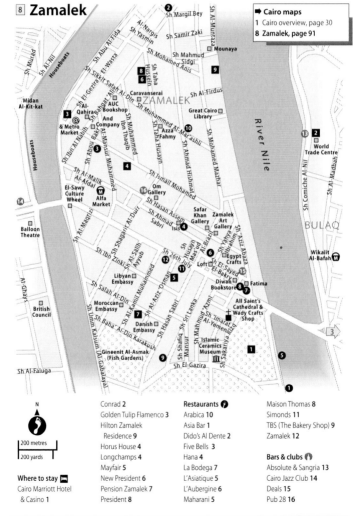

8 Zamalek

➡ Cairo maps
1 Cairo overview, page 30
8 Zamalek, page 91

Where to stay ▭
Cairo Marriott Hotel
& Casino 1

Conrad 2
Golden Tulip Flamenco 3
Hilton Zamalek
  Residence 9
Horus House 4
Longchamps 4
Mayfair 5
New President 6
Pension Zamalek 7
President 8

Restaurants 🍴
Arabica 10
Asia Bar 1
Dido's Al Dente 2
Five Bells 3
Hana 4
La Bodega 7
L'Asiatique 5
L'Aubergine 6
Maharani 5

Maison Thomas 8
Simonds 11
TBS (The Bakery Shop) 9
Zamalek 12

Bars & clubs 🍸
Absolute & Sangria 13
Cairo Jazz Club 14
Deals 15
Pub 28 16

The west bank

The newer suburbs on Cairo's west bank are chiefly comprised of concrete blocks built post-1960, interspersed with the occasional grand villa, crumbling mansion and pleasant green square. There are a few smaller, less frequented museums that have a great deal of charm as well as some good restaurants, which may draw you over this side of the river. **Dokki** (pronounced *Do'ii*, with a glottal stop in the middle) is home to the **Agricultural Museum** and the **Mr and Mrs Mahmoud Khalil Museum**, but not much else that would interest a tourist. **Mohandiseen**, further inland, is a middle-class enclave of swanky boutiques, fast-food joints and decent international and Egyptian cuisine. It is about the only district in Cairo that looks and feels Western (but just on the main drags) with strings of American coffee shop chains, wide palm-lined boulevards, luminous billboards and sleekly fashionable shoppers. In sharp contrast is **Imbaba** to the north, a gritty suburb with great *baladi souks* and where a string of 30 or so picturesque houseboats remain moored along the Nile at Midan Kit Kat. The attractions of **Giza**, apart from the obvious, are the child-friendly **Pharaonic Village** and the zoo, which has attractive botanical gardens adjacent to it.

Agricultural Museum

ⓘ *Adjacent to the Ministry of Agriculture in Dokki at end of 6th October Bridge, T02-3761 6874, Tue-Sun 0900-1400, E£3, cameras 20 pt.*

This has the distinction of being the oldest agricultural museum in world (dating from 1930), with stuffed animals, racks of luminescent birds, Egyptian farming practices and photos of medical anomalies. It might sound tedious, but it is a slice of unspoilt history – the museum itself ought be in a museum – full of waxy wooden display cabinets and housed in glorious buildings engraved with decorative flora and fauna. Downstairs in the main Scientific Museum, countryside scenes are brought to life by statues of farmers at work and gruesome pictures of rural diseases (pay the guard a bit of *baksheesh* to gain entry to the side galleries). The many animals that were worshipped, hunted or eaten – cats, ostrich, Apis bulls and falcons – are here, as mummies or skeletons. Unfortunately the labels, in a variety of languages, give little information if they exist at all.

The ticket price includes entrance to several museums in the grounds, some of which are closed for maintenance and due to reopen soon. The strangely beautiful **Bread Halls** reveal the story of bread in Egypt, with plaster-casts of the various forms of this staple food and interesting old photographs. The **Cotton Museum** surveys cotton-growing in Egypt and the **Ancient Egyptian Agriculture Museum** contains quite a choice range of pharaonic artefacts; both are housed in Soviet-style edifices but are currently closed for renovation. Also on site is the **Palace of Princess Fatma**, daughter of Khedive Ismail, which is accessible to those with special interest. Meticulously maintained on two levels, the museum displays her ornate furniture, many beautiful works of art, and collections of ivory curios, old cameras and Persian carpets. The gardens surrounding the museum are a peaceful place to relax, full of dusty old palms and flowering trees.

Step into the salon

Beauty parlours provide all sorts of treatments. Foot massages and pedicures are lengthy and often public, enjoyed by both men and women; ladies then go on to choose from an array of gaudy nail polish.

Men should head to the barbers, not to risk a radical haircut but for a cut-throat close shave. Not only do they double-shave customers the smoothest they've ever been, there's an invigorating head, face and neck massage afterwards that sets the teeth tingling. Be warned, though, the barber might take it upon himself to start threading your face to remove all stray wisps above the cheekbones, plus eye-wateringly removal of any nasal hairs and shaping of eyebrows. Make sure you are happy with the hygiene standards of the establishment before you let them take a razor to you.

While it's not recommended for women to chance going for a haircut in Egypt (unless it's for bizarre feathering or 'trims' that take 15 cm off) there are other ways to indulge yourself for a small sum. Hair removal is cheap and relatively painless, with lumps of cool sticky melted sugar (*helawa*) being pressed and smeared onto the skin then worked off in jerky tugs. Egyptian women get virtually every hair plucked from their body, and though you might not want a full body wax, lots of foreigners living in Cairo follow the custom to some degree and get their arms sugared. Face 'threading' is an interesting process to watch but not necessarily to participate in, with a stretch of twisted cotton held between the mouth and fingers and drawn across the skin to magically remove the tiny hairs with a pinging sound. *Baladi* women perform these tasks for each other at home, but if you don't have that option, a good places to go is Tarek Nail Centre, 47 Sharia Michel Bakoum, Mohandiseen, T02-3748 7422, quite a public experience for pedicures (but privacy for other things), full leg wax E£50. They also have a salon in Maadi, 73 Road 9, T02-2358 3385.

Mr and Mrs Mahmoud Khalil Museum

① *1 Sharia Kafour, off Sharia Giza, Dokki, T02-3748 2142, www.mkm.gov.eg, Wed-Mon 0900-1730, E£25, students E£12, photo ID required for entry.*

The sumptuous villa of the Khalil's hides a wonderful collection of Impressionist paintings by the likes of Renoir, Monet and Toulouse-Lautrec. It also used to house a Van Gogh, but this was stolen in broad daylight in 2010 prompting a nationwide overhaul of museum security facilities and the imprisonment of the curators of museum. Despite the loss, there are also some fine sculptures, including works by Rodin, and the fact very few visitors make it here mean it's a pleasurably personal experience.

Giza Zoo

① *T02-3570 1552, daily 0900-1700 in winter, 0800-1800 in summer, E£20.*

The zoo has many claims to fame. In particular it is the biggest exhibitor in Africa, having on display the largest number of endangered species. Its situation near the west bank of the Nile at Giza makes it easily accessible over El-Gamea Bridge. The zoo is organized into five huge grottos, one holding statues of rare Egyptian mammals. There are over 6000 animals and birds on display from around 40 species. Features include the Reptile House and the Lion House. The zoo is proud of its record in breeding and returning to the wild barbary sheep, nubian ibex, dorcas gazelle and sacred ibis. **Note** Visitors used to Western zoos may find a visit here very distressing, particularly the lion cages.

Dr Ragab's Pharaonic Village

ⓘ *On Jacob's Island, Giza, 3 km south of the city centre, T02-3572 2533 or T02-35718675/6/7, www.pharaonicvillage.com, daily Sep-Jun 0900-1800, Jul-Aug 0900-2100, E£201, children under 4 years free.*

Numerous actors on floating amphitheatres perform the daily activities of the ancient Egyptians as you cruise and view from a pharaonic boat. The pace is set by the boat tour through the village on the bullrush-fringed Nile so be sure to allow at least two hours. There are 12 museums relating the history of Egypt, plus demonstrations of papyrus-making – it's possible to purchase quality papyrus copies of illustrations and writing found in tombs at the on-site Papyrus Institute. The Nefertari yacht takes you on a one-hour cruise along a scenic stretch of the Nile as part of the ticket price. It's a great place for children who will enjoy the Tut Land amusement park, and a quite bizarre experience for anyone.

Pyramids of Giza

ⓘ *T02-2391 3454, daily 0800-1700 winter, 0800-1800 summer, E£80 (students E£40) to enter the area, additional E£200 (students E£100) to enter the Pyramid of Cheops. The number of tourists who can enter Cheops is limited in order to preserve the monument so arrive early (morning session 0800, then another batch at 1300; 250 at one time in winter, 150 people in summer), additional E£60/30 to enter the second and third pyramids. No cameras permitted inside the pyramid, they have to be left with the guards on entering, and claustrophobics should avoid going inside. For Sound and Light performances, see page 120. A camel ride around the pyramids can be a fun way to take in their splendour, offer no more than E£20 for a short ride – to be paid after your meander. AA and MG stables (past the entrance to the Sphinx) are among the more notable in Giza.*

One of the first things that visitors to the Pyramids will notice is their unexpected proximity to Cairo. The second is the onslaught of hustlers that bombard the awe-struck onlooker. Despite the increased police presence that tries in earnest to subdue the camel and horse hustlers, water and soda hawkers and papyrus and postcard vendors, they still get through. Be firm with your 'no' and they'll get the point, eventually. To get the best out of the experience, it's definitely recommended to be first through the gate or the last person in before the gates close, and strike off into the desert around to view their majesty from afar.

Of the Seven Wonders of the ancient world only the Pyramids are left standing. Those at Giza are by no means the only ones in Egypt but they are the largest, most imposing and best preserved. When Herodotus, chronicler of the Ancient Greeks, visited them in 450 BC they were already more ancient to him than the time of Christ is to us today. That the huge blocks were quarried, transported and put into place demonstrates how highly developed and ordered the Old Kingdom was at its peak. Herodotus claimed that it would have taken 100,000 slaves 30 years to have constructed the great **Pyramid of Cheops**, but it is more likely that the pyramid was built by peasants, paid in food, who were unable to work the land while the Nile flooded between July and November. Happily, the high waters also made it possible to transport the casing stone from Aswan and Tura virtually to the base of the pyramids. The enormous Pyramid of Cheops, built between 2589-2566 BC out of over 2,300,000 blocks of stone with an average weight of two and a half tonnes and a total weight of 6,000,000 tonnes to a height of almost 140 m, is the oldest and largest of the pyramids at Giza. Maybe not surprisingly, it can be seen from the moon. The **Pyramid of Chephren** and **Pyramid of Menkaure** date from 2570-30 BC. There is a theory that the odd plan of the three Pyramids of Giza, progressively smaller and with the third slightly offset to the left, correlates to the layout of the three stars of Orion's Belt. Highly controversial, it suggests that the Ancient Egyptians chose to reproduce, on land and over a great distance, a kind of map of the stars.

A breakdown in the structure of society, and the reduction of wealth, have been proposed as reasons why other pyramids were not constructed on the same scale later in the Old Kingdom. The first thefts from tombs occurred relatively soon after the Pyramids' construction, which was undoubtedly an important factor in the preference for hidden tombs, such as in The Valley of the Kings, by the time of the New Kingdom.

The Great Pyramid of Cheops (Khufu)
Very little is known of Cheops. His tomb, which could have provided some answers, was looted long before any archaeologists arrived. He is believed to have been the absolute ruler of a highly stratified society and his reign must have been one of great wealth in order to afford so stupendous a burial site. Although he was buried alone, his wives and relations may have merited smaller *mastabas* nearby.

Originally the 230 x 230 m pyramid would have stood at 140 m high but 3 m has been lost in all dimensions since the encasing limestone was eroded or removed by later rulers who used the cemeteries like a quarry to construct the Islamic city. The entrance, which

Pyramids of Giza

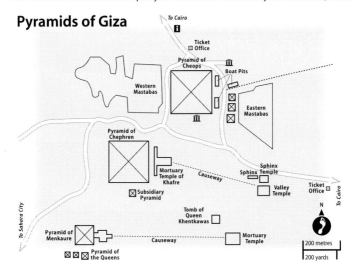

was at the centre of the north face, has been changed in modern times and access is now 15 m lower via an opening created by the plundering Khalifa Ma'mun in AD 820.

Inside the Great Pyramid Going up the 36-m long ascending corridor, which is 1.6 m high and has a steep 1:2 gradient, you arrive at the start of the larger 47-m-long **Great Gallery**, which continues upward at the same incline – the sensation of being under six million tonnes of stone becomes overpowering at this point; it's definitely not for claustrophobics or those who dislike being hustled into moving too quickly by lines of other visitors. The gallery, whose magnificent stonework is so well cut that it is impossible to insert a blade into the joints, narrows at the top end to a corbelled roof and finishes at the King's Chamber, 95 m beneath the pyramid's apex.

The walls of **The King's Chamber** are lined with polished red granite. The room measures 5.2 x 10.8 x 5.8 m high and contains the huge lidless Aswan red granite sarcophagus, which was all that remained of the treasures when archaeologists first explored the site. It was saved because it was too large to move along the entrance passage and, therefore, must have been placed in the chamber during the pyramid's construction. Above this upper chamber there is a series of five relieving chambers that are structurally essential to support the massed weight of the stones above and distribute the weight away from the burial chamber. A visit to the collapsed pyramid at Maidoum (see El-Fayoum, page 149) will illustrate why this was necessary. You may want to wait around a while in the King's Chamber, if you can stand the heat, to let the crowds thin out and you'll start to get a sense of the mystique of the place that prompts some visitors to start chanting.

One of the great mysteries of the massive Pyramid of Cheops is the four tiny meticulously crafted 20-cm-sq shafts, which travel, two from the King's Chamber and another two from the

Pyramid of Cheops (section)

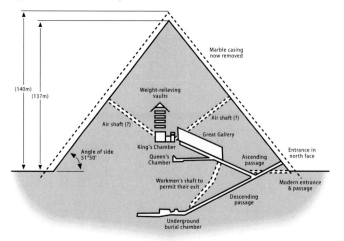

Queen's Chamber, at precisely maintained angles through the body of the pyramid to the outer walls. Obviously serving a significant function, they were originally thought to be ventilation shafts. However, Egyptologists are now more inclined to believe that they are of religious significance and relate to the Ancient Egyptians' belief that the stars are a heavenly counterpart to their land, inhabited by gods and souls of the departed.

The main feature of the ancient night sky was the Milky Way, the bright band of stars that was believed to be the celestial Nile. The most conspicuous of the stars were those of Orion's Belt, whose reappearance coincided with the yearly miracle of the Nile flood and was associated with Osiris, the protector god. The brightest star in the sky (Sirius) was his consort, the goddess Isis, because it was glitteringly beautiful and followed Osiris across the sky. Linked to the creation myth, the texts on the great pyramid's walls repeatedly tell of the dead Pharaoh, seen as the latest incarnation of Horus, the son of Isis and Osiris, travelling in a boat between various star constellations. At an angle of exactly 45°, the southern shaft of the King's Chamber points directly at where Orion's Belt would have been in the sky in ancient times. Meanwhile, the southern shaft of the Queen's Chamber points to Sirius, his consort Isis. The northern shaft of the King's Chamber is directed at the circumpolar stars, important to the Ancient Egyptians as the celestial pole because these stars never disappear or die in the sky. The 'star shafts' thus appear to be directed so that the spirit of the dead Pharaoh could use the shafts to reach the important stars with pinpoint accuracy.

Around the Great Pyramid of Cheops

In accordance with the pharaonic custom, Cheops married his sister Merites whose smaller ruined pyramid stands to the east of his, together with the pyramids of two other queens, both of which are attached to a similarly ruined smaller sanctuary. Little remains of **Cheops' Mortuary Temple**, which stood to the east of the pyramid. It was connected by a causeway, which collapsed only in the last 150 years, to the Valley Temple that stands near the modern village of **Nazlat Al-Samman**. The temples and causeway were built and decorated before Cheops' Pyramid was completed.

West of the Cheops Pyramid is an extensive **Royal Cemetery** in which 15 *mastabas* have been opened to the public after having been closed for over 100 years. A 4600-year-old female mummy, with a unique internal plaster encasement unlike that seen anywhere else, was discovered at the site.

The **Sun Boat Museum** ⓘ *daily 0900-1600, E£60, students E£30*, is at the base of the south face of the Cheops Pyramid where five boat pits were discovered in 1982. The boat on display, painstakingly reassembled over 14 years and an amazing 43 m long, is held together with sycamore pegs and rope. The exact purpose of these buried boats is unclear but they may have been a means of travelling to the afterlife, as can be seen in the 17th to 19th Dynasty tombs at Thebes, or possibly a way of accompanying the Sun God on his diurnal journey. It may not sound like much and is yet another expense in an already expensive day, but the scale and antiquity of the vessel is impressive and makes real the engravings of boats you so often see on temple walls around Egypt.

Pyramid of Chephren ⓘ *E£20, students E£10*, or Khafre as he is sometimes known, was built for the son of Cheops and Hensuten and stands to the southwest of the Great Pyramid of Cheops. Although, at 136.5 m high and an estimated weight of 4,880,000 tonnes, it is actually a few metres smaller than the Cheops Pyramid and its construction on a raised limestone plateau was a deliberate attempt to make it appear larger than that of his father. The top of the pyramid still retains some of the casing of polished limestone from Tura that once covered the entire surface, providing an idea of the original finish and how the pyramid would have appeared to the earliest travellers – gleaming and white as they approached from the desert. The entrance to the tomb was lost for centuries until 1818 when Belzoni located it and blasted open the sealed portal on the north side. Although he believed that it would still be intact, he found that it had been looted many centuries earlier. As with the Pyramid of Cheops there is an unfinished and presumed unused chamber below the bedrock. The entrance passageway now used heads downwards before levelling out to a granite-lined passageway that leads to the burial chamber. To the west of the chamber is the red granite sarcophagus, built into the floor, with the lid lying nearby.

The **Mortuary Temple of Khafre** lies to the east of the pyramid and is more elaborate and better preserved than that of his father. Although the statues and riches have been stolen, the limestone walls were cased with granite, which is still present in places. There are still the remains a large pillared hall, a small sanctuary, outhouses and a courtyard.

A 500-m causeway linked the Mortuary Temple to the **Valley Temple**, which is better preserved than any other because it lay hidden in the sands until Mariette rediscovered it in 1852. It is lined with red granite at roof height that protects the limestone. Two entrances to the temple face east and lead to a T-shaped hall supported by enormous pillars. In front of these stood 23 diorite statues of Khafre. The only one that has remained intact can be found in the Egyptian Museum.

The Sphinx

The Sphinx is next to Khafre's Valley Temple to the northeast. We are extremely lucky that it still exists because it was built of soft sandstone and would have disappeared centuries ago had the sand not covered it for so much of its history. Yet it is equally surprising that it was ever carved because its sculptor must have known that such soft stone would quickly decay. The Arabs call it the Father of Terror (*Abu'l-Hawl*). Nobody can be certain who it represents but it is possibly Khafre himself and, if this is the case, would be the oldest known large-scale royal portrait. Some say that it was hewn from the remaining stone after the completion of the pyramid and that, almost as an afterthought, Khafre set it, as a sort of monumental scarecrow, to guard his tomb. Others claim that the face is that of his guardian deity rather than Khafre's own. The Sphinx was first uncovered by Tuthmosis IV (1425-1417 BC) thereby fulfilling a prophecy that by uncovering the great man-lion he would gain the throne. Recent efforts to conserve the Sphinx are now complete but the rising water table threatens to accelerate its decay. Earlier attempts to restore it caused more harm than good when the porous sandstone was filled, totally inappropriately, with concrete. The Sphinx suffered at the hands at Mamluke and Napoleonic troops who used him for target practice, and a piece of the missing 'beard' is exhibited in the British Museum.

The name 'sphinx', which means 'strangler', was given first by the Greeks to a fabulous creature that had the head and bust of a woman, the body of a lion and the wings of a bird. The sphinx appears to have originated in Egypt in the form of a sun god with whom the pharaoh was associated. The Egyptian sphinx is usually a lion with the head of a king wearing the characteristic wig-cover. There are, however, ram-headed sphinxes associated with the god Amun.

Pyramid of Menkaure (Mycerinus)

This is the smallest of the three Giza Pyramids and marks the beginning of a steep decline in the standards of workmanship and attention to detail in the art of pyramid-building. At the time of Menkaure's death (who was Chephren's successor and later known by the Greek name of Mycerinus) the pyramid was unfinished and the granite encasement intended to cover the poor quality local limestone was never put in place by his son Shepseskaf. The base is 102 x 104 m (the original measurements much reduced by removal of stones) and rises at 51 degrees to 66.5 m high, considerably lower than the earlier pyramids. It also differs from those of Khufu and Khafre in that the lower chamber was used as the burial tomb. The walls are lined with granite hewn into the rock below the level of the Pyramid's foundations. A fine basalt sarcophagus was discovered in the recessed floor but unfortunately lost at sea en route to Britain.

East of the Pyramid of Menkaure lies the **Mortuary Temple**, which is relatively well preserved. The walls were not encased with granite or marble but with red mud bricks and then lined with a thin layer of smoother limestone. It is connected to the Valley Temple via a 660-m mud-brick causeway that now lies beneath the sand.

Subsidiary pyramids

South of the Pyramid of Menkaure are three smaller incomplete pyramids. The largest, to the east, was most likely intended for Menkaure's principal wife. The granite sarcophagus of the central tomb was recovered and was found to contain the bones of a young woman.

The **Tomb of Queen Khentkawes**, who was an obscure but intriguing and important figure, is to the south of the main Giza pyramids. Although she appears to have been married to Shepseskaf, who was the last Fourth Dynasty pharaoh, she subsequently married a high priest of the sun god Re at a time when the male dynastic line was particularly weak. By going on to bear a number of later kings who are buried in Saqqara and Abu Sir, she acted as the link between the Fourth and Fifth Dynasties. Her tomb is an enormous sarcophagus and is linked to a Mortuary Temple cut out of the limestone.

The **Zawiyat Al-Aryan Pyramids** are roughly halfway between Giza and North Saqqara and one has to ride through the desert to see them. A visit would probably only be rewarding to the devoted Egyptologist. There are two pyramids of which the southernmost one is probably a Third Dynasty (2686-2613 BC) step pyramid. The granite of the more northerly suggests that it is Fourth Dynasty (2613-2494 BC) but it would appear to have been abandoned after the foundations had been laid.

Other excursions around Cairo

Birqash Camel Market

ⓘ *35 km northwest of Cairo: getting there via public transport is quite a confusing affair, as there are no direct routes, but if you want to try, take a taxi or minibus to the old camel market in Imbaba (near Imbaba Airport), from there, minibuses run to the the 'souk al-gamal'. Alternatively, hire a taxi for the morning or go with one of the organized tours from a budget hotel. Ismailia and Sun Hotel, in Midan Tahrir, both have weekly trips for E£50 per person, they usually leave around 0630 and return at 1130, the earlier you arrive at the market, the more action you'll see. Tourists are expected to pay a E£20 fee to enter the market.*

Cairo's Friday camel market (there is a smaller version on Mondays) makes an interesting and bewildering morning trip. Shortly after the sun rises, camel traders mill about the smelly grounds in search of the biggest humps and healthiest gums they can find. Larger camels are generally used for transport and farming; smaller ones land up on the dinner table. As the camels have walked from Sudan to Aswan (taking a month) and then been trucked to Cairo, some of them are in a poor state and all of them are hobbled. It is worth bearing in mind an excursion to the market can be distressing as well as fascinating.

Heliopolis
ⓘ *By a/c airport bus from Midan Abdel Moniem Riad (E£2) or by tram from Midan Ramses (50pt), 30 mins.*

Heliopolis (*Masr Al-Gedida*) is a charming and beautiful suburb 12 km northeast of central Cairo, designed in 1905 by the Belgian-born industrialist Baron Empain. He dreamt of

Heliopolis

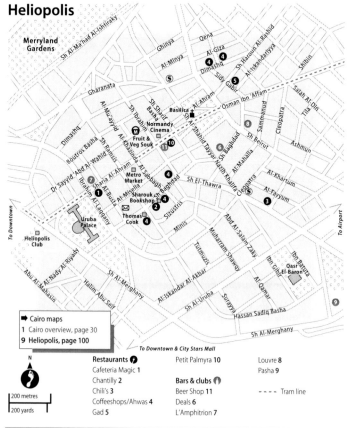

N

200 metres
200 yards

➡ Cairo maps
1 Cairo overview, page 30
9 Heliopolis, page 100

To Downtown & City Stars Mall

Restaurants ⓐ	Petit Palmyra 10	Louvre 8
Cafeteria Magic 1		Pasha 9
Chantilly 2	**Bars & clubs** ⓐ	
Chili's 3	Beer Shop 11	– – – Tram line
Coffeeshops/Ahwas 4	Deals 6	
Gad 5	L'Amphitrion 7	

creating the perfect garden city, a true oasis in the desert, and he succeeded – the tree-lined boulevards of fantastical Oriental architecture became the secluded choice of colonialists and affluent Egyptians in the early years of the 20th century. Today Heliopolis is still a desirable address, with a pervasive air of prosperity and sophistication throughout (and the added enticement of the new City Stars complex), but it is happily totally Egyptian and, come evening, shoppers go crazy and life takes off on the streets. Tiered and arcaded buildings, decorated with ornamental minarets and Islamic emblems, make up much of Heliopolis' whimsical architecture. Particularly fine are the neo-Mamluk buildings along Sharia Ibrahim Al-Laqqany and Sharia Baghdad, and on the residential square behind the Basilica. Though the sprawl of the metropolis has long since encompassed the Baron's little enclave, if you arrive by tram you still get the sense of arrival in another city.

Baron Empain built himself a palace on raised ground with exotic gardens, from which he viewed the construction of Heliopolis below. Known locally as the **Qasr El-Baron**, the palace is a bizarre medley of Hindu and Buddhist architectural styles and motifs. The grounds have recently been cultivated by the Ministry of Tourism, with palm trees and grass being sprinkled around the clock; however, it's off-limits to the public and you'll have to be content with views of Shiva, gargoyles and dragons from behind the railings. From the palace you can see the landmark building of the **Basilica of Notre Dame**. The interior of the Basilica is unspectacular, but its 'jelly mould' exterior is a miniature replica of St Sofia in Istanbul and the remains of Baron Empain and his son are interred within. The Basilica marks the end of Heliopolis' main drag, Sharia Al-Ahram (so-called because at one time the pyramids of Giza could be seen from here), which leads up to another key landmark, the **Uruba Palace**. A monumental and beautiful structure, completed in 1910, the former Palace Hotel was once the most lavish of all the hotels in the region. It became a military hospital during World War II and was for many years the offices of President Mubarak; entry (and even scrutiny) is forbidden.

While a visit to Heliopolis will not be at the top of the list if you've only a few days in Cairo, it is perfect for an afternoon of pleasant yet stimulating strolling followed by good food and drinks, especially if you are tiring of mosque visits and museums.

Trips down the Nile

A trip to Egypt would be remiss without at least an hour's meander on the Nile on an age-old *felucca*. Even if you are planning to go to Luxor or Aswan where *feluccas* are an essential ingredient of any visit, it's still mesmerizing to have a night-time sail while in Cairo when the city is at its most beautiful. Most *feluccas* accommodate up to eight people, and some have seats for far more – the greater number of passengers, the cheaper the fare. Bargaining is the norm, be prepared for a battle, but a standard price is around E£70 per hour. Tips are expected. *Feluccas* for hire dock in front of the Nile Hilton, Downtown, and near the Four Seasons in Garden City.

If you want to sail on a greener part of the Nile, past pastoral islands and away from the city, take a taxi to the nearby suburb of **Maadi** (E£15-20) and ask for the *felucca* dock. Or, an alternative trip closer to the city can be taken around the island of Zamalek on one of the motorboats moored past the houseboats north of Midan Kit Kat. These have neon lights and blare out Egyptian pop; a circuit can be done in about an hour; try to bargain for E£60.

Gardens

Apart from the pinnacle that is Al-Azhar Park (see page 78) the gardens of Cairo are likely to be a disappointment, being criss-crossed with concrete and big on 'Keep Off The Grass' signs. But if you are in need of some tranquillity away from the city bustle, you could try the **Zoological Gardens** ① *0900-1700, but avoid Fri and public holidays*, in Giza, where there are many rare and beautiful trees. In Zamalek, the **Fish Gardens** ① *Sharia Geziret al-Wusta, daily 0900-1630*, has several large aquaria with tropical fish housed in a weird grotto, popular with courting couples strolling the rather scrubby grounds. There's also a string of gardens in Gezira, running north along the river from Tahrir Bridge towards the Marriott Hotel, which cost between E£2 and E£10 to enter. The **Merryland Gardens** in Heliopolis are a splendid place for children, with a dolphin on site, a pedalo lake, a merry-go-round and lots of good restaurants. **Kanatir Al-Khaireya Gardens** (the Good Barrage) about 20 km downstream from the city has some shady parks and is good for a day out with a picnic (but not on Fridays when it is hideously crowded). The journey there is a lot of fun, with a party atmosphere on board the ferry, which leaves from the Maspero Dock in the front of the television building, hourly 0800-1000, returning 1400-1600.

⊙ Cairo listings

For sleeping and eating price codes and other relevant information, see pages 10-14.

⊜ Where to stay

As the largest city in Africa and the Middle East, and one of the world's great tourist destinations, Cairo has hundreds of hotels ranging from the premier de luxe accommodation of major international chains to some really rugged local dives. The listings below, which have sought to avoid the worst and include the extraordinary, provide options to suit varied budgets, though higher end mid-range accommodation is somewhat lacking in Central Cairo. Nearly all the notable budget and mid-range accommodation centres around Downtown (the City Centre) and Zamalek. The most exceptional expensive hotels are also in the City Centre or near the Pyramids. Be sure to check online for discount rates and promotions at mid- and top-range hotels, significantly cheaper than the rack rate.

Credit cards are accepted in higher-end establishments, and some mid-range places. Take into account that the prices of accommodation in Cairo and all over Egypt

fluctuate significantly depending on the season and number of tourists in the country, so use the price codes indicated here as a guide.

For travellers on a budget, Cairo has loads of interesting and decent cheap hotels, which means fierce competition, and brutal hotel touts. Lies are part of the game. You will be told hotels are full, or closed, or have doubled in price. Take control of the situation by choosing a place in advance, or assertively spend some time wandering around the centre exploring your options. Also remember that bargaining is the norm in Egypt, especially if it's summertime or you have plans to stay for a while. Where possible, we have included specific costs for the most budget of choices.

Camping Because Cairo has very little undeveloped earth on which to pitch a tent and since there are so many budget hotels, there is little demand for camping. The only decent real campground is **Salma Camping**, T02-2381 5062. It can be reached by turning off from Harraniya village on the road between the Pyramids and Saqqara. It offers cabins, a camping ground, hot showers, a buffet and a bar. E£30 to pitch a tent; E£100 for a simple double cabin.

Central Cairo *p40, maps p32 and p36*
eeee **Fairmont Nile City**, Corniche El-Nil, Bulaq, T02-2461 9356, www.fairmont.com. One of the newest additions to the 5-star scene, the **Fairmont** is utterly luxurious with rooms that combine contemporary chic with art nouveau styling. The wealth of restaurants and uber-cool bars are a plus point, as is the fabulous spa. It is 10 mins in a taxi from Downtown.
€€€€ **Four Seasons**, 1089 Corniche El-Nil, Garden City, T02-2791 7000. Some of the classiest rooms in town and faultless restaurants – famed for their Fri brunches, E£200 for all you can eat. There is another **Four Seasons** in Giza, 35 Sharia Giza, T02-3573 1212, opposite the zoo, which is somewhat brasher but a hot-spot for belly-dancing, Sufis and entertainments.
eeee **Kempinski**, 12 Sharia Ahmed Rageb, Corniche El-Nil, Garden City, T02-2798 0000, www.kempinski.com. Plush new place, with a level of personalised service equal to that of a boutique hotel despite having 191 rooms (including 54 suites). Interiors are classic modern, blending Egyptian and European styles, with marble bathrooms and expensive fittings. Floor 10 has a champagne balcony, **Jazz Bar**, exclusive restaurant and rooftop pool (which becomes a bar/club at weekends). The other top-quality restaurant, **Osmanly**, serving Turkish food, and the de luxe spa make it a perfect choice if you have money to spend.
€€€€ **Nile Ritz-Carlton**, Corniche El-Nil, Midan Tahrir, www.ritzcarlton.com. On the Nile adjacent to the Egyptian Museum, this Cairo landmark was opened in 1959 by President Nasser and is currently being fully renovated. It's due to reopen soon; check the website for the latest dates.
€€€€ **Semiramis Intercontinental**, Corniche El-Nil, Garden City, T02-2795 7171.

Masses of rooms in an ugly pink building and expensive, but excellent service all around and good views of the Nile overlooking the end of Gezira Island. Outdoor pool. People come for the belly-dancing at the weekends, and the **Bird Cage** Thai restaurant, which achieves absolute perfection in terms of food, service and atmosphere.
eeee **Conrad**, 1191 Corniche El-Nil, Bulaq, T02-2580 8000. What appears to be a fairly uneventful location is actually an interesting mix of teeming markets, old mosques and hammans in the lanes of Bulaq behind the hotel, contrasted with the grandeur of the **Nile City Mall** shops and cafés just north along the river. There's a pool and good healthclub, notable restaurants, and **Sangria** restaurant/**Absolute** nightclub is directly opposite.
eee **Cosmopolitan**, 1 Sharia Ibn Taalab, Qasr El-Nil, T02-2392 3956. In the centre of Downtown in a quiet side street, the elegant building has a fabulous chandelier in the foyer, yet some rooms are pokey for the price – ask for one with a balcony. All have a/c, fridge and TV. The restaurant serves reasonable food, the **Kings Bar** is a good hangout, plus there's a café and nightclub next door. Breakfast included.
eee **Talisman**, 39 Sharia Talaat Harb, T02-2393 9431, www.talisman-hotel.com. This gem of a hotel is hidden down an alley parallel to Sharia 26th July. Look for the **New Minerva** hotel sign and once inside take the left-hand elevator up to rich, warm colours and tasteful Arabesque decor throughout. Each room is unique and the lounge area is festooned with artefacts. This is the only almost-boutique hotel in Downtown, and it's a good idea to book in advance. Free Wi-Fi or broadband.
eee-ee **Grand Hotel**, 17 Sharia 26 July, T02-2575 7700, www.grandhotelcairo.com. In a crowded but central location, it retains a few original art deco fixtures among a mixture of parquet and plastic veneers.

Rooms are clean with new mattresses and spotless marble bathrooms. Breakfast included, TV and fridge in rooms, but there's no bar. Staff are very friendly and helpful.

€€ Cairo Inn, 1st floor, 6 Midan Talaat Harb, T02-2575 9213, cairoinn44@hotmail.com. Offers 7 spotlessly clean rooms with bath. Free Wi-Fi and breakfast. An excellent central location, but noisy.

€€ Carlton, 21 Sharia 26 July, T02-2575 5181, www.carltonhotelcairo.com. 60 airy a/c rooms with high ceilings, dark waxy furniture and wooden floors. Bathrooms need revamping. Near the bustling *souk* El-Tawfiqa and Sharia Alfi with its bars and cheap eats. Hotel has laundry service, restaurant and a nice rooftop *ahwa*. Breakfast is extra. A good place to escape other tourists.

€€ Garden City House Hotel, 23 Sharia Kamal El Dinn Salah, Garden City, T02-2794 8400, www.gardencityhouse.com. On the edge of Midan Tahrir yet this place feels well out of any backpacker scene. Large rooms have plenty of furniture and share huge balconies with a bit of a view. There's a sociable breezy restaurant area and general air of nostalgia throughout. Doubles cost E£130/205 with or without a/c and bathroom (which are clean but old-fashioned), breakfast included. Friendly staff. Long-stay discounts are possible.

€€ Paris Hotel, 15 Sharia Talaat Harb, T02-2395 0921, T012-400 7126, parishotel_2006@hotmail.com. 8 simple, clean rooms with tiled floors, immaculate (but small) en suites. All with a/c and balconies. Free tea and coffee. Slightly dark public areas. Breakfast is extra. (Sister hotel **Le Paris** is 2 buildings away and is a bit pricier but includes breakfast, T02-2390 3815.)

€€ Victoria Hotel, 66 Sharia El-Gumhoriyya, T02-2589 2290, www.victoria.com.eg. A large pink hotel that's been around since the 1930s, but long red carpets, wooden floors and loads of chandeliers make it feel almost Victorian.

High-ceilinged a/c rooms have all amenities, en suites are roomy and have tubs as well as showers. There's an internet café, cosy darkened bar and a pleasant open-air coffee shop with lots of foliage. The best deal for a 3-star in the city, and although not in the 'heart' of Downtown it's an easy walk to Islamic Cairo. Breakfast included.

€€ Windsor, 19 Sharia Alfi Bey, T02-2591 5277, www.windsorcairo.com. Historic and atmospheric, well-run, family-owned hotel with clean a/c rooms. Look at a few as they vary greatly, the de luxe rooms are stacked with antique furniture while others have drawers hanging off. Bathrooms are definitely on the small side, some cheaper rooms have toilet outside. Breakfast included. One of the classiest and cosiest bars in the city, with barrel chairs, plenty of memorabilia and an interesting history. Michael Palin stayed here while going around the world in 80 days. Show your *Footprint Handbook* to receive a 15% discount.

€€-€ Meramees Hotel, 32 Sharia Sabry Abu Alam, near Midan Talaat Harb, T02-2396 2518. Recommended for no hassle and good *felucca* trips, it's a low-key place where single women will feel comfortable. Pleasant airy a/c rooms have either complete bathrooms or shower cubicles only. Beds in nicer-than-average dorms are E£30. Cleaned daily, breakfast included, internet.

€€-€ Pension Roma, 169 Sharia Mohamed Farid, T02-2391 1088, www.pensionroma.com.eg. Among the classiest of budget options, this old-world hotel is impeccably clean with hardwood floors, original fittings and furnishings and high ceilings and fans (pay more for a/c in the new annex). The staff is friendly and informative, lounge has TV, and it attracts an international and age-diverse group of travellers. Doubles start at E£104 with shared bath, with private bath E£170-250, they can accommodate 3 or 4 people in larger rooms, and the singles are the best value in Cairo.

Some excellent balconies look down on the mayhem, breakfast included. Highly recommended, you should book ahead. Free Wi-Fi.

€€-€ Sara Inn Hostel, 21 Sharia Yousef El-Guindi, Bab El-Louq, T02-2392 2940, www.sarainnhostel.com. A quiet, intimate recently renovated hotel, centrally located with friendly staff. Good location as quiet at night and bustling during the day. Rooms have TV and most have balconies. Warmly decorated, communal lounge with TV and internet access. Can pick up from airport if pre-book 2 nights in a double room.

€€-€ Sun Hotel, 9th and 10th floor, 2 Sharia Talaat Harb, T02-2579 7977. An old-timer on the budget scene, Sun has had a refit and the new rooms with a/c, satellite TV and fridge are often booked up. Located in a convenient spot, but with annoyingly infrequent elevators, necessitating walking down 10 floors (and possibly up 2). Rooms are cleaned and sheets changed daily, breakfast included, internet (E£5 per hr). A good place to come for trips to nearby sights like Saqqara or the Camel Market, even if you're not staying here.

€ African Hostel, 3rd floor, 15 Sharia Emad El-Din, T02-2591 7220, T02-2591 1744, www.africanhousehostel.com. 12 clean, simple rooms located in an elegant 1860s building have wooden floors and clean bedding. Rooms on 4th floor have balconies. Public areas are brightly painted but a bit tired looking. Free internet, free Wi-Fi and tea. Super-friendly staff. Doubles with shared bath E£100, private bath E£120. A good choice.

€ Akram Inn, 5 Midan Tahrir, T02-2794 4353, akramsafir@hotmail.com. 4-bed dorms are E£25 a bed Climbing up 3 floors of stairs is painful with luggage, but the location is undeniably top and one room has balcony views over the Midan. No breakfast but there's a kitchen, fridge, internet (E£5 per hr).

€ Alexander Hotel, 165 Sharia Mohamed Farid, T02-2390 1844, alexander.hotel@ hotmail.com. 10 smallish rooms all with a/c and bath are very clean but slightly cramped. A bit overpriced at $22 for a double. Public areas are kitsch with faux leopard skin cushions. Staff are friendly and the location is spot on. Free Wi-Fi and breakfast.

€ Amin Hotel, 38 Midan Falaky, Bab El Louk, T02-2393 3813. Dingy double rooms with acceptable shared baths are about the cheapest in town at E£39, or E£44-49 with private bathroom. Come here for a proper Egyptian vibe, lack of hassle, excellent balcony views and proximity to the Horiyya coffee shop – but not for comfort or good facilities.

€ Bluebird Hotel, 42 Sharia Talaat Harb, 6th floor, T02-2575 6377. Small family set-up in a top-floor hideaway with extremely clean rooms, all with fans. Choice of bathroom (very much) inside the room or spotless shared showers, and a communal kitchen, breakfast included. A cute little place.

€ Canadian Hostel, 5 Sharia Talaat Harb, T02-2392 5794. Recommended for the super-friendly staff who offer good travel advice. Clean airy rooms are a little stark and gloomy, but breakfast is included, there's reliably hot water, cheap laundry (E£10), communal fridge, internet (E£6 per hr) and free Wi-Fi. Double rooms with standing fans are E£130, E£20 more for a/c.

€ Dahab Hotel, 7th floor, 26 Sharia Mahmoud Bassiouny, T02-2579 9104. One of the cheapest beds in town, this rooftop hotel is amazingly successful in offering a little taste of Dahab in the middle of downtown Cairo madness. Small, very simple rooms on the rooftop, some with fans, have clean sheets and decent pillows. Bathrooms are clean and newly tiled. It's the garden that's special; a little oasis overflowing with flowers and plants, you can even hear birds chirping. Pure backpacker vibes, it's a good place to meet people. Breakfast E£8 extra.

€ Dina's Hostel, 5th floor, 42 Sharia Abdel Khalek Sarwat, T02-2396 3902, T010-3025

346, dinahostel@gmail.com. A welcome new arrival on the Cairo hotel scene. Bright spacious rooms have wooden floors and crisp, clean bedding. Free Wi-Fi. Internet E£5. Standard breakfast but the hard-boiled eggs are fresh and warm. An 8-bed dorm offers the cleanest budget accommodation around. (E£40 per bed). The 2 bathrooms are pristine and beautifully tiled. (More are being planned.) No a/c or fans yet. If arriving at night there's a buzzer downstairs.

€ **Hotel Suisse**, 8th floor, 26 Sharia Mahmoud Bassiouni, T02-2574 6639. Rooms here are spacious and bright, have sinks and fans, some have balconies. Staff are very pleasant, it's an all-round winner in terms of atmosphere, location and value for money.

€ **Ismailia House**, 8th floor, 1 Midan Tahrir, T02-2796 3122. A classic budget hotel in the middle of Midan Tahrir, entrance hidden in an alley behind the book stand. It's a friendly place with good management, clean rooms but grubby shared baths, reliable cheap tours (available to non-guests), and an absolutely flabbergasting view of Midan Tahrir. News crews film from the balconies when there's action in the main square. Laundry, internet, shared kitchen, lounge with CNN always on. Some rooms have a/c, all others have fans. Request one with a balcony. Breakfast included. Dorms E£35, doubles E£90, with bath and fan.

€ **Juliana Hotel**, 8 Sharia Ibrahim Naguib, Garden City, T012 4249 896, www.juliana-hotel.com. With just 9 simple, immaculate, quiet en suite rooms all with satellite TV, a great place to stay. The only problem may be finding it, but they provide excellent directions on their website. There's free Wi-Fi and use of the kitchen. A good central location that feels peaceful and away from it all.

€ **Lialy Hostel**, 8 Midan Talaat Harb, 2nd floor, T02-2575 2802. Right in the heart of everything, spotless, private, and homely – though rooms are very simple. The staff is young, well-informed and friendly. Hearty breakfast included, there's a great view over Midan Talaat Harb from the lounge. Internet, laundry (E£1 per piece) and free use of the kitchen. All bathrooms are shared.

€ **Lotus Hotel**, 12 Sharia Talaat Harb, T02-2575 0966, www.lotushotel.com. 50 rooms, some with bath and a/c, in a drab but clean and centrally located hotel run by the same family as **Windsor**. Some rooms have balcony. Breakfast included. Restaurant is OK and the uneventful **Polo Bar**, which is a real blast from the past, has a small balcony way above Talaat Harb. Reception is on the 7th floor. Show your *Footprint Handbook* for a 15% discount.

€ **Ramses II Hotel**, 37 Sharia Talaat Harb, Downtown, T02-2395 0745. All 18 rooms have private bath, a/c, satellite TV, some have glimpses of the silver dome of the Citadel but all have good views as it's on the 12th floor. Rooms are new and staff are friendly, not bad for E£160 a double. Breakfast is on the terrace with superb views across the city, it feels more Egyptian than some backpacker haunts. Free Wi-Fi. Internet E£4.

€ **Richmond**, 41 Sharia Sherif, T02-2393 9358. The glossy orange and green paint is a little startling, but 4 front rooms have good balconies and get lots of light. You won't see many other tourists there. Smells a bit smoky. Breakfast included and friendly management.

€ **Safari Hotel**, 4 Sharia Souk El-Tawfikia, 5th floor, T012-446 9010. The funk and flavour of the colourful *souk* outside makes up for the filth of the building, meaning the Safari and **Sultan** are perennially popular with backpackers. Dorm beds going for E£20 (men and women separate), using 2 shared but clean showers, but don't expect clean sheets. Safari has plenty of bustle, is friendly and popular with Japanese backpackers.

€ **Sultan Hotel**, 4 Sharia Souk El-Tawfikia, T02-2577 2258. This is where it's at for backpackers on the tightest of budgets. Cheap dorm beds for E£20 on the 1st floor (separate for men and women), shared baths are rather grimy, but many folk make it home for a while. Kitchen facilities and laundry, plus gaudy murals to welcome you in the reception area.

€ Venice Hotel, 4 Sharia Souk El-Tawfikia, T02-2773 5307, www.venicehosokawaya.net. Venice has undergone a re-vamp in the last year, and all rooms are freshly painted with new mattresses and bedding, and consequently higher prices. Clean dorm beds are E£35. Run by Japanese and Egyptians. Kitchen, washer and dryer.

Islamic Cairo *p48, maps p49 and p51*

If you like things noisy and crazy, stay in the immediate vicinity of the Khan and get properly immersed in Islamic Cairo. If you're here during the Moulid of Al-Hussein (booking imperative) don't expect to get any sleep and bear in mind that multiple mosques and the call to prayer are literally on the doorstep in all events.

€€€€ Le Riad, 114 Sharia Muizz li-Din il-Allah, T02-2787 6074/5, www.leriad-hotel decharme.com. With a lovely roof garden and tea shop, this new 'boutique' hotel has 17 spacious themed rooms (Umm Khalsoum, pharaonic, etc) with flagged stone floors, artwork on the walls, rich colours and modern amenities. The bathrooms are fabulous. It's just a shame that it is so expensive. Breakfast included and free internet.

€€-€ El Hussein Hotel, Midan El-Hussein, T02-2591 8089. In the heart of Khan El-Khalili, entry via an alley at the front (right-hand side) of the Khan. A gloomy old-fashioned hotel but, if you can handle the noise, the location makes it worthwhile. The large rooms with private bath have great balconies overlooking Midan Hussein. It's worth shelling out to avoid the shared bathrooms, though the private ones are on the dank side too. Rooms with a/c are a bit more expensive (double E£180). Great view from the cafeteria.

€ El-Malky Hotel, 4 Sharia El-Hussein, T02-2589 0804, www.elmalky.com.

Unquestionably the best value of the 3 hotels around Midan Hussein, at E£110-130 per room. You'll definitely need to book in advance. Except for the El-Hussein mosque, which sounds periodically, street noise isn't a problem. Rooms and baths are reasonably clean and include TV, telephone and fan, some with a/c. Breakfast included. Make sure you request a room with a balcony, as some have no windows, and check out the view from the roof.

€ Radwan, 83 Sharia Gawhar El-Kaaid, Midan Al-Azhar, T02-2590 1311. Though rooms are pretty scuffed they are clean, as are the private baths. The hotel has quite a nice vibe and there are seating areas on each floor. Go between 1000-1200 to view a few rooms, and check the a/c works (a few have balconies). Noisy but vibrant location. No breakfast. Friendly staff.

Roda Island *p88*

€€€€ Grand Hyatt Cairo, Corniche El-Nil, Garden City, T02-2365 1234. Excellently located on the north tip of Roda Island, looking down on *feluccas* circling on the river. There's a range of restaurants, and an adjacent **Hard Rock Café**, plus one of the best views of Cairo from the revolving restaurant bar. They are serving alcohol again (but only in the restaurant) after the furore caused in May 2008 when the Saudi owner turned the hotel dry and up to US$1 million of liquor was poured into the Nile.

€ Youth hostel, 135 Sharia Abdul Aziz Al-Saud, El-Manial, Roda Island, near University Bridge, T02-236 0729, T02-2362 4593. Location is inconvenient, though connected to the city via public transport. Stunning Nileside views.There's a shared kitchen with prepared meals available, family rooms and laundry. E£16-25, depending on if you share a room with 3 beds or 8-10. Doors closed 2400-0800. Book in advance. Places for disabled. Handy ATM outside.

Zamalek and Gezira *p90,*
maps p32 and p91

€€€€ Cairo Marriott Hotel and Casino, 16 Sharia Saray El-Gezira, Zamalek, T02-2728 3000, www.cairomarriotthotel.com. Over 1000 rooms, mainly in 2 high-rise towers, around a lavish 19th-century Gezira Palace built to commemorate the opening of the Suez Canal and still retaining much of its splendour. Restaurants are average, but the garden terrace is simply perfect for a drink, **Harry's Bar** is reassuringly familiar, and there's the **Omar El-Khayyam** casino. Also has own sporting facilities – tennis court, health club, etc – and though day-use of the pool is very expensive, it has possibly the nicest settings in the city. Classic and palatial, the **Marriott** makes a good place to unwind from the bustle of Cairo.

€€€€ Hilton Zamalek Residence, 21 Sharia Mohamed Mazhar, Zamalek, T02-2737 0055, www1.hilton.com. Due to open soon, this Hilton Zamalek Residence has a perfect location next to the Nile in a quiet area of the city. Lovely new pools, fresh furnishings, oriental and international restaurants – it will be worth looking into.

€€€€ Sofitel El Gezirah, 3 Sharia El Thawra Council, Gezira, T02-2737 3737, www.sofitel.com. Ignore the uninspiring exterior because the **Sofitel** has been stylishly revamped by a French interior designer and is now worthy of its prime location at the southern tip of the island. Luxurious and tasteful rooms, truly high-class restaurants, a decadent spa and a bar floating on decking over the Nile.

€€€€-€€€ Golden Tulip Flamenco Hotel, 2 Sharia El-Gezira El-Wasta, Zamalek, T02-2735 0815/6, www.goldentulipflamenco. com. Most rooms have a good view of houseboats on the Nile and are of a decent standard. There's a 24-hr café, **Carmen** lounge bar is quiet and friendly, and a beer in the 10th floor Spanish restaurant affords marvellous sunset views (though it is not

open air). Doubles are US$140, US$20 more for a Nile view, some suites, it's always busy with businessmen so best to book ahead.

€€€ Horus House Hotel, 21 Sharia Ismail Mohammed, T02-2735 3634, www.horus househotel.4t.com. 1 floor under **Longchamps**, this is a marginally cheaper and less appealing choice. Rooms have all the extras and have been freshly decorated, the staff are friendly and there's a (very cheap, 24-hr) bar and restaurant but, compared to its bright upstairs neighbour, the hotel feels old and dreary. However, you are guaranteed to meet some interesting long-stay residents over breakfast (which is included).

€€€ Longchamps, 21 Sharia Ismail Mohammed, T02-2735 2311, www.hotel longchamps.com. Long-standing family-run hotel that is about the quirkiest in Cairo. Always popular, it's imperative to book in advance. 2 shaded terraces offer peace, greenery and a cold beer, the restaurant is pleasant, the breakfast buffet highly recommended and there is a library. Rooms (standard, superior, executive) are very comfortable with new furniture, a/c, TV, fridge and a hint of the colonial flavour that permeates the public areas.

€€€ President Hotel, 22 Sharia Taha Hussein, T02-2735 0718. Awesome views over the island, new bathrooms and huge rooms with good facilities compensate for the shabby public areas and generic decor. Some rooms have enormous balconies overlooking the Nile, and the **Cellar Bar** down in the basement is delightfully dark and atmospheric. The French patisserie is famed. The adjacent **New President Hotel**, 20 Sharia Taha Hussein, T02-2737 2780. Has some rooms that have been tastefully renovated, standard ones are dated though clean and spacious. It's not a bad mid-range option, and slightly cheaper than the original President.

€€ Mayfair Hotel, 9 Sharia Aziz Osman. T02-2735 7315, www.mayfaircairo.com. Unspectacular but clean rooms (try for one with a balcony) in a quiet location. Breakfast included, served on the pleasant flowery balcony with free Wi-Fi. Show your *Footprint Handbook* for a 10% discount. Doubles are around E£250, with a/c and bath, it's always busy so call ahead.

€€ Pension Zamalek, 6 Sharia Salah Al-Din, T02-2735 9318. Spacious, warm old-fashioned rooms, some with a/c and heater, most with balconies, in very tranquil nook off Zamalek's main drag. A family-run super-friendly hotel, every 2 rooms share a spotless bath. Laundry service and TV in the eerie salon. Breakfast included. Phone ahead as they're often booked up with long-stayers (who get a discount).

The west bank *p92, map p32*
Most tourists staying in Giza will have been pre-booked into one of the many high-end hotels as part of a package deal. With the obvious exception of the pyramids, Giza is too much out on a limb to be convenient for main attractions of the city.

€€€€ Mena House Oberoi, 6 Sharia Pyramids, El-Ahram, T02-3377 3222, www.oberoihotels.com. An exquisite old-style hotel built in 1869, with sublime views of the Pyramids and set in luxuriant gardens. Excellent Indian (and other) restaurants, disco, casino, largest outdoor pool in Cairo (you can see the Pyramids as you float around), tennis, a nearby 18-hole golf course, horse and camel riding with experienced instructors. Take a room in the renovated older part for preference. If out of your budget, it's still a delightful place to enjoy breakfast opposite the Pyramids.

€€€ Havana Hotel, 26 Sharia Syria, Mohandiseen, T02-3749 0758, www.havanahotelcairo.com. Modest, friendly Anglo-Egyptian hotel, breakfast included.

€€€-€€ Saqqara Country Club & Hotel, Saqqara Rd, Abu El-Nomros, T02-3381 1307. 20 rooms outside the city near the Saqqara pyramids, well run with good food and excellent horse-riding facilities. Temporary

club membership available. Day use, including a drink, is E£120.

Trips down the Nile *p124*

Maadi
€€€€ Villa Belle Epoque, Near Rd 9, T02-2516 9656, Maadi, www.villabelle epoque.com. A 1920s villa with 13 period rooms, delightful gardens, pool, excellent restaurant and charming bar. It is a true boutique hotel, in a residential suburb 8 km south of the city centre.

❷ Restaurants

Cairo is a cosmopolitan city with an increasingly diverse and eclectic population. The cuisine reflects huge variety. You can find Japanese, vegetarian, Chinese, Italian, Indian and French, in addition to superb Middle Eastern cuisine. At the most chic restaurants (often found in the chicest of hotels), expect to pay what you would at home for a classy meal. It's also possible to dine deliciously on the cheap. You can fill up on tasty local fare (*fuul*, *taameyya* and *koshari*) for less than a dollar.

Do pay attention, though, especially when buying food on the street. If things don't seem too clean and there isn't a quick turnover of custom, it's better to move on and find some establishment where the flies and the heat are less menacing. Opening times and menus may change during Ramadan as some restaurants focus on providing a slap-up *iftar* meal, and *koshari* also becomes impossible to find during this period. Most restaurants home-deliver, which also applies to hotels.

Central Cairo *p40, maps p32 and p36*
€€€ The Bird Cage, Semiramis Intercontinental, Corniche El-Nil, Garden City, T02-2795 7171. Open 1230-2400. Thai cuisine complete with live (caged) birds, neo-feng shui design and sheer curtains separate tables for privacy. Ask for 'spicy' otherwise you might find dishes toned down, all the entrées

are excellent, and so is the service. Very expensive and very good.

€€€ Maharaja, Ramses Hilton, 1115 Corniche El-Nil, T02-2577 7444. Open 1300-1600 and 1900-2400. Modern decor within a small space, the Maharaja serves up some marvellous Indian cuisine, specializing in tandoori. There's a non-smoking section.

€€€ Pane Vino, Semiramis Intercontinental Hotel, Corniche El-Nil, T02-2795 7171. Open 1300-0100. Serves top-notch antipasta and pizza (the Da Vinci is recommended), in modern metal and glass surroundings. A lively place with music and lots of shouting coming from the show kitchen.

€€€ Paprika, 1129 Corniche El-Nil, T02-2578 9447. Open 1200-0100. Paprika-based dishes of mixed Egyptian and Hungarian food. Near the TV and Radio Building, it's not uncommon to spot local Egyptian celebrities on the premises.

€€€-€€ Alfi Bey, 3 Sharia El-Alfi, Downtown, in pedestrian precinct, T02-2577 1888. Open 1300-0100. Authentic Egyptian food since 1938, especially kebabs, koftas, lamb chops and shank, grilled and stuffed pigeon with pastas and rice. Smart waiters provide an efficient and friendly service, but custom is declining as the place feels dated and no alcohol is served.

€€€-€€ Kowloon, Cleopatra Hotel, 1st floor, Midan Tahrir, T02-2575 9831. Open 1100-2300. Authentic Korean cuisine that delights even Korean patrons, with some Chinese dishes thrown in. The place feels retro in a good way.

€€€-€€€ Peking, behind Diana Cinema, 14 Sharia Saraya El-Azbakia, T02-2591 2381. Open 1200-0100. Warm atmosphere and friendly service with a mix of Asian and Oriental decor, extensive Chinese menu though not the most authentic. Some say ketchup is the secret ingredient of the sweet and sour sauce. It's reliable, however, and there are a few vegetarian options. Several chains around Cairo, they also home deliver.

€€€-€€ Taboula, 1 Sharia Latin America, Garden City, T02-2624 5722. Open 1200-0130 daily. Romantic subterranean lounge space, with dim lighting and faithfully Lebanese decorations, cushions, and pictures all around. The hot and cold *mezza* suit vegetarians and meaty mains are as authentic as the interior and the menu vast. Highly recommended. Serves alcohol.

€€ Abu Shakra, 69 Sharia Qasr El-Eini, Downtown, T02-2531 6111. Open 1200-0200. Among the most reputable and oldest of all local grills in Egypt (since 1947), pigeon, leg of lamb and grilled chicken all to be recommended. Vegetarians limited to delicious soups and salads. The late-lamented Muslim missionary Mohammed Mitwalli El-Shaarawi was said to order here frequently. A recent refit has left it rather soulless and with TVs in the main dining area.

€€ Arabesque, 6 Sharia Qasr El-Nil, Downtown, T02-2574 8677, www.arabesque-eg.com. Open 1200-0200 daily. A chance to try less common Egyptian dishes: *mezza* includes *besara* (a tasty bean dip) and mains include tagines and stuffed pigeon. Old tiled floors, stella bottle lampshades, lit alabaster on the bar, Orientalist art and very dim lighting make it a cool hideaway. It's a handy location just off Tahrir.

€€ El-Bahrain, 123 Sharia El-Roda, by the Fatima Hamada Cinema, Manial, T02-2532 2175, daily 1300 until late. Their grandfathers were fishermen, and for the last 4 years this restaurant has been serving up the freshest of the day's catch. Pick your fish from the ice (ask for it to be cooked *mistakawi* style), accompanying salads are excellent and the shrimps some of the best you'll ever taste. The 1st-floor restaurant is nothing flash, the usual marble and plastic surrounds, but it's great value. They will feed large groups for E£25 per head.

€€ El-Nil Fish Restaurant, 25 Sharia Al-Bustan, near Midan Falaki. Open 1200-0100. Fish fresh off the ice is grilled or fried, either to take away or eat upstairs. Served with the standard salads, it's always delicious and is very reasonably priced.

€€ Felfela, 15 Sharia Hoda Sharawi, Downtown, T02-239 2833. Open 0830-0130. One of Downtown's most popular tourist restaurants, serves good, clean, local food and beer in a dimly lit, strangely funky cave-like environment. A good place for a first experiment with Egyptian food on arrival, there is also a branch in Giza near the pyramids and others around the country. Also see page 111, for **Felfela Takeway**.

€€ Greek Club, 3 Sharia Mahmoud Bassiouni, Downtown, T02-2575 0822. Open 0700-0200. Above **Groppis** on Midan Talast Harb, this is a deserved classic of the Cairo scene. Grand neoclassical interior, complete with moose head, there's no menu but dishes are standard kebab, salad, soups, nothing truly special, but the terrace (only open in summer) is a splendid vantage point over the Midan. Beer is reasonable at E£12.

€€ Le Bistro, 8 Sharia Hoda Sharawy, T010-507 0078. Open 1200-2400, their bar (next door) is open till 0200. Good French food in a modern little blue and white space, intimate tables, no pretensions. Fillet steaks (E£55), chops, fish and chicken are all done to a high standard.

€ Abu Tarek, 40 Sharia Champollion, corner of Sharia Maarouf, T02-2577 5935. Open 0800-2400. Serving up what is arguably the best *koshari* in town since 1950. A good place to land with an empty belly after hours of aimless wandering. If you've been worried about trying it on the street for fear of stomach upsets, rest assured that Abu Tarek is among the cleanest of *koshari* establishments. It's more expensive than your average *koshari* joint with a small dish starting at E£E5.

€ Akher Sa'a, 8 Sharia El-Alfi. Open 24 hrs. An all-Egyptian vegetarian's heaven. Lentil soup is excellent, as is *shakshouka* and all other local favourites. Eat-in or take-out.

€ El-Tabei el-Domiati, 31 Sharia Orabi, T02-2575 4391. Open 0700-0100. Another cheap and famed local favourite serving up *mezze* galore and, of course, *fuul* and *tameyya*. Especially recommended for its trustworthy salad bar, though there is less choice in recent years.

€ Fatatri El-Tahrir, 166 Sharia Tahrir, 1 block east of Midan Tahrir. Serves delicious *fatir* both sweet and savoury; favoured with locals and travellers alike for being cheap, filling and open all night long.

€ Felfela Takeaway, 15 Sharia Talaat Harb, T02-2392 2833. Near to the Downtown restaurant of the same name, this takeaway joint also has a few seats inside. A great, cheap introduction to local flavours, the lentil soup is delicious, but there's also *koshari*, grilled meats, salads and sandwiches.

€ Gad, several locations across the city, but most convenient Downtown is 13 Sharia 26th July, T02-2576 3583. Open 24 hrs. Always heaving; tasty, cheap local grub includes excellent *fuul*, *taamiyya*, and acclaimed liver sandwiches. Seating upstairs and deliver almost anywhere.

€ Sayed Hanafi, 5 Midan Orabi, on Sharia El-Alfi, T02-2576 9162. Constantly packed with Egyptians. Serves excellent, authentic, cheap staples.

€ Shabrawi, Sharia 26 July. Near the junction with Sharia Ramses, look for the crowd milling around outside waiting to be served with the freshest, juiciest *shawarma* sandwiches in town.

Ahwas and cafés

Arabica, 1st floor, 20 Sharia Marashly, corner of Sharia Ahmed Heshmat, Zamalek T02-2735 7982. Open daily 1000-0200. One of few cafés still to offer free Wi-Fi, this place has a large selection of *fatir*, decent Western breakfasts, omelettes on toast (try the goat's cheese), salads and OK juices. Prices are more reasonable than most and it's popular with students from the nearby AUC residence. Walls are decorated by customer's artwork –

there are crayons for sketching on the paper tablecloths.

Cilantro's, 31 Sharia Mohammed Mahmoud, opposite the old AUC campus. For a Western-style coffee Downtown, the most pleasant environment is still upstairs at **Cilantro's** despite the competition from **Costa** and **Beano's** nearby. There are a couple of tables out on the balconies and velvet 'snugs' for couples, it's unpretentious and has a clean toilet. They charge for Wi-Fi, however.

Groppi's, Midan Talaat Harb, Downtown. This landmark used to be the place to meet, but renovations have dimmed the classic café's former charm. The coffee isn't great but the pastries are OK, and it's handy when you're ready for a break. A more agreeable location is the branch on Sharia Adly, which has a garden terrace that is genuinely peaceful.

Islamic Cairo *p48, maps p49 and p51*
€€€ Citadel View Restaurant, Al Azhar Park, Salah Salem, T02-2510 3868, www.alahzarpark.com. Daily 1200-0100. A little expensive, but the views are so worth it and it's an ideal way to round off a day in Islamic Cairo. An excellent mix of Oriental and Western mains, or on weekend evenings there's an all-you-can-eat buffet.
€€€ Naguib Mafouz Coffee shop and Khan El-Khalili Restaurant, 5 Sikkit El-Badestan, Khan El-Khalili, T02-2593 2262. Open 1000-0200. The classiest place to relax after a day's wander through Islamic Cairo, has a/c, serves Western and Egyptian *mezze* and meals. Prices for tea and coffee are inflated, but the surroundings justify going. Live Oriental music is featured on occasion. Minimum charges apply.
€€ Egyptian Pancake House, 7 Midan Al-Azhar. *Fiteer* galore, savoury and sweet. Tuna, cheese, eggs, meat, chicken, cream, and even turkey cock are available fillings. Price range from E£15-25 depending on size and filling.

€€ Taj Al Sultan, Al-Hussein, T02-2787 7273/5, www.tajalsultan.com. Open 1000-0200. Strange to find an Indian restaurant in the heart of Islamic Cairo, but typical British-Indian dishes (*rogan josh*, *murg masala*, *sag aloo*) are done very well. There is also an extensive Arabic menu plus a couple of international dishes. The old building, with a rooftop with great views, decorated in Orientalist style is pleasing, the coffee shop is attractive, and the prices are not outrageous considering the location.
€ Gad, Sharia Al-Azhar. Open daily 0900-0200. The famous fast-food chain is perfect for tasty soup and staples if you're hungry round the Khan but don't want to pay tourist prices. There is seating upstairs.
€ Mohamed Ali's *fuul* cart, behind the Palace of Amir Bashtak, Sharia Al-Muizz, Midan Hussein. Undoubtedly some of the best *fuul* going, as the queues further testify. Handy for basic refuelling north of the Khan, and an interesting place to take a break among dilapidated mansions.
€ Zizo, Midan Bab El-Futuh. Open 1200-0700. Facing the north wall of Islamic Cairo. Said to have the best liver sausage and fried brain in town, if that's your thing. This tiny takeaway joint is a local landmark, very cheap and open through the night.

Ahwas and cafés
Fishawi's, smack bang in the middle of Khan El-Khalili. Open all the time. **Fishawi's** is Cairo's longest standing *ahwa*, claiming never to have closed since it first opened in 1773. If you only go to one coffee shop in Egypt, let it be this one. The place is filled with atmosphere, dangling chandeliers, mottled mirrors and characters that have been here for decades. Plus heaps of tourists and hawkers adding to the cacophony of noise. *Sheesha*, fresh juice, tea and Turkish coffee are all good, but at a steep price.

Zamalek and Gezira *p90,*
maps p32 and p91

€€€ Abu El-Sid, 157 Sharia 26th July, in an alley behind **Maison Thomas**, T02-2735 9640. Open 1300-0200. Intimately lit sumptuous decor makes you feel like you've entered a harem, the cuisine is authentically Egyptian and it's a rare chance to smoke *sheesha* and drink alcohol at the same time. Egyptian men admit that Abu El-Sid is as close as it gets to their mum's cooking, try the *molokhia*, a unique slimy green soup. However, it's not great for vegetarians and can get annoyingly busy (when the staff try to hurry you along; essential to book a table at weekends).

€€€ Asia Bar, **Blue Nile Boat**, Sharia Saraya El-Gezira, T02-2735 3112. This floating restaurant is a recommended haunt, for sushi and a beer you can't go wrong. There's a very cool bar to hang out in.

€€€ Hana, 25 Sharia Hassan Asem Sayed Bakri, T02-2738 2972. Open 1200-0030. Recently reopened in a new venue, this is an authentic Korean restaurant that also serves some Chinese dishes. The *kimchi* and hot-and-sour soup are good, and the beef *bartogi* (cook up the slices on your own personal hot plate) comes recommended. One of the few restaurants in town that makes edible tofu. Serves beer and other alcohol, and has a very loyal clientele.

€€€ L'Asiatique, Le Pacha 1901, Sharia Saraya El-Gezira, T02-2735 6730. Open 1900-0200. Superb sushi and Thai cuisine on the floating, not cruising, **Pacha**, a delightful, albeit pricey dining experience.

€€€ La Bodega, 157 Sharia 26th July (1st floor), T02-2735 0543. Open 1200-0200. Arty international in a venue that's as chic and spot-on as it gets in Cairo. There's a choice between the mustardy and colonial room or the newly refurbished cuisine 'Aperitivo' section that specializes in Italian for dining, plus a separate lounge with plush leather chairs as well as private rooms. The bar is lively, dark and well-stocked with quite a mixed clientele, and it's one of the few places that serves alcohol during Ramadan.

€€€ Maharani, Le Pacha 1901, Sharia Saraya El-Gezira, T02-2735 6730. Open 1400-2400. A 5-star Indian floating restaurant set to the sound of sitars. Something for everyone on the menu, a decent vegetarian section, the yellow dahl is strongly recommended.

€€€ Sequoia, 3 Sharia Abou El-Feda, T02-2736 6379. A beautiful setting on the northern tip of Zamalek makes this a good place for sunset nibbles and a drink, overlooking houseboats and Imbaba bridge. The food has improved greatly in recent years, although the service can still be slow, but it's more the location and stylishly spacious outdoor setting that make it. No minimum charge before 1700.

€€€-€€ Chili's, Nile City Boat, Sharia Saray Al-Gezira, T02-2735 3122, delivery T19002. True, it's purely a Tex-Mex restaurant that serves up American-style food, but the setting on the **Nile City Boat** with outdoor seating on deck is just superb. Meals are reliable, vegetarians will find things of interest on the menu, and the prices are not outrageous.

€€€-€€ Five Bells, corner of sharias Ismail Mohamed and El Adel Abu Bakr, Zamalek, T02-2735 8635. Indoor and garden seating in an old villa with old-style atmosphere, serves tasty dinners though vegetarians will be limited to soups and *mezza*. Be prepared for persistent attention from neighbourhood cats.

€€€-€€ Maison Thomas, 157 Sharia 26 July, T02-2735 7057. Open 24 hrs, and good for home delivery. Continental-style deli atmosphere, serving pretty authentic Italian pizza. The caramel chocolate cake and cheesecake are scrumptious if you have room for dessert. The place can use a better ventilation system, but the decor works and it's a real institution. Good for breakfast. Branches also open in Heliopolis, Maadi and Mohandiseen.

€€ **Crave**, 22a Sharia Taha Hussein, T02-2736 3870. Open 1100-0200. A café/restaurant with cool decor, slouchy leather sofas and good food if you're craving something Western. The sort of place that suits a leisurely breakfast or when you need a/c.

€€ **Dido's Al Dente**, 26 Sharia Bahgat Ali, Zamalek, T02-2735 9117, www.didospasta.com. Open 1300-0500. This little pasta place can use more space, but if you're in the mood for tasty cheap Italian fare, it's worth the cram: the penne arrabiatta is a winner, the pizzas are great and portions are generous. However, the service can be abominable if they're busy. Popular with AUC students who live in the hostel nearby. They also home deliver.

€€ **L'Aubergine**, 5 Sharia Sayed El-Bakry, T02-2738 0080. A mellow little restaurant, with a wide drinks menu, and vaguely Italian food that's very acceptable. A good selection for vegetarians, one of the best in the city. Upstairs is a bar/club that gets going at around 2200 which is quite fun.

€ **TBS (The Bakery Shop)**, 4D, Sharia Gezira, T02-2736 0071/3. A surprisingly good Western-style sandwich bar, with paninis, German bread, ciabatta, etc, all freshly made, plus some good pastry items. Choose from a great mix of sandwich fillings, and they can toast the end product for you. Takeaway only.

€ **Zamalek Restaurant**, 118 Sharia 26 July, near intersection with Sharia Al Aziz Osman. Open 0600-0200. A sit-down meats and grills joint on Zamalek's main drag.

Ahwas and cafés

Mandarin Koueider, 17 Sharia Shargarat Al-Dor, Zamalek. This place has the best ice cream and sorbets in Cairo. Mango and mandarin flavours come out on top.

Simonds, Sharia 26 July, Zamalek, T02-2735 9436. Open 0730-2130. One of the oldest stand-up coffee shops in Cairo, it unfortunately underwent a soulless refit in 2008 and little of the 1898 charm remains. Even so, it is still a good

place to read the paper, observe classic Cairo characters, and have decent cappuccino. The mini-pizzas and OJ are a great pick-me-up.

The west bank p92, map p32

Mohandiseen

There are several good restaurants in Mohandiseen that can make the trip to the concrete suburbs worthwhile, but bear in mind most do not serve alcohol.

€€€ **Bukhara**, 5 Sharia Lebnan (entry from Sharia Hegaz), T02-3302 5669. Great Indian cuisine, many people reckon it's the best in Cairo. There's also a branch in Maadi (43 Sharia Misr Helwan, T02-2380 5999) and they deliver.

€€€ **Charwood's**, 53 Sharia Gamat El-Dowel El-Arabiya, T02-3749 0893. Open 1300-0030. Recommended for a laid-back atmosphere, quality steaks and great oven-baked pizzas. Faultless service. A good little hideaway, though the decor is spartan, it's tasteful. Serves alcohol.

€€€ **Raousha & Kandahar**, 3 Sharia Gamat El-Dowal, T02-3303 0615. Open 1200-2400. An Oberoi-owned restaurant split in 2 to serve excellent Lebanese or Indian cuisine. Overlooks one of the busiest streets in Cairo. Attentive service.

€€€-€€ **Ataturk**, 20 Sharia Riyadh, T02-3347 5135. Open 1000-0200. Turkish food, all the *mezzas* are fab, it's worth getting the mixed platter, served with fresh bread. No alcohol.

€€€-€€ **Cortigiano**, 44 Sharia Michel Bakhum, T02-3337 4838. Open 1300-0100. Pizzas, soups and Italian specialities continue to delight customers. Hefty portions and a good choice of desserts. No alcohol. Has a branch in Heliopolis (T02-2414 2202).

€€ **Maroush**, 64 Midan Lebanon, T02-3345 0972. Open 0900-0200. Restaurant and *ahwa*. Large comfortable outdoor seating area overlooking the midan. Authentic Lebanese cuisine. Most people come here for *sheesha* and tea, and order some *mezza* to accompany. A very local place. No alcohol served.

€€-€ El Omda, 6 Sharia El-Ghazza, behind Atlas Hotel, T02-3336 7596. Open 1200-0200. Famed for traditional Egyptian food, especially *fuul* and *koshari*, served very speedily. For carnivores, try the kebab, *kofta* and *shish tawook*.

Imbaba

€€€-€€ The Swiss Club, Villa Pax, 90 Sharia El Gehad, off Sharia Sudan, Midan, Kit Kat, T02-3314 2811, www.swiss-club-cairo.com. Palm trees and banyans surround grassy lawns, a children's play area, and a pseudo-Swiss villa. It's an odd but delightful enclave in the heart of Midan Kit Kat's back-alleys. The cuisine encompasses rosti and fondues, but there's plenty of other decent Western choices and a kid's menu. Entrance is E£10 (children under 6 free), open 0900-2000 for food and drinks (alcohol served), though private parties often continue in the hired rooms late into the night. The service, however, is mediocre.

€ El Embrator, before the post office on Sharia Sudan, Midan Kit Kat. Possibly the best *koshari* chain in town and they're extremely generous with their toppings. Finish with *ros bi-laban* (rice pudding) if you've got room. Worth stopping in if you've come this way to look at the houseboats.

Giza

€€€ Moghul Rooms, Mena House Oberoi, T02-3383 3222. Open 1200-1445 and 1930-2345. Authentic Indian food, sophisticated atmosphere, live Indian entertainment every evening. A fabulously plush experience in a historic hotel, but does serious damage to your wallet.

€€€-€€ Barry's Oriental Restaurant, 2 Sharia Abu Aziza, T02-3388 9540. Follow the road (Sharia Abu El-Houl) past the entrance to the Sphinx (on your right) to the

very end, Barry's is above **AA Stables**, just ring the bell. Go for drinks, meat grills or *mezza* (if you're vegetarian, great *besara*) and the best view of sunset behind the pyramids in the world. You can even just about hear the Sound and Light show from the roof terrace. It's best to check the price of Saqqara and juices before you order them. There's also a shop with some old and interesting curios.

€€€-€€ Christo, 10 Sharia El-Haram, T02-3383 3582. Open 1100-0300. A choose-your-own-seafood restaurant with a view of the pyramids. Often busy at lunchtimes with tour groups, the service is good but the decor is getting scruffy.

€€ Andrea, 59 Mariuteya Canal Rd, T02-3383 1133. Known for its pigeon dishes and still the best place for grilled chicken. Outdoor eating on a plant-filled patio shaded by awnings. A family-friendly place with lots of open space for children to play.

Heliopolis *p100, map p100*

€€€ Chantilly, 11 Sharia Baghdad, Korba, T02-2414 5620. Open 0700-2400. In the centre of Heliopolis, a long-standing Swiss establishment popular with wealthier locals and expats, Chantilly has a nice atmosphere and good patisserie at the front. Continental mains are heavy and very meat orientated (vegetarians are restricted to soup or salads) but their cheese fondue is excellent for a splash out (E£165). Serves alcohol, and has a pleasant shady terrace out the back.

€€€ City Stars, Sharia Omar Ibn Al-Khatab, T02-2480 0100. Restaurants generally open 1100-2400. For a massive choice of every kind of food you could be missing, trek out to **City Stars**: **Wagamama**, **Eatalian**, **Shogun**, **Bellini Cocktail Lounge** and plenty more.

€€€-€€ Chili's, 18 Sharia El-Thawra, T02-2418 8048. Open 1100-0100. Spicy Tex-Mex food served up in huge portions, try their fajitas and awesome black beans. The large outdoor patio with cooling fans make it a popular hangout in Heliopolis after the sun sets. Extensive dessert menu, including banana splits and brownies. No alcohol. Branches in Mohandiseen and Gezira.

€€€-€€ Petit Palmyra, 27 Sharia Al-Ahram, T02-2417 1720, www.palmyra groups.com. Open daily 1100-0100. This piano restaurant has been operating since 1949, and has a mix of Lebanese, oriental, and international food (pigeon, veal, chops) plus a separate vegetarian selection. Old-fashioned ambiance. Alcohol served, piano music from 2030.

€ Cafeteria Magic, 131 Sharia Al-Ahram (El-Nouzah). Reliable *fuul*, *taamiyya*, *shwerma* and other staples, either to eat in or take away. Handily opposite L'amphitrion.

€ Gad, Sharia Haroun Al-Rashid. Super-cheap takeaway Egyptian sandwich favourites from the countrywide chain. A safe bet for those with sensitive stomachs.

Trips down the Nile *p124*

Maadi
Red Onion, 27A Road 276, T02-2520 0240.
Villa 55, 55 Road 9, T02-2380 9592. The quiet garden setting seems a million miles away from the hustle of Cairo, while there is a tastefully decorated a/c interior for those steamy days. Food is international.

🎧 Bars and clubs

Central Cairo *p40, map p36*
Cairo has plenty of intriguing and diverse places to go for a drink, from strictly functional via classic vintage to bijou expensive. Some of the upmarket bars have room to dance and they morph into discos later on, plus there are plenty of 'nightclubs' that put on a floorshow or belly dancing. Some 5-star hotels also have discos that appeal to a range of affluent and Westernized Egyptians. Bear in mind most places don't serve alcohol during Ramadan, only top-end hotels and a couple of bars in Zamalek. Look out for Drinkies beverage shops, which also deliver (T19330).

Absolute, Casino El-Shargara, Corniche El-Nil, Maspero, Bulaq, T02-2579 6512, www.deyafa.net. Weekend nights see hectic club music, and there are chiller nights during the week. It's a cool-looking venue on the river, with the excellent **Sangria** bar upstairs for pre-party drinks and Italian/Lebanese food.

After Eight, 6 Sharia Qasr El-Nil (past a kiosk down an unlikely looking alley), T010-339 8000. Open 1200-0300, sometimes later. A hotspot on the Downtown scene, this smoky little dive is one of few places in Cairo to hear good live music. Currently *Sahra* play *rai* favourites and originals you can dance to on a Thu to a packed house, other nights have a swingtime thing going on, and DJ Dina (a woman) is on the decks on Tue, or Bashir and his band on a Nubian vibe on Sun. Cover charge of E£100 on Thu and E£50 on Sun. Fully stocked bar, standard menu serving variety of meats and pastas through the night.

Café Riche, 17 Sharia Talaat Harb, T02-2392 9793, www.caferiche.com. Open 1000-2400. Classic café that has seen the face of virtually every Arab intellectual and artist of the last century. Renovations have altered the feel of the place and now it's less of a revolutionary den, but it's still worth a visit, especially if you can get the story from an old timer, and the beer is reasonably priced.

Estoril, 12 Sharia Talaat Harb, T02-2574 3102. Cold beer, nibbles, and surprisingly good food – vegetarians should try the *fattah*. A place where artists and intellectuals still gather to work and play.

Fontana Hotel, Midan Ramses, T02-2592 2321, has an open-air bar on the top floor looking down on the mayhem of the Midan far below with *sheesha* and Stella at reasonable prices. There's also a 24-hr disco – one of the kitschiest you will ever see.

Grand Hyatt Hotel, Garden City, has spectacular views over the city from the lounge bar on the 40th floor. There is no minimum charge before 1900, or E£95 per person after that. You can stop for a drink or

just have a wander round, and there's also a revolving restaurant upstairs open from 1900.
Happy City Hotel, 92C Sharia Mohamed Farid, T02-2395 9333. This bar on the rooftop has views over a busy Downtown street, reasonably priced booze, decent food is available, plenty of seating to accommodate big groups or lone drinkers having a beer over their book.

Hard Rock Café, by the **Grand Hyatt Hotel**, Corniche El-Nil, T02-2532 1277/81/85. Open 1200-0400. Provides all you expect from the place: standard tex-mex specials, celebrity guitars, funky costumes, live shows, karaoke, and theme nights. The dance floor gets kicking after midnight. No minimum for foreigners.

Kings Bar, **Cosmopolitan Hotel**, 1 Sharia Ibn Taalab. Open 1000-0200. A fairly salubrious, relaxing yet local-feeling choice, warmly lit by yellow lanterns, generally peopled with *pasha* types shooting the breeze. It's a good place to snack or dine while you're drinking, with grills, salad, fish and steaks at quite reasonable prices. Stella E£13, all in.

Le Bistro, 8 Sharia Hoda Sharawy, T012-849 1943. A nice little bar open 1900-0200, with a restaurant of the same name next door.

Le Grillon, 8 Sharia Qasr El-Nil, Downtown; T02-2576 4959. Open 1100-0200. Pleasing indoor garden, restaurant, bar and *ahwa*, very popular spot for local intellectuals and artists. Conversations about revolutions and poetry continue into the wee hours over excellent *sheesha* and beer. The food is mid-priced and quite good, lots of meats, soups and salads, fairly standard Egyptian fare. It's a local place that is comfortable for single women and somewhere you will see Egyptian women enjoying a drink.

Odeon Rooftop Bar, **Odeon Palace Hotel**, 6 Sharia Abdel Hamid Said. Open 24 hrs and offers a great view of the city. A nice place to come to wind down after a rowdy evening, or where the hardcore carry on past dawn.

Tamarai, Nile City Towers, www.tamarai-egypt.com. This rooftop restaurant morphs into a club as the night wears on. It is genuinely chic, a high-society spot and place to glimpse celebrities. People get properly dancing. Every Tue is Nostalgia Night.

Windsor Hotel Barrel Lounge, 19 Sharia Alfi Bey, T02-2591 5277, is a truly delightful place for a drink, although the prices are a bit steep these days. The ambience is charming despite, or perhaps because of, the fading Anglo decor of polished wood, antlers and mottled mirrors.

Local drinking holes

Locals' bars are generally patronized by men only, and women on their own will probably feel uncomfortable although should be perfectly safe. As the government forbids the word 'bar' in the names of establishments, most go under the guise of 'cafeteria'.

Cafeteria Honololo, Sharia Mohammed Farid across the street from **Pension Roma**, Downtown. A taste of Cairo's seediest: Stella, *sheesha*, Heinekein, and bar girls.

Cafeteria Irabi, Sharia Orabi, Downtown. A miniature Stella-themed den that is friendly and allows glimpses of the world through the open door.

Cafeteria Stella, next to **Felfela** restaurant, Downtown. This tiny hole-in-the-wall of a bar is as local as it gets. On offer: basic *mezza*, E£9.50 Stella, and rum and brandy that is probably best avoided.

Carrol Restaurant, 12 Sharia Qasr El-Nil, Downtown. The food is expensive and the ambience extraordinarily gaudy. After midnight, there's a live show, performed by the only women who frequent the place.

El-Horriya, Midan Falaki, Bab El-Louk, Downtown. About the only local *ahwa* that serves beer, Horriya is a true Cairo institution. Everyone comes here, old and young, foreign and local, to spew thoughts on the state of the country, play chess, and get rowdy as the night wears on. It's become a bit over-run with AUC youth in recent years, but still should feature on any Cairo itinerary.

New Arizona, Sharia Alfi Bey, Downtown. They have removed the wallpaper of Swiss mountain posters, but this is about as local as it gets. Probably best not venture into the nightclub upstairs.

Zamalek *p90, map p91*

Buddha Bar, Sofitel El Gezirah, T02-2737 3737. Dominated by a gargantuan gold Siddhartha, the decor is plush (dark red velvet) great food downstairs (terrace with amazing Nile views, Asian and sushi) and upstairs gets into a dancing groove later on, good music and environment. Take plenty of cash.

Cairo Jazz Club, 197 Sharia 26 July, Mohandiseen, T02-3345 9939. Many rate it as the best place in town for live local music. Each night has a theme or regular act, check www.icroc.com for what's on. Loungey feel with a small dance floor that doubles as a stage. On occasion there's real jazz, and it's often quite good.

Deals, 2 Sharia El-Sayed El-Bakry, Zamalek. Closes at 0200. A noisy buzzing basement-like bar with cheapish beer and lots of Western food on the menu (try their shrimp provençale if you find yourself here at dinnertime). Also have branches in Mohandiseen and Heliopolis, but this one's the busiest.

Marriott Hotel, 16 Sharia Saray El-Gezira. Offers the drinking choices of **Harry's Pub** and the **Garden Promenade**. The first is a British-style wood-panelled pub with karaoke some nights, while the garden terrace is people-watching central and surrounded by shady trees and birds. Both serve OK continental food.

Pub 28, 28 Sharia Shagar Al-Durr, Zamalek. One of the oldest pubs in Zamalek, it attracts a more matured expat crowd as well as *pashas* quaffing large quantities of whisky in the smoky darkness. Cheap-ish beer and bar food (great French onion soup) means it's always crowded.

Purple Lounge, 6 Imperial Boat, Saray El-Gezira, Zamalek, T02-2736 5796.

Expensive and plush club playing house and retro sounds. If you're planning on dropping a lot of cash, it's worth it to be in one of very few places where people really get dancing.

Restaurants that double as late-night bars (see Restaurants, page 113) include: **La Bodega**, a cool yet not too pretentious, place for a drink, and **L'Aubergine**, a black box bar popular with students and local expats, which starts kicking around 2200 and is heaving on a Thu.

Heliopolis *p100, map p100*

Deals, 40A Sharia Baghdad, T02-2291 0406. Open 1600-0200. Very dim, cosy and functional, this is a more laid-back version of the **Deals** in Zamalek. The food (steaks, pasta, *mezza*) is tasty enough and there's a DJ every night from 2000.

L'Amphitrion, Sharia Al-Ahram, T02-2258 1379. Open 0800-0100. Nothing remains of the original 1922 fixtures but, now the Palmyra nightclub down the road has been turned into a Starbucks, this is the only place left in Heliopolis to have a beer in the outdoors and remember the allied forces who did likewise. Stella is E£20 and good *sheesha tuufah* E£8.50. Alcohol has to be drunk in the back courtyard with a curious water feature, complete with a Buddha statue. Plus there's an interesting clientele of higab-ed ladies, lone drinkers and old-school gentlemen. Slow service despite the plentiful cheery waiters. Food is available in the adjacent restaurant.

The Louvre, in the **Beirut Hotel**, 43 Sharia Baghdad, T02-2415 2347. Open 1200-0100. Feeble reproductions of the Mona Lisa don't really justify the name, but this is a stalwart for local expats. Serves acceptable food.

Pasha Bar, Baron Hotel, T02-2291 5757, www.baronhotels.com. With an attempt at oriental decor and views to the Baron's Palace, it's not a bad spot for a quiet drink before the DJ comes on at 2230.

Cairo *p40, maps p30, p32, p36, p49, p51, p78, p81, p91 and p100*

Belly-dancing shows

For a slick belly-dancing performance by one of the famous stars, head to one of the ritzy 5-star hotels. There's usually a cover charge (E£300-600, depending on the venue), which includes the show and a multi-course meal. Otherwise, progressively cheaper venues exist in floating restaurants (particularly the **Nile Maxim**, in front of the Marriott, T012-738 8888), in the strip of dodgy nightclubs along Pyramids Rd and tucked away in seedy alleyways Downtown. Of the latter, the **Palmyra**, and the **Miami**, both down an alley

at 16 Sharia 26th July, are as sleazy as they come and give a taste of Cairo's underworld. Women are fine to visit these places but only when accompanied by men, and everyone must be wary about being ripped-off for drinks or snacks and should query the price of anything and everything before consuming it. **Semiramis Intercontinental**, T02-2795 7171, at present hosts Dina, one of the most acclaimed dancers in town, every Thu night at 2330-0300, entrance includes dinner and taxes E£500-740 depending on proximity to stage.

Casinos

Found in the following hotels, see Where to stay, page 102; make sure you bring your passport with you:
Cairo Marriott, Mena House Oberoi, Nile Hilton, Ramses Hotel, Semiramis Inter-continental and **Sofitel El Gezirah**.

Cinemas

Current information on cinema performances can be found on www.icroc.com, in *Al-Ahram Weekly*, www.weekly-ahram.org.eg, the *Egyptian Gazette*, and the monthly glossy *Egypt Today* magazine. Commercial cinemas change their programmes every Wed and screenings are generally at 1030, 1330,

1530, 1830 and 2130 and sometimes at 2400, especially on weekends. Cultural centres have 1 or 2 screenings per week. Arabic films rarely have subtitles.
The following cinemas show films in English:
Al Tahrir, 122 Sharia Al-Tahrir, Dokki, T02-2335 4726.
Cairo Sheraton, Midan Galaa, Dokki, T02-3336 9700.
Cosmos, 12 Sharia Emad El-Din, Downtown, T02-2574 2177.
Family Land, Osman Towers, Corniche El-Nil, next to Maadi Hospital, Maadi, T02-2524 8100.
French Cultural Centre, 1 Sharia Maddraset El-Huquq El-Faransiya, Mounira, T02-2794 7679.
Galaxy, 67 Sharia Abdel Aziz Al-Seoud, Manial, T02-2532 5745, www.galaxycairocinema.com.
Goethe Institute, 5 Sharia El-Bustan, Downtown, T02-2575 9877.
Good News First Mall, Sharia Giza (opposite Giza Zoo), T02-3571 7803.
Karim, 15 Sharia Emad El-Din, Downtown, T02-2592 4830.
Metro, 35 Sharia Talaat Harb, Downtown, T02-2393 7566.
Odeon, 4 Sharia Dr A Hamid Said, Downtown, T02-2576 5642.
Ramses Hilton, 7th floor of the hotel's shopping annexe, Corniche El-Nil, Downtown, T02-2574 7435.
Renaissance Nile City, Nile City Towers, Corniche El-Nil, T02-2461 9101/2/3.
Stars/Golden Stars, City Stars Mall, Sharia Omar Ibn Al-Khatab, Heliopolis, T02-2480 2012/3, www.citystarscinema.com.
Townhouse Gallery, 10 Sharia Nabrawi, off Sharia Champollion, Downtown, T02-2576 8086, www.thetownhouse gallery.com, occasionally has programmes screening foreign films.
Villa Grey, 24 Sharia Abdallah Al Kateb, Dokki, T02-3338 2184. A cine-club showing art-house and foreign films, Wed at 2030.

Galleries

Cairo Opera House Art Gallery, Gezira, T02-2739 8132. Sun-Thu 1000-1430 and 1630-2030.

French Cultural Centre, 1 Sharia Maddraset El-Huquq El-Faransiya, Mounira, T02-2794 7679. Also at 5 Sharia Chafik El-Dib, Ard El-Golf, Heliopolis, T02-2417 4824, F02-2419 9143.

Gezira Art Centre, 1 Sharia El-Marsafy, Zamalek, T02-2737 3298. Interesting exhibitions by contemporary artists.

Hannager Arts Centre, Opera House Grounds, T02-2735 6861. Daily 1000-2200.

Khan El-Maghraby Gallery, 18 Sharia El-Mansour Mohammed, Zamalek, T02-2735 3349. Mon-Sat, 1200-2200.

Mashrabia Gallery, 8 Sharia Champollion, T02-2578 4494, www.mashrabiagallery.com. Exhibitions by foreign and Egyptian artists. Daily, except Fri and Mon 1100-2000. Contemporary art.

Safar Khan Gallery, 6 Sharia Brazil, Zamalek, T02-2735 3314. Sat-Thu, 1000-1300, 1700-2000.

Townhouse Gallery of Contemporary Art, 10 Sharia Nabrawi, off Sharia Champollion, Downtown, T02-2576 8086, www.thetown housegallery.com. Sat-Wed 1000-1400 and 1800-2100, Fri 1800-2100, closed Thu. Probably the best space in town to see interesting and adventurous exhibitions. Gift and bookshop opposite.

Zamalek Art Gallery, 11 Sharia Brazil, T02-2735 1240.

Sound and Light show

2 performances daily at the Sphinx and pyramids, Giza, www.soundandlight.com.eg at 1830 and 1930 in winter; 2030 and 2130 in summer. E£75, no student discounts. The voice of the Sphinx narrates the story of the pyramids in the following languages: Arabic, English, French, German, Italian, Japanese, Russian and Spanish. Call for specific schedules, T02-3383 8823/3587 6767.

Theatre, music and dance

Current information for performances is given in the *Egyptian Gazette* and *Al-Ahram Weekly*, www.weekly-ahram.org.eg. Apart from the *Opera House*, all theatrical performances are likely to be in Arabic.

Arab Music Institute, 22 Sharia Ramses, Downtown, T02-2574 3373. Classical Arabic music performances, twice a week.

Balloon Theatre, Sharia Corniche El-Nil, El-Agouza, nr Al-Zamalek Bridge, T02-2347 1718.

Beit Al-Suhaymi, Darb Al-Asfar, Al-Hussein, Islamic Cairo, T02-2591 3391. Folk music and songs every Sun at 2000, free, for 2 hrs, and occasional special events and performances, particularly during Ramadan.

El-Genena Theatre, Al-Azhar Park, Salah Salem, T02-2362 5057. Great venue to hear music, sometimes international.

El-Gomhouriya Theatre, 12 Sharia El-Gomhouriya, Abdin, T02-2390 7707.

El Mastaba Center for Egyptian Folk Music, El Tanbura Hall, 30A Sharia Balaqsa, Abdin, T02-2392 6768. Performances every Thu by Rango and on Fri by El Tanbura at 2130, cost E£20 and last around 1½ hrs. A visit is strongly recommended, particularly on a Thu when Rango get people out their seats and perform some haunting ensembles.

El-Sawy Culture Wheel, Sharia 26 July, Zamalek, T02-2736 6178, www.culture wheel.com. Bands and concerts most nights in a great venue under 15th May bridge, varying from Bedouin folk, to Arab rap, to Ghanaian flutes.

Makan, 1 Sharia Saad Zaghloul, Al-Mounira, T02-2792 0878. *Zar* performance by the Mazaher band every Wed, involving drumming and chanting (traditionally to drive out evil spirits), and Nass Makan every Tue at 2100, which is folk music from around Egypt. An essential night out and best on Wed. Tickets can be reserved by phone 48 hrs in advance, which gives a E£10 discount (or buy for E£30 on the night). Performances last about 2 hrs.

The National Theatre, Midan Ataba, T02-2591 7783.

Opera House, Gezira, info T02-339 8144, box office T02-2739 0132, www.cairoopera.org. Has a hall with 1200 seats for opera, ballet and classical music performances, a 2nd hall with 500 seats for films and conferences and an open-air theatre. For grandeur, get tickets to the main hall show; advance booking recommended. Men must wear jacket and tie.

Puppet Theatre, Ezbekiah, El-Ataba, T02-2591 0954, traditional puppetry shows which might appeal, Thu and Fri 1930, Fri 1030.

Whirling dervishes On Mon, Wed and Sat, 2030, during Ramadan 2100, in Wikala El-Ghuri, near Midan Hussein, Islamic Cairo. Tickets are given out at 1830 and it is advisable come at that time to collect one; least busy on a Mon night. Free. Cameras (but not video) permitted. Sponsored by the Ministry of Culture, the **El-Tanoura Dance Troupe** puts on a spectacular show in the restored *wikala*, which makes a great setting. Just hearing the vibrant music and staring at the colourful spinning can put you into a trance. The performance lasts about 1½ hrs and is a Cairo must-see (if you suspend any desire for authenticity for a while).

✿ Festivals

Cairo *p40, maps p30, p32, p36, p49, p51, p78, p81, p91 and p100*

Jan International Book Fair at the Exhibition Grounds in Nasr City, 0900-1900. **Christmas**, Coptic Church. **Epiphany**, Coptic Church.

Mar International Fair: Annual Spring Flower Show.

Apr Easter, Coptic Church. **Annunciation**, Coptic and Roman Catholic.

Jun Pentecost, Coptic Church.

Jul International Festival of Documentary Films.

Aug International Song Festival. Nile Festival Day at Giza.

Sep International Festival of Vanguard Theatre. Nile Festival Day in Cairo.

Nov International Children's Book Fair at Nasr City.

Dec Festival for Arab Theatre. Festival of Impressionist Art (alternate years). International Film Festival.

○ Shopping

Cairo *p40, maps p30, p32, p36, p49, p51, p78, p81, p91 and p100*

Bookshops

As the largest publisher of Arabic books in the world, Cairo is a haven for Arabic literature enthusiasts. For second-hand books (some of which are in English) try the book market in the northeast corner of Ezbekiya Gardens, by Midan Ataba. The following are shops selling books and periodicals in European languages:

Al-Ahram, 165 Sharia Mohammed Farid, Downtown. Sat-Thu 0900-1700.

American University in Cairo (AUC) Bookstore, Sharia Kasr El-Aini, Downtown, on the old campus, T02-2797 5929, www.aucpress.com. Open Sat-Thu 1000-1800 (-1500 in Ramadan). On 2 floors, Cairo's biggest and best collection of fiction and books on Egypt (and everywhere else). They no longer stock textbooks, which have been moved to the campus in New Cairo. There's also a store next to the **AUC Hostel**, Zamalek, T02-2739 7045, open Sat-Thu 0900-1800, Fri 1300-1800. Note that it's 20% off everything the first Sat of the month.

Anglo-Egyptian Bookshop, 165 Sharia Mohammed Farid, Downtown, T02-2391 4337. Mon-Sat 0900-2000. Fairly intellection selection, classic fiction but better for non-fiction, plus some guidebooks.

Dar El-Bustan, 29 Sharia Faggala, Downtown. Open 0900-1700, Fri 1000-1500, closed Sun.

Diwan, 159 Sharia 26 July, Zamalek, T02-2736 2578, www.diwanegypt.com. Open 0900-2330. Coffee shop inside, children's books section. French, English and Arabic books on offer, occasional cultural events in the evenings, definitely one of the best selections in the city. Also has a branch in Maadi, 45 Rd 9, T019-8887 326, and Heliopolis at 105 Sharia Abou Bakr El-Seddik, T02-2690 8184.

L'Orientalist, 15 Qasr El-Nil, Downtown, T02-2575 3418, www.orientalebooks.com. Rare books and maps, original David Roberts lithographs, and other beautiful antique items.

Lehnert & Landrock, 44 Sharia Sherif, T02-392 7606, daily 1000-1900, and in the mall next to **Naguib Mahfouz Coffeeshop** in the Khan el-Khalili. Also has branches at Giza and in the Egyptian Museum. Books in German and English, but best known for the black and white prints by Lehnert & Landrock who documented the Middle East in the early 20th century.

Librairies Renaissance, 20 Sharia El-Sawra, Mohandiseen, T02-3761 5835. Best for French books. They also have branches in Heliopolis (T010-1662012) and Maadi (T02-25199684).

Livres de France, 17 Sharia Brazil, Zamalek, T02-2735 1148. Open 1000-1900, Sat 1000-0130, closed Sun. Ma'adi branch at 2 Road 23, near Ma'adi Grandmall, opens Mon-Sat 1100-1900.

Madbouli, 6 Midan Tala'at Harb, Downtown, T02-2575 6421, www.madboulybooks.com. Open 0900-2300. Down in the basement they have a decent selection of books in various European languages.

Shorouk, 1 Midan Talaat Harb, Downtown, T02-2393 0643. Open 0900-2200. Has a good fiction section. Also in Heliopolis at 15 Sharia Baghddad, Korba, and in **City Stars Mall**.

Virgin Megastore, City Stars Mall, Heliopolis, T02-2480 2244. One of the biggest book departments in Cairo.

Crafts and souvenirs

Among the most attractive areas to shop is the **Khan El-Khalili Bazaar** and **Sagh** comprising an array of shops dating from the 14th century. Renowned for craftsmanship in silver and gold, embroidered cloth, copperware, leather and mother-of-pearl inlaid goods. (Remember that the import of ivory is forbidden into most Western countries.)

The Kerdassa village, east of Giza, is noted for its embroidered cotton and silk dresses, and good-quality carpets at a cheaper price than you will find in the bazaars (E£120 for simple organic colours, up to E£300 for more complex and colourful designs). Haraneya, west of Giza, is another main centre for quality carpets. See page 16 for more information on shopping. Listed below are fixed-price shops in Cairo selling good-quality crafts and souvenirs from around Egypt.

Abd El-Zaher Book Binders, 31 Sharia Sheikh Mohamed Abdou, behind Al-Azhar Mosque, T02-2511 8041, www.abdel-zaher.com. Open 1000-2200. Notebooks, photo albums, folders, etc, are beautifully bound in leather and handmade paper. They can cover books or diaries to order, and can initial them in gold, though it might take a few days. Also has a small selection of books on Egypt.

Al Ain Gallery, 73 Sharia El-Hussein, Dokki, T02-3749 3940. Bedouin textiles, cushions, ceramics, and 1000 filigree and metalwork lanterns.

Al-Khatoun, 3 Sharia Mohamed Abdou, Islamic Cairo, T02-2514 7164, www.al khatoun.com. Open 1100-2100 (1200-2300 in Ramadan). Fabulous swathes of cloth, pots, beaten copperware, iron lamps, old film posters, cushions, pop art and other items of homeware that are all in impeccable taste. Their new branch in Zamelek is called

Al Qahira, 1st floor, 6 Bahgat Ali, T011-3133 932, www.alqahiracrafts.com. Open 1100-2100 except Sun. Housed in an attractive apartment.

And Company, 3 Sharia Bahgat Ali, Zamalek, T02-2736 5689. Open 0900-2300, daily. This is where to come for superior Egyptian cotton, specializing in clothing, sheets, etc of a contemporary rather than ethnic bent. Also sells quality jewellery, pottery, candles and the like, plus works by local artists.

Atlas, near Nagib Mahfouz Café in Khan El-Khalili, T02-2590 6139. Moiré silk handmade shoes.

Azza Fahmy Boutique, 15C Sharia Taha Hussein (corner of Sharia Mohamed Marashli), T02-2735 8351, www.azzafahmy.com. Open 1000-2200. Celebrated jewellery designer.

Caravanserai, 16 Sharia Marashly, Zamalek, T02-2735 0517. Open Mon-Sat 1000-2000, Sun 1000-1730. Well-known for its fabulous lighting, which remains unique among all the pretenders. They also have some mirrors, ornaments and ceramics. A visit here could result in a major purchase to take home.

Egypt Crafts, 1st floor, 27 Sharia Yahia Ibrahim, Zamalek, T02-2736 5123, www.fairtradeegypt.org. Sat-Thu 0900-2000, Fri 1000-1800. Helping to revive traditional crafts throughout Egypt, this non-profit fairtrade shop has a good selection of pottery, basketry, hand-woven scarves and rugs, jewellery and much more. A very stress-free as well as worthy place to indulge yourself.

Fatima, 157 Sharia 26 July, Zamalek, T02-2736 9951, in an alley of the main road next to Abu El-Sid restaurant. A cubby-hole selling intricate embroidered textiles and clothing from Egypt and central Asia.

Khan Misr Touloun, Sharia Touloun, facing the main entrance of Ibn Touloun Mosque T02-2265 3337. Daily 1000-1700, except Sun. Handicrafts from the villages and oases of Egypt (and countries further afield). They pretty much have something for everyone – books, glassware, textiles, clothes, pots, woodwork – although some shoppers feel the selection is not as attractive as it once was.

Loft, 12 Sharia Sayed El-Bakri, Zamalek, T02-27366931, www.loftegypt.com. Open 1000-1500. An eclectic selection of oriental furniture, metalwork, friezes, over-the-top lighting, icons and antiques are displayed in a boudoir-like setting – worth visiting in itself.

Markaz, 1b Road 199 (entrance on Road 233), Maadi, T02-2754 7026, T010-240 5858.

Open 1000-2100, daily. Working with NGOs and small enterprises all over Egypt, exquisite crafts, rugs, drapes, cushions, scarfs and more are discerningly selected and worth paying a bit more for.

Mounaya Gallery, 14 Sharia Montazah, Zamalek, T02-2737 7726, www.mounaya. com. Stocks an interesting range of textiles, metalwork and ornaments.

Morgana, Road 9, Maadi, T010-125 0441. Fabulous antique colonial and Egyptian furniture plus a smattering of nick-nacks, pictures, old clocks, etc.

Nagada, 13 Sharia Refa'a, Dokki, T02-3748 6663, www.nagada.net. Open 1000-1830. An exquisite selection of fabrics, textiles, clothing, and ornaments, as well as exclusive pottery creations from their workshop in Tunis in Fayoum (see page 153), High-quality goods at high-end prices.

Nomad, 1st floor, 14 Saraya Al-Gezira, Zamalek, T02-2736 1917. Open 1000-2100. Tasteful goods from all over Egypt, the original jewellery made to traditional designs is especially good. They also have a smaller branch in the **Marriott**.

Om Gallery, 14 Sharia Hassan Assem, Zamalek, T02-2736 3165. This small gallery has an eclectic array of handmade leather and wrought-iron artworks, alabaster lamps and curios.

Oum El-Dounia, 1st floor, 3 Sharia Talat Harb, just off Midan Tahrir, T02-2393 8273. This delightful shop keeps getting bigger and better, with goods selected from all over Egypt at reasonable prices. If you can't find anything in here then something's wrong. Large selection of books, mainly in French. Open 7 days a week, 1000-2100. There's also a branch in Maadi on Rd 23 (off Sh El-Nadi), T02-2753 0483, daily 0930-2030.

Shahira Mehrez and Companions, 3rd floor, 12 Sharia Abi Emama, Dokki, T02-3748 7814. Open Sat-Thu 1000-2000. An intriguing shop with some lovely antiques (rugs, pots, calligraphy, etc) and faboulous *galabiyyas* made by seamstresses from around Egypt to the owner, Shahira's, designs.

Souk Al-Fustat, Sharia Saydi Hassan Al-Anwar, Old Cairo. Open 1000-2200. A bit pricey, but it showcases traditional crafts (some of which are made in the workshops of the complex). Sadly, this exceptionally high-quality *souk* doesn't have the air of being the great commercial success that was hoped for, with shop units sitting empty, but it's a good place to get handmade metal lanterns with arabesque motifs in all sizes and designs, curios, unique jewellery, handwoven fabrics and such like. Haggling is still possible in many shops.

Swellams, 30 Sharia Adly, T02-2393 9470, *the* place to buy cotton pyjamas in Cairo. Family-run for 55 years, **Swellams** has made clothes for former presidents and still sells beautifully made garments and, in addition to their classic pyjamas, can tailor shirts and suits.

Wady Craft Shop, All Saint's Cathedral, 5 Sharia Michel Lutfalla, Zamalek, T02-2735 4350, www.wadycrafts.com/shop. Open 0930-1700, Sun and Fri 1100-1600. Handicrafts made by disadvantaged and disabled persons, as well as Sudanese refugees, all proceeds go to these charitable causes.

Supermarkets
Metro markets are scattered around Cairo and have a good variety of stock, hotline T19619. There are branches of **Carrefour** in 6th October City and Maadi. **Alfa Market**, 4 Sharia El-Malek El-Afdal, Zamalek, T02-2736 6265, which is good for toiletries as well as groceries, and **El Tamimi** supermarket, 116 Sharia 26th July, Zamalek, T02-2738 0274, are open 24 hrs and seem to be able to produce almost anything out of their storerooms. **Isis**, 8 Ahmed Sabry, Zamalek, T02-2738 2724, is a small health food store that might be helpful for those with specific dietary requirements.

⚠ What to do

Cairo *p40, maps p30, p32, p36, p49, p51, p78, p81, p91 and p100*

Diving
Maadi Divers, 18 Road 218, Maadi, T02-2519 8644, www.maadi-divers.com. The 1st PADI dive centre in Cairo.
Nautilus Diving, 4 Sharia Omar Shabban, off Sharia El-Nozha, Ard El-Golf, Heliopolis, T02-2417 6515, www.nautilusdiving.com.
Seascapes Diving and Safari, 1/2 Sharia Lasilky, New Maadi, T02-2519 4930. PADI courses, diving trips and desert safaris.

Golf
Katameya Heights Golf Course, 23 km southeast of Cairo, www.katameyaheights. com. 2 courses, 1 with 18 holes and another with 9 holes.
   Mena House Oberoi, Gezira Sporting Club and the **Marriott Hotel** at Mirage City also have 18-hole courses.

Gym and health clubs
Cairo Sheraton Health Club, Galaa Sq, Giza, T02-3336 9700/800 ext 599/177. Fully equipped gymnasium and other facilities.
Golden Tulip Flamenco Hotel Health Club, 2 Sharia El-Gezira El-Wosta, Zamalek, T02-2735 0815. Mon-Sat 0800-2200. Gymnasium, sauna, jacuzzi and massage.
Gold's Gym, 8th and 9th floor, Maadi Palace Mall, T02-2378 5592. Includes a mixed-gender gym, a ladies-only gym and 2 pools.
Samya Alloubah Dance and Fitness Centre, 6 Sharia Amr, off Sharia Syria, Mohandiseen, T02-3302 0572. Gym, steam room, gymnastics, martial arts and dance and fitness classes for both adults and children.
Spa and Wellness Centre, Four Seasons Hotel Cairo at the First Residence, T02-2567 2040. Full-service spa, 8 treatment rooms and extensive facilities. Specializes in Cleopatra milk baths, Nefertiti facials, papyrus wraps and private spa for couples.

Horse riding

It's very pleasant to ride in the desert by the pyramids, particularly for sunrise or sunset. Avoid the haggard-looking horses lined up for tourists by the pyramid's gate and head for the stables in Kafr El-Gebel (straight on past the entrance to Sound and Light show). **AA Stables**, T012-153 4142, and **MG Stables**, T02-3385 1241 are the most highly recommended, have regular Western clients, and offer a variety of excursions from the standard hour-long ride around the pyramids (E£50), riding lessons, to a trip to Saqqara. More elaborate excursions and night rides need to be booked in advance. See also Saqqara Country Club, below.

Swimming

Heliopolis, and **Gezira** sporting clubs have pools that you can pay daily or monthly memberships to use. The **Mohamed Ali Club**, on the banks of the Nile, by Mounib metro stop, has a great pool, day use is E£60 or on Fri E£80. It's possible to use the pools at some hotels, those in the 5-star establishments obviously cost more. The **Atlas Hotel**, Mohandiseen (E£35 minimum charge, enough for a couple of drinks as well) and the **Fontana**, Midan Ramses (E£25) both have small and unappealing pools.

Other hotels with good pools include: **Grand Hyatt**, Garden City, for E£200 per day 0700-1900; **Marriott**, Zamalek, which has hiked its prices to E£240 per day, or Thu-Sat E£305; the **Nile Hilton** charges E£150 and the pool is large though the surroundings a bit tacky; **Semiramis Intercontinental** is good for E£137 per day. The **Saqqara Country Club**, at the end of Saqqara Rd, Giza, T02-3381 1307, costs E£120 per person including lunch and a drink, day-use of a room E£220. If you go early at the weekend it will be mostly empty, later on it gets crowded with Egyptians. Plus there is horse riding, tennis courts, a restaurant and bar lounge. It's a great place to get away from it all.

Tennis

Katameya Tennis Resort, www.katameya heights.com, 23 km southeast of Cairo. Has 10 clay and 2 grass courts but you have to know a member.
Marriott Hotel, has hard courts for rent by the hour, and adequate racquets.

Tour operators

Abercrombie and Kent, 18 Sharia Youssef El-Guindy, El Bustan Centre, Downtown, T02-2393 6255, www.akegypt.com.
American Express, 21 Sharia Giza, Nile Tower Building, T02-574 3656.
Astra Travel, 11 Midan El-Missaha, Dokki, T02-3749 1469, www.astratravel.com. Also have branches in Heliopolis and Maadi.
Egypt Rays, 18 Sharia Hassan Shawi, Nasr City, www.egyptrays.com. Can cut your costs by booking budget accommodation, entry tickets to all sites included.
Isis Travel, 48 Sharia Giza, Orman Bldg, T02-3749 4325, www.isistravel.com.
Mena Tours, El-Nasr Bldg, Sharia El-Nil, Giza, T02-3574 0864, and 14 Sharia Talaat Harb, T02-2396 2497, www.mena-tours.net.
Misr Travel, 1 Sharia Talaat Harb, T02-2393 0010, and 7 Sharia Talaat Harb, T02-2393 0168, www.misrtravel.net.
See Real Egypt, El Obour Building, Sharia Salah Salem, Nasr City, T018-305 0677, www.seerealegypt.com. Customized or standard tours, mainly visiting the big sights in Cairo and down the Nile Valley.
Spring Tours, 11 Sharia Talaat Harb, T02-392 2627, and 3 Sharia Sayyid El-Bakry, Zamalek, T02-2393 2573, www.springtours.com. Open 0900-1800.
Travco, 12 Sharia Mahmoud Azmi, Zamalek, T02-2736 2024, www.travco.com.
Thomas Cook, 7 Sharia Baghdad, El-Korba, Heliopolis, T02-2416 4000; 17 Sharia Mahmoud Bassiouny, Downtown, T02-2574 3955/67/776, daily 0800-1700; 10 Sharia 26 July, Mohandiseen, T02-3346 7187, www.thomascookegypt.com.

Cairo *p40, maps p30, p32, p36, p49, p51, p78, p81, p91 and p100*

Air

Cairo International Airport, is about 22 km northeast of downtown Cairo. **EgyptAir**, www.egyptair.com, which operates from Terminal 1, offers regular flights to the following domestic destinations: **Abu Simbel**, **Alexandria**, **Assuit**, **Aswan**, **Hurghada**, **Luxor** and **Sharm El-Sheikh**.

Airline offices **Air Canada**, 26 Sharia Mahmoud Bassiouny, T02-2575 8402, www.aircanada.com. **Air France**, 2 Midan Talaat Harb, T02-2770 6250, www.airfrance.com, Sun-Thu 0830-1630. **Austrian Airlines**, 6 Sharia El-Sheikh El-Marsafi, Zamalek, T19404, www.austrian.com, Sun-Thu 0800-1600. **British Airways**, Intercontinental Residence Suites, City Stars Complex, Sharia Al Forsan, Heliopolis, T02-2480 0380, Sun-Thu 0900-1700. **CSA Czech Airlines**, 9 Sharia Talaat Harb, T02-2393 0395, www.csa.cz. **Cyprus Airways**, 4th Floor, 17 Sharia Qasr El-Nil, T02-2395 4770, www.cyprusair.com. **Delta**, 17 Sharia Ismail Mahmoud, Zamalek, T02-2736 2039, www.delta.com. **EgyptAir**, 9 Sharia Talaat Harb, T02-2393 2836, 6 Sharia Adly, T02-2392 7649. **El-Al**, 5 Sharia El-Makrizi, Zamalek, T02-2736 1795, www.elal.co.il. **Emirates**, 18 Sharia El-Batal Ahmed Abdel Aziz, Mohandiseen, T19899, www.emirates.com. **Lufthansa**, 6 Sharia El-Sheikh El-Marsafi, Zamalek, T19380, Sun-Thu 0800-1700, www.lufthansa.com. **Saudi Arabian Airlines**, 5 Sharia Qasr El-Nil, T02-2574 1200, www.saudiairlines.com. **Singapore Airlines**, 22nd Floor, Infinity Towers, 8 Sharia Geziret Al-Arab, Mohandiseen, T02-3749 2879, www.singaporeair.com. **Swiss**, 6 Sharia El-Sheikh El-Marsafi, Zamalek, T19380, www.swiss.com, Sun-Thu 0800-1700. **Syrianair**, 25 Sharia Talaat Harb, Downtown, T02-2393 6232, www.syriaair.com. **Turkish Airways**, 17 Sharia Sabri Abu Alem, Midan Taalat Harb, Downtown, T02-2396 0454, www.turkishairlines.com, daily except Fri 0900-1800.

Bus

Local Only recommended for the truly adventurous or extremely broke traveller, public buses in Cairo guarantee an experience to write home about. That said, the public bus network succeeds surprisingly well in connecting the labyrinth of streets that make up Cairo's many boroughs. Before setting off, beware: except for the main hubs in **Midan Abdel Mouneim Riad** (by MidanTahrir), behind **Midan Ramsis** and next to **Midan Ataba** where the lines start and stop, the buses often fail to come to complete stops and require extraordinary agility to mount and descend. However, when the driver sees a foreigner flagging down the bus he may make a special exception and come to a halt. When mounting a bus, get on from the back, pay your ticket to the attendant and plan to descend from the front. Since they're so cheap and the way most Cairenes get around, buses are always crowded – especially during commuting hours from 0700-1000 and 1500-1900. Be mindful of yourself and your belongings as pickpockets and groping may occur. Note that bus numbers are generally posted above the dashboard or on a plate in the window. Do not confuse the vehicle identification number (sometimes in English) with the route number. As bus numbers are not in English, it's a good idea to learn the numerals (read as in English from left to right). Some bus routes have slashes through the digits, which indicate a wholly different route. The slightly smaller and newer public buses are a bit more manageable since there is no standing room and only 1 door (not to be confused with the even smaller private microbuses that look more like vans). Buses operate daily from 0530 to 0030 with extended hours during Ramadan and cost 50 pt, minibuses cost E£1-2. If in doubt, just ask the person next to you how much it costs to your destination.

The **CTA** a/c buses are more comfortable and a good way to get to the airport, though they take a detour through Heliopolis, which can mean a journey time of well over an hour. They cost a flat E£2, no matter how far you ride. When in doubt, ask a station chief located in a box in the middle of all main bus hubs. They may not speak English, but state your destination and they'll point you in the right direction.

Long distance Cities in Egypt are well connected by buses that are quite comfortable and inexpensive. When tourist season is high, it's wise to buy tickets in advance, especially to key destinations like the Sinai, Siwa or Hurghada. You must buy tickets at the bus station; phone reservations are still not possible. The following schedules are for your reference. Do not rely too heavily on them as times and prices change constantly in Egypt depending on the number of tourists and a million other variables. You can always call the respective bus station to enquire about departure times – try to have an Arabic speaker nearby as few operators are proficient in English. Note that some prices are quoted in ranges because later buses tend to be a few pounds more expensive than early morning buses. There are several bus stations in Cairo that cover different regions of Egypt.

Turgoman/Cairo Gateway is the main terminal, on Sharia Shanan in Bulaq, now signed as the 'Cairo Gateway' although no one calls it that. Recently rebuilt and modernized, there are electronic boards above the ticket counters showing destinations and times. It's huge and offers services to virtually everywhere in Egypt (except El-Fayoum). Ironically, though, it's not readily connected to public transport, but is within walking distance of Midan Ramses (500 m). By taxi, it's a E£5 ride from Midan Tahrir. 4 bus companies operate from Turgoman:

East Delta, T02-2577 8347, have daily buses to the following destinations in Sinai: **Taba**, then on to **Nuweiba** 0600, 0930,

2300 (E£70-E£80, 7 hrs); **St Catherine** 1100 (E£45, 8 hrs) via **Wadi Feiran** (E£40, 7 hrs); **Sharm El-Sheikh** 0630, 1030, 1630, 2300, 0145 (E£60-80, 8-9 hrs); **Dahab**, 0715, 1330, 1930, 1215 (E£90, 8 hrs); **El-Arish** 2 daily (E£27-37, 5-6 hrs); **Ras Sudr** 0715, 0815, 1930 (E£30, 3 hrs). The Sinai-bound buses also pick up passengers at **Abbasiya** terminal, 3 km north of Ramses, 30 mins after leaving Turgoman, and at **Al-Maza** terminal past Heliopolis, 15 mins after Abbasiya. Buses leave for **Ismailia** and **Suez** every ½ hr from 0600-2000 (both destinations E£9, 1½-2 hrs); for **Port Said** buses leave every hour from 0545-2130 (E£17, 3 hrs). The Canal Zone buses also pick up passengers from Al-Maza.

West & Middle Delta, T02-2575 2157/ 2415 6597, operates buses every hour to **Alexandria** 0430-0100 (E£30-35, 3 hrs); **Marsa Matruh** at 0615, 0630, 0730, 0830, 1100, 1515, 1945, 2130 (E£50-60, 6-7 hrs); **Salloum** at 2330 (E£65, 9-10 hrs); **Siwa** 1 bus daily at 1945 (E£65, 7-8 hrs). They also have buses to destinations in the Delta: **Tanta** and **Mahalla** every hour between 0700-2000 (E£8-10, 2-2½ Hrs).

Upper Egypt Travel, T02-2576 0261, operates buses to the **Western Desert**: **Bahariyya** daily at 0800 (E£30, 5 hrs); **Farafra** (E£55, 8-9 hrs) and **Dakhla** at 0700, 1800 (E£75, 12 hrs), via **Bahariyya**; **Kharga** 2130, 2230 (E£65, 10-11 hrs). The **Red Sea Coast**: daily to **Hurghada** at 0800, 1200, 1330, 1700, 1830, 2100, 2200, 2330, 0100 (E£70-75, 6 hrs). The 1700 continues to **Aswan** (E£100, 14 hrs) and the 2100 continues to **Luxor** (E£100, 11 hrs), both go via **Safaga** (E£80-85); the 1330, 1830 and 2330 continue to **El-Quseir** (E£81, 8 hrs) and **Marsa Alam** (E£91, 11 hrs) and to **Shalatein** (E£96). Buses to **Wadi Natrun** (E£7, 2 hrs) leave from bus station on Sharia Shubra, call first at **Sadat City** (E£6, 1½ hrs).

Metro stops of particular interest

Sadat: Tahrir; Downtown.
Mubarak: Midan Ramses; Ramses Train Station.
Attaba: closest stop to Islamic Cairo, can walk to Al Azhar and Khan El-Khalili from here.
Mar Girgis: in the heart of Old Cairo, definitely the best way to get here.
Maadi: lots of expats live in this accessible suburb, some good restaurants and access to services not as available in other parts of Cairo; good library and prettiest part of the Corniche with lots of Nile-side restaurants and coffee shops; also a good spot to commence a *felucca* ride (take a taxi from the metro stop – about E£4 to the Nile).

Tickets for international buses to **Saudi Arabia** (3 per week) can be bought from the same office, though the staff who deal with these are only present on Sat.

Superjet, T02-2579 8181, operates buses to prime tourist destinations and are a step above others in terms of quality and price. To **Hurghada** at 0730, 1430, 2315 (E£65, 6 hrs); **Sharm El-Sheikh** at 0730, 1515, 2345 (E£85, 6 hrs); **Luxor** at 2345 (E£100, 9-10 hrs); **Port Said** every hour from 0645-2000 (E£23, 3 hrs). Also runs international buses 4 times a week to **Libya**, **Jordan**, **Syria** and **Saudi Arabia**. Buses for international destinations leave from the **Al-Maza terminal**, T02-2290 9013, at the far end of Heliopolis except for the Libya bus, which starts at Turgoman. Superjet buses to **Alexandria** leave from Sharia Al-Galaa near Midan Abdel Mounim Riyad, every hour from 0600-2300 (E£25, 3 hrs).

Aboud Station is on Sharia Ahmed Helmi, 3 km north of Ramses – a E£5 taxi ride from Ramses, E£10 from Downtown, or a quick microbus hop. From here, 3 companies operate daily buses at least once an hour from 0600 to 2000 to **El-Fayoum**, the **Delta**, **Middle and Upper Egypt**, and **Alexandria** (Specific cities: **Alexandria**, **Damanhur**, **Tanta**, **Benha**, **Mansura**, **Damietta**, **Zagazig**, **Fayoum**, **Minya**, **Assiut**, **Sohag**, **Luxor** and **Aswan**). Note that those going to Middle and Upper Egypt may want to opt for the comparably cheap

and significantly more comfortable and convenient train.

Calèche

Horse-drawn carriages are generally found south of the **Marriott** hotel on Zamalek. Not a way to get around, but nice for an evening's exploration. Expect to pay about E£30 per hr.

Car hire

Al Arabia, 13-71 Sharia Ahmed Orabi, Mohandiseen, T02-3304 9776. **Avis**, 16A Sharia Ma'amal El-Soukkar, Garden City, T02-2794 7081. **Hertz**, www.hertzegypt. com, at the airport, T02-2265 2430.

Ferry

Small ferries cross between Imbaba on the west bank of the Nile and Zamalek, at the north end of the island. The fare is 50 pt and it's a pleasant 10-min trip. The boats don't operate on a Fri.

Metro

Marked with big red 'M' around the city. Signs are clearly marked in both English and Arabic. There are 2 functioning lines: **El-Marg–Helwan** and **Shobra–Giza**, with a 3rd still in construction that will link the airport to the west bank of the city. It's easy, efficient, relatively clean and cheap (E£1 to go anywhere). Every train has a women-only carriage, where children are of course also permitted. Make sure you hold on to your ticket, you'll need it to exit. During rush hours (0700-1000, 1500-1900) it can be uncomfortably crowded, hot and pushy. Still, the metro is more manageable and reliable than the buses and often quicker than a taxi.

Taxi

There is a profusion of the black and white taxis in Cairo. They're ramshackle, but easy to use and by Western standards, extraordinarily cheap. There are now newer white and black cabs (mainly white with small black checks on the side). These should all have a/c and functioning meters, which start with E£2.50 on the clock and go up in increments of 25pt. They are a real life-changer for tourists, taking much of the stress and arguments out of travelling by taxi. To hail a taxi, simply wait on the side of the street, extend your arm, and say 'taxi'. But you will find they pull up alongside you beeping and shouting 'tax' at you anyway, whenever you walk along the side of the road. Before entering, tell the driver your desired destination and establish that they know the way. The older black and white cabs never have a functioning meter, or if it does function the price is so antiquated it is completely irrelevant. If you want to avoid a haggling fuss, agree on a fare before entering the taxi. Otherwise, be prepared for a struggle. Most locals know the fair charge from one place to another. It's best to enquire at your hotel or with the tourist authority to

Cairo Metro

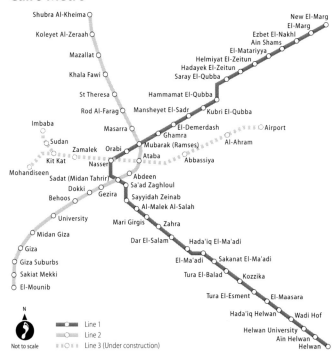

get an idea of the standard rates. In general, travelling from one point of the centre to another shouldn't cost more than E£5. From one borough to another, E£10-15. To the **Giza Pyramids**, from Downtown expect to pay at least E£20 and to the airport, E£30-40. In general, taxis waiting outside hotels expect more money so it's best to walk 100 m and hail a taxi from the street.

There are a few yellow cabs and blue cabs circulating Cairo that have a/c and working meters. These can be booked by calling T16516 or T19155, and are good for travelling longer distances (say to the airport, which is around E£35 in a yellow cab) but they work out more expensive for short hops.

Note In Egypt, there is basic etiquette when riding in a taxi. Single women always sit in the back seat, at a diagonal to the driver. If a man is present, he generally sits in the front, next to the driver. Note that it is not uncommon for people going to different destinations to share taxis. If you do not want to share, simply notify your driver if he slows to pick someone up, bearing in mind he may expect more money.

As well as private and shared private taxis, there are service taxis (pronounced *servees*), which follow specific routes and carry up to 7 passengers. They function in the same way as microbuses and can be flagged down from anywhere en route. Fares range from E£1-2.

Train

The main railway station in Cairo, **Ramses Station**, T02-2575 3555, in Midan Ramses, is a E£4-5 taxi ride from Tahrir and easily accessible via **Mubarak** metro station. Train timetables and fares can be checked online at www.egyptrail.gov.eg, although it's not yet possible to book online. Ramses Station is a bit confusing, with several different ticket counters selling tickets for different destinations. There is a tourist office at the back of the station (T02-2579 0767, open

0830-2000) who can advise on train schedules and ticket counters. There are plenty of tourist police hanging around who are willing to point you in the right direction. There are ATMs inside the station.

In short, if you're facing the main platforms, tickets to **Alexandria** are purchased in the back left corner; to **Middle** and **Upper Egypt**, from the counters by platform 11 outside to the left, via the underpass; to **Port Said/Ismailiya**, outside the main door behind you.

Trains go to **Alexandria** almost once an hr, first departure at 0600 and last departure at 2230 taking around 2½ hrs. So-called express trains, which have fewer stops, leave at 0800, 0900, 1200, 1400, 1800, 1900 and 2230, costing E£50 1st class, E£35 2nd class; slower trains at 0815, 1100, 1510, 1600, 1700 and 2000 cost E£35/£19. There are 3 trains daily to **Port Said** (E£22, 2nd class a/c) at 0615, 1445 and 1915, via **Ismailia** (E£16, 2nd class a/c), plus 3 to Ismailia only at 1300, 1845 and 2100, but they are slow and the journey is far quicker by bus. For **Suez**, trains leave from Ain Shams Station rather than Ramses, but the journey is easier by bus or service taxi. Trains also cover **Delta** destinations (daily, at least once an hr).

Travel to **Upper Egypt** is restricted for foreigners to 1 train per day, leaving at 2200 from Ramsis (2210 from Giza). Foreigners will only be sold 1st-class tickets which cost E£167 for either **Luxor** and **Aswan**. Tickets can be booked up to 1 week in advance, and it's recommended to book at least 48 hrs in advance. It might be possible to board other trains for destinations in Middle and Upper Egypt, but this is best attempted from Giza rather than Ramsis station; it is better to pay on board than trying to buy a ticket in advance, when authorities will be alerted to your presence. **Sleeping Trains**, T02-2576 1913, also travel to **Luxor** and **Aswan** daily at 2000 and 2130, departing from Giza station. The central booking office is in

Ramsis station, however, open 0900-2300, where they demand payment in US$, euro or pounds sterling only (credit cards and Egyptian pounds are not accepted). During peak season, it's wise to buy your ticket in advance, which can be done up to 2 weeks before travel. Price US$60 per person; US$45 for children aged 4-9 years – prices include dinner and breakfast. The sleepers are a clean, comfortable way to travel. Each train has a 'club' area (a very smoky but kitsch bar) and restaurant. They also run trains in the summer (Jul and Aug, but not during Ramadan), to **Marsa Matruh**.

ⓘ Directory

Cairo *p40, maps p30, p32, p36, p49, p51, p78, p81, p91 and p100*

Cultural centres

American, US Embassy, 5 Sharia America Al-Latiniya, T02-2794 9601. Open Sun-Thu.
British, British Council, 192 Sharia El-Nil, Agouza, T19789, www.britishcouncil.org.eg. Open Mon-Sat. Has an excellent library that can be joined for a minimum of 6 months, E£120, plus 1 photo and ID.
Cervantes, 20 Sharia Adly, Kodak Passage, Downtown, T02-2399 04639.
CSA, 4 Road 21, Maadi, T02-2358 5284, www.livinginegypt.org. Open Sun-Wed 0900-2100, Thu 0900-1700. Provides information and support for the expat community in Egypt. Gym, library, outings, courses and coffee shop.
Egyptian Centre for International Cultural Cooperation, 11 Sharia Shagaret El-Dor, Zamalek, T02-2736 5419.
French, 1 Sharia Madraset El-Hoquq El-Faransia, Mounira, T02-2794 4095, T02-2794 7679 and 5 Sharia Sharfiq El-Dib, Heliopolis, T02-2417 4824.
German, Goethe Institute, 5 Sharia Bustan, Downtown, T02-2575 9877.
Indian, 23 & 37 Sharia Talaat Harb, Downtown, T02-2393 9152. Has yoga classes, a library and screens Bollywood movies.

Italian, 3 Sharia Sheikh El-Marsafi, behind Marriott Hotel, Zamalek, T02-2735 8791. Open Sun-Thu.
Japanese, 3rd Floor, Cairo Centre Building, 106 Sharia Qasr El-Aini, Garden City, T02-2792 5011.
Swiss Club, Villa Pax, Sharia Gehad, off Sharia Sudan, Imbaba, T02-3314 2811.

Embassies and consulates

For embassies and consulates in Egypt, see www.embassiesabroad.com.

Emergencies

Ambulance: T123. **Fire**: T125. **Police**: T122.
Major police offices: at Railway Station, Cairo Airport, Midan Tahrir, Sharia 26 July/Mansour Mohammed, Pyramids. **Tourist Police**: T126.
Tourist Police Head Office: T02-390 6027.

Immigration

Visa extensions can be obtained at the grey monstrosity of the Mugamma building on Midan Tahrir, Downtown, Sat-Thu 0800-1700. This generally involves taking your documents in 1st thing in the morning and collecting in the afternoon around 1300 (or the next day before 1200). You need a photocopy of the last page of your passport, a copy of the last stamp of entry, 1 passport photo (photocopying and photo booths available in the foyer of the Mugamma). For a 6-month tourist visa it currently costs E£11, to add multiple entry is E£60. If you overstay your visa, there is a 15-day grace period during which you can pay a fine at the Mugamma of E£153 or the same amount is payable at the airport on leaving the country. To extend your visa go up to the 1st floor, walk down the long corridor after the X-ray machine, head for window 12 to collect a form. Go to window 44 to pay and take the stamps you will be given back to number 12. You leave everything there and collect it when they tell you from window 38.

Internet

The vast majority of hotels have internet services, and in budget hotels they are as cheap as going to an internet café.

Language schools

Arabic classes available at: **International Language Institute**, 4 Sharia Mahmoud Azmy, off Ahmed Orabi, Mohandiseen, T02-3346 3087, www.arabicegypt.com; **Kalimat Language & Cultural Centre**, 22 Sharia Mohamed Mahmoud Shaaban, Mohandiseen, T02-3761 8136, www.kalimategypt.com, very well regarded, set up a few years ago by former teachers at the British Council; **Egyptian Centre for International Cultural Cooperation**, 11 Sharia Shagarat El-Dor, Zamalek, T02-2736 5419, cheapest (48 hrs for E£950) but not the best.

Medical services

Hospitals and clinics Anglo-American Hospital, by Cairo Tower, Gezira, T02-2735 6162. **As-Salam International Hospital**, Corniche El-Maadi, T02-2524 0250; **Cairo Medical Centre**, 4 Sharia Abou Obeida El-Bahr, Midan Roxy, Heliopolis, T02-2258 1003/0566; **Dar al-Fouad Hospital**, Sixth of October City, has excellent facilities though it is a E£50/45-mins ride in a taxi from central Cairo, T02-3835 6030/40; **El-Salam Hospital**, 3 Sharia Syria, Mohandiseen, T02-3302 9091-5, also the place to go if you need an X-ray; **Dr Neveen El-Hafnawy Clinic**, 10 Sharia Souria, Mohandiseen, T02-3761 6905, for gynaecological issues; **Shaalan Surgicenter**, 10 Sharia Abd El-Hamid Lotfi, Mohandiseen, T02-37485479, Sat-Thu 0900-2200.

Pharmacies El-Esaaf Pharmacy, next to Nasser metro, Sharia Ramses, T02-2574 3369, open 24 hrs, no delivery; **Seif**, 76 Sharia Qasr Al-Ainy, Downtown, T02-2794 2678, open 24 hrs, delivery; **New Universal Pharmacy**, 12 Sharia Brazil, Zamalek, T02-2735 4896, 0900-2400, delivery; **Zamalek Tower Pharmacy**, 134 Sharia 26 July, Zamalek, T02-2736 1338, 1030-1530, 1800-2300, delivery.

Post office

Cairo's main post office is in **Midan Ataba**, open Sat-Thu 0800-2100 (Ramadan 0900-1600). The post office at **Midan Ataba** also has a *poste restante* office that will hold mail for a month, free. Enter via Sharia El-Badek and look for the 'private boxes' counter. There are other branches, but they tend to be more crowded. Major hotels often provide the same services. If you have an American Express card, you can send mail via AmEx on Shari Qasr El-Nil. Stamps are available at post offices and from hotel shops and cigarette kiosks.

Telephone

Mobile sim cards are cheap and easy to buy in Cairo, available from Vodaphone, Etisalat and other companies who have stores all over the city. Re-charge cards can be bought at any kiosk or you can top-up your credit in the official stores. Besides the international telephone and fax services at all major hotels, there are several public telecom centres where it's possible to make international phone calls for cheaper, but the wait can be long.

Contents

Footprint features

Around Cairo & the Nile Delta

At a glance

🚌 **Getting around** Microbuses are frequent and convenient.

⏱ **Time required** 2-3 days will give you a taster. El-Fayoum alone can be thoroughly explored in a couple of days.

🌧 **Weather** Much like Cairo, but slightly cooler in the Delta and slightly hotter in El-Fayoum.

✖ **When not to go** El-Fayoum can be affected by sandstorms in Apr.

Around Cairo

There are several interesting day- or half-day trips that can be made from Cairo. South of the city lie a series of pyramids which, due to their desert location, many visitors find more rewarding and evocative than a visit to the great pyramids at Giza. Peace and tranquility can be found around Lake Qaroun in El-Fayoum oasis, where village life is easily accessible. To the north of Cairo, the living monasteries at Wadi Natrun allow insight into the Coptic tradition and have beautiful paintings on the interior walls.

Saqqara

ⓘ *Open daily 0800-1600, E£60, students E£30, camera/video free, parking E£2.*

Saqqara, which faces Memphis (the oldest known imperial city on earth) across the Nile, was the enormous necropolis for the first pharaohs. With many tombs believed to be still undiscovered it is Egypt's largest archaeological site, spanning more than 7 sq km. From its inception it expanded west into the desert until the Fourth Dynasty (2613-2494 BC) when the Giza plateau superseded it. At the end of the Fifth Dynasty (2494-2345 BC) a more systematic construction of pyramids and *mastabas* began, which resulted in many splendid monuments around Saqqara and some of the most gorgeously decorated private tombs in Egypt. The approach through a forest of date palms and the sweep of the desert beyond are as breathtaking as the multitude of hidden *mastabas*, ruinous courts and causeways, and the sand-strewn rungs of the step pyramid itself.

Arriving in Saqqara

Getting there Given the relative proximity to Cairo, and the distance between tombs in Saqqara, it is worth hiring a taxi for the day (E£130-180 for Giza and Saqqara; E£180-200 if you include Dahshur). Most travel agencies book tours to the area for about E£100 or more per person and budget hotels often transport groups for less. Tours generally do not include ticket prices. Public transport can be a bit fiddly, though very cheap – and you are left with the problem of how to get between the various sites within the area of Saqqara itself. If you choose to brave public transport, take any microbus going to Giza from Sharia Gala'a (Downtown), change at Midan Giza to a microbus headed for the Pyramids (in Arabic, 'Haram') and ask to get down at the Marioteya canal. Cross the Pyramids Road and walk down the side street to the south. From there you can get a micro to Saqqara. Get off on the main road by the sign for Saqqara antiquities and walk the remaining 1.5 km to the site. (Getting back is less complicated. Once you get to the Pyramids Road you can very likely catch something all the way to Midan Tahrir without changing in Giza). Giza to Saqqara by camel or horse can be a rewarding journey. A round trip with waiting time costs around E£300-400 per person, but one way is usually more than enough as it takes two to four hours (horses are faster) plus a good couple of hours at Saqqara. Bring water and food for the day, as the restaurants surrounding the area tend to be overpriced and bare in their offerings and if you are walking between tombs you won't get much time for a proper meal break. Soft-drink sellers operate around the main attractions.

The journey to Saqqara, though short in terms of actual distance, can be like stepping back in time. On the far side of the Marioteya Canal rural life goes on as it has for centuries. Early in the morning, the fields and palm groves are partially obscured by a romantic mist and in the afternoon you will see donkeys and water buffalo being led home, indifferent to the passing cars and microbuses after a hard day's work. If you have no plans to visit anywhere else outside Cairo, then the road to Saqqara can show you a different side to life in the city.

Note Saqqara can be easily visited as a day trip from Cairo. See page 102 for Cairo accommodation. Public transport can sometimes be difficult to come by late at night, so plan your trip accordingly.

Imhotep Museum

A ticket includes entrance to the excellent new Imhotep Museum (past the ticket booths), which should not be missed. Building blocks and artefacts are put into context using scale diagrams, the main hall being dominated by an impression of how Zoser's tomb would have looked in its heyday. Stunning green-blue faience tiles, textured to resemble reeds, line the walls. Vessels, statues (some so detailed that the pleats in the fabric can be seen) and friezes have been intelligently selected. On display is the mummy of King Merenre I; the oldest, most complete royal mummy known. Simply wrapped, the king's bare toes protrude from the linen strips. A decorated block from the causeway of Unas shows emaciated figures, with their ribs clearly outlined, during a time of famine. There is a fascinating room detailing the life and work of Jean-Philippe Lauer, who spent 75 years working and restoring the site. This room also houses his library of marvellous volumes on early exploration of Egypt's antiquities. Sadly, these are too precious to be handled.

Zoser's Funerary Complex

This complex, the largest in Saqqara, is an example of some of the world's most ancient architecture. The whole complex, including but not confined to the **Step Pyramid**, was designed and built for Zoser (2667-2648 BC), the second king in the Third Dynasty, under the control of his chief architect Imhotep who many regard as the world's first architect. At its heart is the **Step Pyramid**, the first of its kind, which can be seen as a prototype for the Giza Pyramids. This marked the evolution of burial tombs from *mastabas* with deep shafts for the sarcophagus to imposing elevated mausoleums. Although the external fine white limestone casing, brought from quarries across the Nile at Memphis, has disappeared over time the step structure is still clearly visible. The pyramid eventually reached a height of 62.5 m on a base 109 m by 121 m, which, although small by comparison with those at Giza, is still an amazing feat. The advances represented by Zoser's Pyramid were not in the building techniques or materials, which were already established, but the concept, design and calculations involved that made such a monument possible.

The shaft, leading 28 m vertically down to the Royal Tomb, was sealed with a three-tonne granite block but this still did not prevent the tomb from being looted. Another 11 shafts were found, 32 m deep, under the east side of the Pyramid, which led to the tombs of the queens and royal children. Unfortunately these are no longer open to the public and the area is currently under restoration.

The whole funerary complex was completely surrounded by buttressed walls over 544 m long, to deter intruders and thieves and to provide space for the Pharaoh's *ka* (spirit) to live in the afterlife. Although 14 fake doors were built, only the one in the southeast corner, which leads into the colonnaded **Hypostyle Hall** actually gives access to the site. Before entering the colonnade, observe the fake door complete with hinges and sockets in the vestibule on the right. The Colonnade leads through to the **Great Court**, on the south side of which there is a frieze of cobras similar to the one found in the museum. This represents the fire-spitting goddess of destruction Edjo who was adopted as the Uraeus, the emblem of royalty and of protection, and worn on the pharaonic headdress.

Further along this south wall is a deep shaft at the bottom of which lies **Zoser's Southern Tomb**, which some believe held the king's entrails. More importantly there is a relief, depicting the king running the Heb-Sed race, which illustrates the purpose of the surrounding buildings and monuments. Some of them are mere façades like a Hollywood film-set, simply representing a pastiche of this crucial ceremony for the afterlife. Their intended purpose was to eternalize the symbol of the unification of a greater Egypt and the power of the pharaoh even in death.

This symbolism is echoed in the lotus and papyrus capitals on top of the columns fronting the **House of the South** and the **House of the North**, which represent the heraldic emblems of Upper and Lower Egypt, respectively. The House of the South is interesting because its columns, precursors of the Greek Doric style, and its New Kingdom graffiti offer a fascinating reminder of the continuity of human civilization.

On the north side of the Step Pyramid there is a stone casket, known as the **Serdab** (cellar), containing a copy of a life-size statue of Zoser. The original is in the Egyptian

North Saqqara

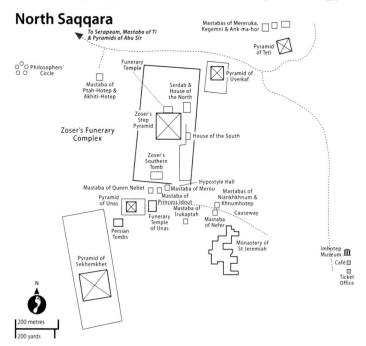

Philosophers' Circle

To Serapeum, Mastaba of Ti & Pyramids of Abu Sir

Mastabas of Mereruka, Kegemni & Ank-ma-hor

Pyramid of Teti

Funerary Temple

Mastaba of Ptah-Hotep & Akhiti-Hotep

Serdab & House of the North

Pyramid of Userkaf

Zoser's Step Pyramid

Zoser's Funerary Complex

House of the South

Zoser's Southern Tomb

Hypostyle Hall

Mastaba of Queen Nebet
Mastaba of Merou
Mastaba of Princess Idout
Mastaba of Irukaptah

Mastabas of Niankhkhnum & Khnumhotep

Pyramid of Unas

Funerary Temple of Unas

Mastaba of Nefer

Causeway

Persian Tombs

Monastery of St Jeremiah

Imhotep Museum

Café

Ticket Office

Pyramid of Sekhemkhet

N

200 metres
200 yards

The sacred scarab

Scarabaeus sacer, a dung beetle, is the celebrated beetle held sacred by the ancient Egyptians. They were fascinated by the beetles' strange habit of fashioning perfectly round balls from animal droppings. (These balls, larger than the insect itself, are moved backwards using the rear legs, the head being thrust against the ground to give purchase. The balls are then buried with newly laid eggs and provide food for the developing larvae.)

The scarab was used as a symbol of the sun god as Egyptians thought the sun was pushed around the heavens just as the beetle pushed the ball of dung.

The dung beetle is called *Kheper* in the Egyptian language and is associated with the verb *kheper*, which means to come into being. Models of the beetle made in clay were supposed to have healing powers while live beetles, secured by a small chain through the wing-case, were actually worn as decoration.

The scarab seal was used to stamp letters into the clay seal on letters, bottles, wine jars, and so on, with the owner's mark.

Museum in Cairo. The Serdab has two cylindrical holes to enable the statue to communicate with the outside world and to preserve the Pharaoh's *ka*. To the west of the Serdab the **Funerary Temple** is in ruins but some of the walls and the entrance can still be seen. A tunnel originally linked it with the royal tomb. At the time of writing this was closed for restoration.

South of Zoser's Funerary Complex

The Pyramid of Unas, which was built for the last pharaoh of the Fifth Dynasty (2494-2345 BC), appears from the outside to be a heap of limestone rubble but the inside of the burial chamber has a star-covered ceiling and the passage has beautiful green hieroglyphs of magic formulae for the pharaoh to ease his passage into the afterlife. These are the first decorations ever made inside a tomb and formed the basis for the *Book of the Dead*. The pyramid was opened as a tourist attraction in 1881 by the director of antiquities Gaston Maspero with financial sponsorship from Thomas Cook & Son, but is now permanently closed to prevent greater deterioration. To the east, a few remnants of the **Funerary Temple** can be seen, some granite columns with palm capitals and pieces of granite floor. Beyond this the remains of a causeway linking the Funerary Temple to the Valley Temple 700 m away has been uncovered, which conjures up a real feeling of walking back in time.

North and south of the causeway are a sprinkling of tombs worth looking into, as well as two 45-m-long troughs of Unas' boat pits. The fascinating and well preserved **Mastaba of Queen Nebet**, Unas' wife, contains some rare scenes of Nebet in the women's quarters, or harem, in the palace. The **Mastaba of Princess Idout** has 10 rooms, of which five are decorated to give a glimpse of life in Idout's day with many rural and domestic scenes. The **Mastaba of Merou** contains some exceptionally well-preserved tableaux; in the Grand Offerings Room the paint scarcely seems to have faded at all. The **Saqqara New Tombs** ① *requires a separate ticket, E£30, students E£15, either purchased from the main ticket office or from the shed near the car park by the Step Pyramid*, are equally vivid and include the adjoining tombs of **Niankhkhnum and Khnumhotep** and the **Mastaba of Irukaptah**, with deeply colourful depictions of the royal manicurists at work, scenes of fishing, and activities at the dairy – look out for the cow giving birth.

The remains of the **Pyramid of Sekhemkhet**, which was at the centre of an unfinished and unused funerary complex very similar to that of his predecessor Zoser, were only discovered in 1950 and there is no public access. To the east of the Pyramid of Sekhemkhet can be seen the remains of the **Monastery of St Jeremiah**, which was founded in the fifth century but destroyed by the Arabs five centuries later. Following its discovery in 1907 many of the paintings and extraordinary carvings were removed and are now on display in the Coptic Museum in Cairo.

North of the Funerary Complex

The **Pyramid of Teti**, the founder of the 6th Dynasty (2345-2181 BC), was discovered by Mariette in 1853 but is now little more than a pile of rubble in constant danger of being submerged by sand. It is possible to enter up the steep pathway leading to the funerary chamber, where the ceiling is decorated with stars.

To the north are a number of well-preserved *mastabas*. The most outstanding of which is **Mereruka**, who was Teti's vizier, chief judge and inspector – an important person in Sixth Dynasty society. This is one of the largest Old Kingdom *mastabas* to have been found and its 32 rooms are divided into three parts for Mereruka (21 rooms), his wife (six rooms) and his son (five rooms). In the main entrance passage Mereruka is depicted at an easel, painting the three seasons. The following room contains interesting hunting scenes, revealing the types of animal they stalked and the techniques that they used. Scenes of everyday life are beautifully depicted throughout the tomb, giving a valuable insight into contemporary life. The largest room, with six pillars, has a statue of Mereruka to the north and some unusual mourning scenes, while on the left are scenes of him being carried by his son and surrounded by dwarfs and dogs.

To the east, the **Mastaba of Kagemni**, also a vizier and judge of the Sixth Dynasty, has some excellent reliefs and paintings of a much a higher standard, but unfortunately less well preserved. Further east is the **Mastaba of Ankh-ma-hor**, also known as the Doctor's Tomb because of paintings depicting circumcision and an operation on a broken toe. Other rooms show the usual scenes of the preparation and transportation of the offerings and various representations of hunting and daily life. Look on the south wall for the mourners fainting at the burial ceremony.

One of the finest of all the *mastabas* is the double **Mastaba of Ptah-Hotep and Akhiti-Hotep**, which contains some of the finest Old Kingdom art and some fascinating unfinished work clarifying the techniques used in painting reliefs. Ptah-Hotep was a priest of Maat in the reign of Djedkare, Unas' predecessor, while his son Akhiti-Hotep was vizier, judge, and the overseer of the treasury and the granaries.

The red paint of the unfinished agricultural scenes in the entrance corridor reveals how preliminary drawings were made before the wall was carved and painted. The outstanding masterpiece, however, is in the **Sanctuary** dedicated to Ptah-Hotep. On the walls behind the entrance Ptah-Hotep is seated watching a concert while his servants wash and manicure him. Other walls bear scenes of Ptah-Hotep receiving offerings. On the left wall, which is the most interesting and impressive, the figure in the first boat is being given water by a boy. The inscription describes him as the Chief Artist, who is thought to have been Ankhen-Ptah, and this scene may well represent the first known example of an artist's signature.

The Serapeum The bizarre Serapeum was a burial place for the sacred Apis Bulls, believed to be manifestations of Ptah's blessed soul and were identified with Osiris after his death. They were given full honours in a ceremony worthy of any pharaoh, embalmed, and then the mummified body placed in a sarcophagus and sealed off from the main gallery by means of a richly decorated wall. The high priests would then start searching for the new Apis Bull within the sacred herd. It had to be the only calf of its mother, black in colour except for a white diamond-shaped marking on the forehead, and have a scarab symbol on its tongue. The cult of the Apis Bulls was significant enough to last well into the Ptolemaic period, and the gloomy passageways of the Serapeum are in fact two and a half millennia younger than the Step Pyramid of Zoser – an interval as long as that which separates the Serapeum burials from our own time.

The long, sloping path down to the Serapeum leads to the three galleries, where 24 surviving sarcophagi are set in small galleries on either side of the main one. Each sarcophagus, from the quarries of Aswan, was made from a single piece of rock and weighed around 65 tonnes. Only three of the enormous basalt or granite sarcophagi bear inscriptions, and these are marked with the cartouches of different pharaohs, Amasis, Cambyses and Khababash. The Serapeum was discovered in 1851 but, with the exception of one tomb, most had already been looted. The artefacts discovered are now displayed in the Musée du Louvre, Paris. At the time of writing the Serapeum was closed for restoration.

The Mastaba of Ti One of the wonders of the Old Kingdom, the beautiful reliefs in Ti's *mastaba* provide fascinating insights into life at the time. Ti was a Fifth Dynasty royal hairdresser who married well and became steward of the sun temples of Neferikare and Nouserre and whose children later bore the title of 'royal descendant'. The reliefs in the courtyard have been damaged but their representations of daily life – breeding birds (north wall left), Ti on his litter with dogs and dwarfs (east wall, centre), and Ti with his wife (west wall centre) – are still worth seeing. In the centre of the courtyard an undecorated shaft leads to the tomb. On the left of the corridor joining the tomb to the main shrine, just after the door, servants are depicted bringing offerings while on the right are musicians and dancers. The main hall of offerings and shrine have an abundance of scenes depicting daily life, from the brewing of beer and the baking of bread to illustrations of boat construction (note the extreme simplicity of the tools used). You can't miss Ti's immense sarcophagus filling the recess in which it stands.

The south wall holds the **Serdab**, where a copy of Ti's statue, the original being in the Cairo Museum, can be peeped at through the slit. Around the two slits there are scenes of daily market life, carpenters, tanners, and various other artisans. Around the second slit, Ti is entertained by musicians while servants burn incense. These paintings should be taken on one level as literal depictions of Egyptian life but it is also important to realize the importance of symbolism and allegory. The north walls show Ti in a boat observing a hippopotamus hunt in the Delta region, but as the hippopotamus was symbolic of evil there is probably more to the picture than meets the eye.

Nearby is the Ptolemaic **Philosophers' Circle**, a collection of seven badly degraded statues arranged in a semi-circle and protected by a concrete enclosure.

South Saqqara

This completely separate necropolis, founded by the pharaohs of the Sixth Dynasty (2345-2181 BC), is about 1 km south of the Pyramid of Sekhemkhet in North Saqqara. Currently this whole area is off limits to casual tourists and can only be visited by written permission from the Supreme Council of Antiquities in Cairo. Should that situation change, or if you choose to scope out the area without official permission, there are stupendous pyramid views of Saqqara to the north and Dahshur to the south. Downsides are a lot of wading through sand, and the relative lack of impressive remains. It has a few interesting tombs, based on the Pyramid of Unas as an architectural model, but sadly has been plundered by unscrupulous stone masons or their suppliers. The pyramids of **Pepi I** and **Merenre** are in ruins.

To the east of the latter lies the **Pyramid of Djedkare**, known in Arabic as the Pyramid of the Sentinel, which is 25 m tall and is open to visitors. The entrance is on the north side through a tunnel leading into the funerary chamber but there is comparatively little to see.

The most important and interesting tombs are further south. The **Pyramid of Pepi II** is surrounded by an entire funerary complex. The inside chamber is decorated with stars and funerary inscriptions. Within the complex are a number of other smaller pyramids belonging to his queens. They are all based on the same design as Pepi's pyramid and contain a miniature funerary complex. The **Pyramid of Queen Neith** has some wonderful inscriptions and decorations.

To the east is the **Mastaba Faraoun**, the tomb of **Shepseskaf**, the last pharaoh of the Fourth Dynasty (2613-2494 BC). The inside is interesting but undecorated and the walls are made from large blocks of granite. From the outside the tomb looks like a gigantic sarcophagus and the exterior was originally covered in a thin layer of limestone. About 1 km further south are two more pyramids. The first is the brick **Pyramid of Khendjer**, which has a funerary chamber made out of quartzite. The second is larger, but unfinished, and bears no inscriptions or signs of use. It has impressive underground white stone chambers and a quartzite funerary chamber.

The Pyramids of Abu Sir and Sun-Temples of Abu Ghura

Pyramids of Abu Sir

ⓘ *Due to reopen to tourists after several years of closure. Daily 0800-1600 winter, and until 1800 summer. A pain to access by public transport, you can pass by on your way to Saqqara either by taxi or camel from Giza.*

The site originally contained 14 Fifth Dynasty pyramids but only four are still standing, and are worth visiting for their isolated beauty more than any impressive scale or their state of preservation. The **Pyramid of Neferefre** was never finished and is now in very poor condition. The next (also unfinished) pyramid to the north was built for **Neferikare** and towering over the others is, at 68 m, the tallest of the group. To the northeast, the **Pyramid of Nouserre** is worth noting for its **Funerary Temple** which, although originally built for the Neferikare, was used by Nouserre because of Neferikare's premature death. About 100 m to the northeast lies the tomb of **Ptah-Cepses**. The *mastaba* is not in good condition but from outside the columns with lotus capitals (which are the oldest so far discovered) can still be seen. Inside is a huge granite sarcophagus and the remains of a few decorated columns.

Sahure's Pyramid, is directly north and its **Funerary Temple** is not too severely damaged. Excavation work around it has led to the discovery of the remains of a 240-m ramp that connected it to the **Valley Temple**. Sahure was brother to Userkaf whose pyramid is at Saqqara. The ceilings are decorated with yellow stars on a blue background and the reliefs carved on the limestone walls showed the king's defeat of his neighbours in the desert and those from Asia. Some have been removed and placed in museums, but a few remain and are quite well preserved.

Sun-Temples of Abu Ghurab

A short distance northwest of Abu Sir's pyramids, the sun-temples were built in the Fifth Dynasty when the solar cult had been declared the state religion. Unlike earlier temples their purpose was solely devotional and the pharaohs who built them were not buried here. Originally twin temples, only the **Sun-Temple of Nouserre** remains with the **Sun-Temple of Userkaf** being little more than rubble. Fortunately because they were identical little is lost.

At the western end of an enclosed courtyard a massive 70-m obelisk once stood. The obelisk was the symbol of the primordial mound, the sun's resting place at the end of the day. An alabaster altar stands in the centre of the courtyard, and animals were sacrificed at the northeast corner from where channels cut in the paving carried the blood to 10 alabaster basins, nine of which survive.

Dahshur

ⓘ *Daily 0800-1600 winter, until 1700 summer, E£30, E£15 for students. Microbuses run from the Marioteya Canal off Pyramids road, direct to Dahshur village 7 km south of Saqqara (or you can change microbuses at the turn off for Saqqara). From the village you can find transport to take you the final 2 km to the site. However, as it's a further 1 km between the sites and public transport gets trickier late in the day, it is easier to hire a taxi there and back from Cairo (E£120).*

If you were surprised by the proximity of Cairo to the Giza Pyramids, or annoyed by the crowds of tourists and hawkers, come to Dahshur. Here, surrounded by nothing but the grey and gold desert, are two sublimely shaped looming monoliths and no one in sight but a few bored policemen. This is how pyramids appear in one's imagination. In the middle of the desert, miles away from civilization, free from tour buses and weighty with a sense of history. A sunset overlooking the pyramids, where there's a small shimmering lake that appears in winter and disappears in summer, is enhanced by the striking separation of the desert landscape and the linear agricultural fields around. Snefru (2575-2551 BC), first ruler of the Fourth Dynasty at the time of great pyramid construction, built the two pyramids in Dahshur and was perhaps responsible for the pyramid at Maidoum. His constructive tendencies were continued by his son Cheops. The monoliths of the Red Pyramid and the Bent Pyramid loom mightily at Dahshur,

After the ticket office, you arrive first at the **Red Pyramid** to the north, named after the reddish local limestone used in the core. It is thought to be the first true pyramid to be constructed with sloping sides rather than steps, and is second in size only to the Great Pyramid of Cheops at Giza. Some of the original Tura limestone facing stones remain on the eastern side and limestone fragments of the monolithic pyramidion still exist. A 28-m climb leads to the entrance, from where you plunge down a shaft to two corbelled antechambers, their sides as smooth as if they were built yesterday. A wooden staircase takes you up to the burial chamber, which was unused by Snefru or anyone else. Claustrophobics who balked at the thought of entering the Great Pyramid should give it a go, as there are no other bodies pushing and shoving to induce anxiety on the descent.

Scheduled to open the public this year, the **Bent Pyramid** (also known as the Southern Shining Pyramid) was constructed of local limestone with a casing of polished Tura limestone; the casing blocks slope inwards making them more stable and also more difficult to remove. At the base the pyramid measures 188.6 m and the height is 97 m (originally 105 m). If construction had continued at the original angle it would have been 128.5 m high.

The pyramid is unique on two counts. First, the obvious change in angles giving the pyramid its unusual shape, for which there are a number of theories put forward. Some think that the builders got tired and changed the angle to reduce the volume and so complete it sooner, others suggest that the change in slope indicated a double pyramid – two pyramids superimposed. It is further hypothesised that the architect lost his nerve, as this pyramid was being built when the pyramid at Maidoum collapsed. That too had an angle of 52° so a quick rethink was necessary. The pyramid is also unique in having two entrances. The first entrance in the middle of the north face is about 12 m above the ground and leads to the upper chamber. The second in the west face is only just above ground and leads to the lower chamber. Both chambers are corbelled and the floors of both were built to a depth of 4 m with small stone blocks.

There are three other pyramids here (from north to south) belonging to the 12th Dynasty Kings, Amenemhat II, Senusert III and Amenemhat III, of which only the latter is more than a pile of rubble.

Memphis

ⓘ *Daily 0800-1600, E£35, students E£20, camera/video free. Reaching Memphis by public transport can be a confusing and time-consuming affair, as is moving on from here to sites nearby. Much better to make a whistle-stop here as part of a taxi-tour to the other sites.*
Just 15 km south of Cairo, Memphis was founded in the First Dynasty (3100-2890 BC) by Menes. The pharaohs' capital city throughout the Old Kingdom (2686-2181 BC), it was inhabited for four millennia. Eventually the old city was abandoned by the Moors and has now returned to the Nile silt from which it was originally constructed. Very little remains today, just some odd bits of statuary and stelae dotted about a garden. Most notable are a giant alabaster sphinx weighing 80 tonnes and a prostrate limestone **Colossus of Ramses II**, both of which may have stood outside the huge Temple of Ptah. He is a much photographed and beautifully preserved Ramses; Murray's guidebook from 1900 recommends visitors stand on his chest to appreciate his expression fully, though today there's a raised walkway around him to facilitate viewing. Also in evidence are the remains of the Embalming House, where there are several alabaster tables, weighing up to 50 tonnes, used to embalm the sacred Apis Bulls before burial at Saqqara. Beyond these, Memphis's former glories can now only be imagined.

El-Fayoum → *For listings, see pages 152-154.*

Although usually described as an oasis, El-Fayoum is not fed by underground water like the Western Desert oases, but by Nile water transported to this natural triangular depression by a series of canals. The water comes from the Ibrahimeya Canal at Assiut, via the Bahr Yusef, which itself feeds into a number of smaller canals west of Fayoum City. Having irrigated the oasis the water runs into **Lake Qaroun** which, despite having dramatically shrunk over the past few thousand years, is still Egypt's largest natural salt-water lake. About 70,000 years ago the Nile flood first broke through the low mountains that surround El-Fayoum to form Lake Qaroun and the surrounding marshes. This is believed to be one of the first, if not *the* first, sites of agriculture in the world as plants that grew around the lake were collected, land was fenced in, and dry and guarded storage areas were built. Even today El-Fayoum is still famous for fruit, vegetables and chickens and to describe food as *fayoum* means that it is delicious.

Arriving in El-Fayoum
Getting there Fayoum City is the main town in the oasis and the province's capital, 103 km southwest of central Cairo and 85 km from Giza, a one- to 1½-hour journey along the four-lane carriageway. Buses leave from Aboud Terminal in Cairo every 15 minutes from 0600-2000 or from El-Mouneeb every 30 minutes, from 0600-1900. Tickets cost E£10-12 and can be purchased in advance, though this isn't necessary. Service taxis bound for Fayoum (E£10-12) congregate around Midan Ramses, Midan Orabi and Midan Giza. There are three daily trains from Ramses to Fayoum City, but only third class and it can take up to four hours. Another option is to hire a private taxi from Cairo to chauffeur

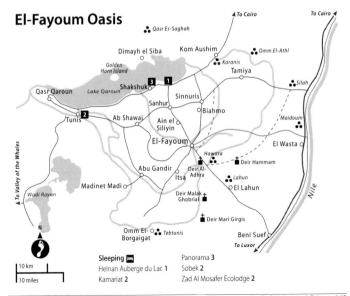

El-Fayoum Oasis

Sleeping 🛏
Helnan Auberge du Lac **1**
Kamariat **2**

Panorama **3**
Sobek **2**
Zad Al Mosafer Ecolodge **2**

Fayoum portraits

While excavating in a cemetery in the vicinity of the Hawara pyramid Sir Flinders Petrie found 146 quite remarkable hand-painted portraits varying in quality of style and preservation. These funeral masks, or portraits, were executed in tempera, or encaustic – a mixture of paint and wax – on slices of cedar or other wood. They were of children, men and women of all ages. They date from Graeco-Roman times, 30 BC to 395 AD, and are among the earliest portraits known. It is assumed that they were commissioned during the person's lifetime and used as decoration in the home until required. When the deceased was embalmed the portrait would be attached to the coffin or mummy case. Examples can be seen in the Egyptian Museum in Cairo.

you around, which is definitely the best idea for day trips if you can afford it, as the sights are quite spread out. Private taxis to Fayoum City should cost around E£350 per day.

Getting around The Bahr Yusef canal bisects Fayoum. Buses and taxis from Cairo terminate at the main bus station on the southwest side of the city. Service taxis to Ab Shawai, from where you can travel on to Tunis, are found at the Ab Shawai terminal to the south of the Bahr Yusef canal. Services to Beni Suef leave from the station 1.5 km northeast of the city centre. If you don't want to walk, you can hire a *hantour* (horse-drawn carriages, E£10-15, depending on where you're going) to your destination. Private taxis cost about E£30 per hour. Taxis around Fayoum city centre are a E£2 flat rate.

Information The **main office** ① *T084-634 2313, 2 km north of town,* is accessible by minibus No 5, where the head of staff can help with arranging tours of the oasis. There's also a **small office** ① *next to the 4 waterwheels in the city centre,* but the staff's English is somewhat lacking, and at present all they offer is a fairly useless map and the usual glossy pamphlet.

Background

The 12th Dynasty pharaoh Amenemhat I (1991-1962 BC) first drained part of the marshes to develop the area for agriculture and also dug a large canal from the Nile. The result of this and further developments by Amenemhat III (1842-1797 BC), who showed great interest in the area and built a pyramid at Hawara (see page 149), was Lake Moeris (Great Lake), twice the present size and teeming with fish, and an agricultural area to the south renowned for its rich and varied crops.

The Romans, who called the area Crocodilopolis (because of the ever-present crocodiles) changed Fayoum's previous system of crop rotation and forced the area to supply grain exclusively to the Roman market. Muslims believe that the prophet Joseph developed the area during his captivity in Egypt through the canalization of the Bahr Yusef River and by building the world's first dam. And although Fayoum's national strategic importance diminished with the canalization of the Nile Delta it remains one of the most productive agricultural areas in the country.

The water level in Lake Qaroun had been falling for about 2000 years until the construction of the Aswan High Dam led to far greater stability in the level of the Nile.

The groaning waterwheels of El-Fayoum

Because the land in the El-Fayoum oasis varies from +26 m to -42 m in three main steps, self-powered waterwheels were essential and the construction of one particular type, which is exclusive to El-Fayoum, began in pharaonic times.

There are often whole series of these *sawaqih al-Hadir* (roaring waterwheels), which produce a perpetual groaning noise. There are over 200 in the oasis,

which has adopted the waterwheel as its official symbol.

In January each year every canal is cleaned and repaired. The sluices are shut, silt is dredged, walls are strengthened and the waterwheels, now white with dead algae, are lifted and overhauled. Although the wheels are considered to be ancient, in fact no part is more than about 10 years old.

Indeed, by medieval times the lake had become far too salty to sustain freshwater fish and new species had to be introduced. It appears that the water table is rising again as houses and fields at the lakeside have been flooded in recent years, and guests have to step up to raised sills to gain access to hotels along the lake shore.

Despite its stagnant and polluted water the beach resorts around Lake Qaroun still attract affluent visitors, mainly Egyptian, to the region. The oasis is declared free from bilharzia (schistosomiasis), a recommendation in itself. The season runs all year round, but from January to April it is considered too cold to swim. The summers are not as hot as Luxor/Aswan and the winters are not as cool as Cairo or the Delta. In the quieter areas there is a rewarding amount of wildlife to observe. While the fox is common in the town, the wolf is found only on the desert periphery. Sightings of wild cat are very rare. Thousands of egrets roost in the oasis, herons are common and many migrating birds take a rest here in spring and autumn.

Fayoum City

The majority of the oasis' population of 1.8 million people are not Nile Valley Egyptians but settled and semi-nomadic Berber people who are related to the Libyan Arabs. There is comparatively little to see in Fayoum City itself, and visitors are not advised to stay in the city for long but rather to enjoy the peace and tranquillity of the oasis' gardens and the lake. Two kilometres north of the town centre is the 13-m red granite **Obelisk of Senusert I**, estimated to weigh over 100 tonnes, standing in the middle of a traffic roundabout. The covered *Souk Al-Qantara* and the adjacent street of goldsmiths, **Es-Sagha**, found across the fourth bridge to the west of the central tourist office, are refreshingly authentic and well worth visiting. A little further west is the attractive **Mosque of Qaitbay/Khawand Asal-Bey**, possibly the oldest in the oasis, often – and erroneously – attributed to the Mamluk Sultan Qaitbay (1468-1498) who was noted as a warrior, a builder and a torturer. It was built for Asal-Bay, his favourite concubine. Remains of its impressive structure, most of which fell into the Bahr Yusef in 1892, include the dome supported by ancient pillars, some with Corinthian capitals, the rather plain *mihrab* and the gilded teak *minbar* elaborately carved and inlaid with ivory from Somalia.

Other mosques nearby are also worth visiting, particularly during the *moulids* (see box, page 156). The **Mosque and Mausoleum** in honour of local sheikh **Ali El-Rubi** is the scene of his birthday feast (around the middle of *Shabaan*). It attracts crowds from around the oasis who sleep in the streets, perform *zikrs* in the courtyard, and revel in the funfairs around. Up a small street north of Bahr Yusef is the **El-Moalak Mosque** or **Hanging Mosque**, so-called because it is built above five arches each of which housed a workshop. It was constructed in limestone in 1375 by Prince Soliman Ibn Mouhamed.

The locals are particularly proud of their **waterwheels**, which are indeed a magnificent sight. They were first introduced by the Ptolemies and are used now as the official symbol of El-Fayoum province (see box, page 145). There are over 200 to see in the region, about 4-5 m in diameter and black with layers of protective tar. Besides the four large ones behind the tourist office on the main Sharia Gumhoriyya, the most famous is the series of **Seven Waterwheels** ⓘ *3 km north along the Bahr Sinnuris, a 30-min walk, take the west bank on the way there and come back along the east.* A solitary wheel at a farm is followed by a spectacular group of four and then the final two wheels by a bridge. They are continuously powered by the fast-flowing water of the stream, which just runs back into the main channel when it's not required for irrigation.

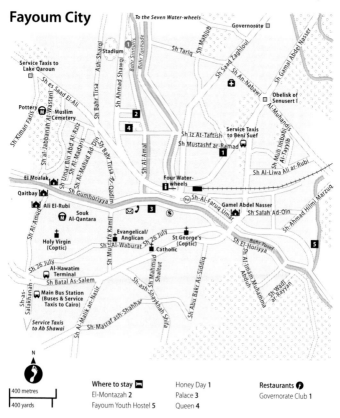

Fayoum City

Where to stay 🛏		Restaurants 🍴
El-Montazah **2**	Honey Day **1**	Governorate Club **1**
Fayoum Youth Hostel **5**	Palace **3**	
	Queen **4**	

Maintenance takes place each spring but should an urgent repair be required it takes a team of strong men to stop the wheel rotating.

There are four **churches** in the town, that of the Holy Virgin (Coptic Orthodox) is the oldest, dated at 1836. Notice the large altar screen decorated with light and dark wood inlay work and the Bible stand and Bishop's throne both inlaid with ivory. The church also contains a shrine to Anba Abram who died in 1914, one time Bishop of Fayoum and Giza, and revered as a local saint.

Excursions from El-Fayoum → *For listings, see pages 152-154.*

Lake Qaroun and Tunis

Lake Qaroun, 'Lake of the Horn', is a favourite local beach resort despite the stagnant and salt-encrusted water. Although it is calm much of the time, in winter it can be quite rough and teeming with ducks and geese that bring the hunters to the lakeside hotels. It is possible to negotiate a rowing boat from the Auberge du Lac to the barren **Golden Horn Island** or to the north shore. There lie the ruins of **Dimayh El-Siba**, which would have been on the edge of the lake but, due to the retreat of the waters, are now almost 3 km away. This old Ptolemaic city with ruins of a small temple dedicated to Soknopaios (crocodile) was once the starting point of a camel trade route to the oases of the Western Desert. The goods first crossed the lake by boat, which still a good way to reach the site.

On the southwest corner of Lake Qaroun is **Tunis** village, a picturesque little enclave and now the heart of the Fayoum potting community whose designs are frequently displayed in Cairo's shops. It is an idyllic place to relax and enjoy lovely walks to absorb rural life, with a couple of charming eco-lodges (see Where to stay, page 153), which are perfect getaways. It's interesting to visit the pottery workshops, where local artists create traditional vessels and homewares under the tutorship of skilled pottery artists. Prices are considerably lower than in the shops and it's possible to commission special orders that take about a week to deliver.

Qasr Qaroun ① *daily 0900-1600, E£32 students E£16*, to the west end of the lake, has the remains of the Graeco-Roman city of Dionysias, and a well-preserved limestone Ptolemaic temple dedicated to a crocodile god and decorated with a symbol of a winged sun. The date is not certain as there are no inscriptions. It is a compact structure but inside there are many small rooms, corridors, cellars and tunnels. It is fun to explore – take a torch. Watch out for scorpions. There are two spiral staircases to the roof, which provide a superb view.

Wadi Rayan and the Valley of the Whales

① *Entrance US$3, overnight camping E£10, vehicles E£5. Accessible only by private vehicle; a taxi from Fayoum City costs E£200-300 depending on whether or not you include the Valley of the Whales.*

A protected area since 1989, Wadi Rayan contains rare wildlife, 169 species of bird, ancient Roman and pharaonic ruins, plus the surreal Valley of the Whales. The dramatic landscape, with three blue man-made lakes contrasting against golden sand and mountains, mean it's a beauty spot popular with Cairo's ex-pats and Egyptians. Hiking in the hills is possible, where you can see churches engraved into the mountains and gain momentous views of the lake and desert beyond. Also here are Egypt's only waterfalls, rather piddling affairs, but an extremely crowded destination on public holidays and

Fridays (best avoided). As well as the wealth of birdlife (mostly spotted during winter), the wadi is home to the world's smallest fox, the Fennec Fox, and a small population of the threatened Docras Gazelle. A visitor centre provides a background to the area, while several lodges and restaurants accommodate for basic needs.

A recently constructed road leads to the **Valley of the Whales**, now making access by non-4WD vehicles possible from Wadi Rayan. Designated a World Heritage Site by UNESCO in 2005, the hulking skeletons of 40-million-year-old marine mammals lie scattered over the desert floor. The fossils validate the evolution of whales from land-based animals to ocean-going mammals, and new remains are still being uncovered. A wilderness campsite is available, with fire pits and toilet facilities, and trails have been marked out for vehicles and walkers in order to protect the area from degradation.

Karanis

ⓘ *Daily 0900-1600 in winter and 0900-1700 in summer, E£32, students E£16. Museum: T084-501825, Tue-Sun 0900-1600 in winter and 0900-1700 in summer, E£16.*

To the east of the lake and 25 km from the city on the main road towards Cairo, the modern village of **Kom Aushim** is adjacent to the site of the ancient city of **Karanis**. Karanis, founded in the third century BC and inhabited by mercenaries of Ptolemy II, was once the centre of a large agricultural area exporting cereals to Rome via Alexandria. Of the two Roman temples, the **Temple of Pnepheros and Petesouchos** (yet more crocodile gods) is bigger and more interesting. Look for the oil/wine presses, tank for crocodiles, Roman baths with evidence of heating pipes, a row of headless sphinxes and the former residence of British High Commissioner Sir Miles Lampson. The results of excavations carried out in the 1920s by the University of Michigan are displayed, together with exhibits from other sites around the Fayoum, in a small circular **museum**. The most interesting exhibits are the carefully restored pottery and glassware, two of the famed Fayoum portraits, the central mummy, the necklaces and the minute statues. Trips to **Qasr Es-Saghah**, a small limestone temple containing seven shrines, and the ruins of the Ptolemaic settlement of Soknopaious Nesos, which used to be on the lakeside but is now 11 km away, 65 m above water level, can be arranged from the museum but it's best to phone a day in advance.

Omm El-Athl, east of Karanis is the ruins of Bachias city, 700 mud brick houses and a small mud-brick temple dedicated to a crocodile god. The Pedestals of **Amenemhat** – two 6-m-high crumbling stone pedestals that once supported a seated colossus of Amenemhat III, can be seen in Biahmo village, 7 km north of Fayoum. Records suggest that each statue of red quartzite was 13 m above the top of its pedestal and each colossus and pedestal was surrounded by a huge solid wall. However, the scant remains are only really of interest to enthusiasts with a lot of imagination.

Madinet Madi

ⓘ *Access is by car, or the El-Qasmiya bus/micro departing from Al-Hawatim southwest of Fayoum city centre can drop you off.*

Madinet Madi, about 30 km southwest of Fayoum City, contains the ruins of a 12th Dynasty temple, built by Amenemhat III and Amenemhat IV dedicated to Sobek the crocodile god and Renenutet the serpent goddess. This site retains an attractive avenue of lions and winged sphinxes. The walls are constructed of limestone, a soft medium for the many reliefs including one of Sobek on the outside wall at the back. The cartouches of both Amenemhats are in the sanctuary with the elegant feet and ankles (all that remains) of several statues. Ongoing excavations have uncovered many new finds, and mean that the site will soon be charging an entrance fee.

Omm El-Borgaigat, with the ruins of **Tebtunis**, is 30 km south of Fayoum. This temple was dedicated to Sobek and was constructed of locally quarried coarse limestone. Little remains of the walls though some paving remains. A cache of mummified crocodiles was found here at the beginning of the last century.

The pyramids of El-Fayoum

There are four separate pyramid sites in the vicinity. **Hawara** ① *daily 0900-1600, E£32, students E£16*, about 10 km southeast from Fayoum, is a mud-brick pyramid 58 m high with a base measuring 100 m, all the decorative casing long since removed. Contrary to normal practice the entrance was positioned on the south side in an unsuccessful attempt to confuse looters. Adjacent to this pyramid is the legendary **Labyrinth**, a mortuary temple also built by Amenemhat III, covering an area of 105,000 sq m. It was half carved into the interior of the rock and was composed of over 3000 rooms but today few traces remain of this spectacular construction. Nearby is the tomb of his daughter Princess Sobek-Nefru Ptah, which was discovered intact in 1956. The poorly preserved necropolis at Hawara are where the famous Fayoum Portraits were discovered.

The ruined **Pyramid of Senusert II** (1897-1878 BC) ① *daily 0900-1600, E£32, students E£16*, near **Lahun** was built by Amenemhat III's grandfather. It was built on a rocky outcrop on which limestone pillars were constructed and then covered over with mud-brick and finally encased in stone. A 'sponge' made of sand and flint was placed around the base in order to prevent any flooding. Once again the unusual south-facing entrance did not deter the tomb robbers who looted Senusert's sarcophagus but left some wonderful jewellery that's now in the Egyptian Museum and New York's Metropolitan Museum. The walled pyramid complex also includes the ruins of a subsidiary pyramid for the queen, the mortuary temple and the *mastaba* tombs of other members of the royal family.

The collapsed **Maidoum Pyramid** ① *daily 0900-1600, E£32, students E£16, to the northwest of El-Wasta on the Nile, and most easily reached from there by a 1-hr early morning train journey followed by a 15-min taxi ride to the village of Maidoum and a short walk*, was originally 144 m sq and 42 m high. However, over the centuries this imposing pyramid, which is built on the edge of an escarpment above the cultivated area, has collapsed leaving only a central three-stepped core of stone standing 65 m high that looks rather like a medieval fort. The difficult entry is up a 30-m stairway on the north side from which visitors descend into a long 57-m sloping passage that levels out to reach a short vertical shaft leading to the limestone-lined and corbel-roofed burial chamber on the same level as the pyramid's foundations.

While it is generally agreed that the Maidoum Pyramid housed the first Fourth Dynasty (2613-2494 BC) pharaoh Snefru, because he also had two other pyramids at Dahshur, it is now believed that it was started by his father Huni and completed by Snefru. The theory as to why it collapsed is that, unlike the pyramids at Giza, which distributed the stresses inwards, it has incorrectly calculated outward stresses – part of the trial and error evolution from the early step-pyramid to the later standard pyramid.

Slightly further north are the rubble remains of the **Seila/Silah** step pyramid of limestone from Second Dynasty and adjacent rock tombs, thought to be Christian. This excursion requires 4WD, a guide and a short walk.

The monasteries of El-Fayoum

Saint Anthony (AD 251-356) acted as an inspiration for hermits and there were soon numerous monasteries throughout the country including the Fayoum depression. A number still stand today. The 12th-century **Deir Al-Adhra** (Monastery of the Virgin), just off the road to Beni Suef about 6 km outside Fayoum City, is the most accessible. It was inhabited until the 18th century then fell into disuse. Bishop Anba Abram was buried here in 1914. The *moulid* of the Virgin is celebrated here each August and the number of pilgrims, already large, is increasing each year. Further south is the beautiful seventh-century Coptic **Deir Malak Ghobrial** (Monastery of the Angel Gabriel) on the desert escarpment at Naqlun above the cultivated lowlands. There is a large number of cells in the area – cut into the hillside – which were accommodation for the monks. The last rebuilding/refurbishment took place this century, so today pilgrims to the annual celebration find more comfortable places to stay in the monastery buildings that surround the church. The church is of a simple classic design. Elements of older buildings have been incorporated giving an impression of greater antiquity. There are icons from the 19th century. **Deir Hammam**, which was originally built in the sixth or eighth century, is 6 km northeast of Lahun and Coptic **Deir Mari Girgis** (Monastery of St George) can be reached by boat from Sidmant Al-Gabal which is 15 km southwest of Lahan. Even more isolated is **Deir Anba Samwail** (Monastery of St Samuel) which is about 30 km south of the rim of the Fayoum depression and can only be reached by pack animal or 4WD.

Wadi Natrun

Wadi Natrun is a natural depression of salt lakes and salt flats lying in the desert west of the Nile Delta, situated off the Giza–Alexandria desert road at approximately Km 100. It is a birdwatchers' paradise brimming with age-old Coptic monasteries, and makes for an excellent day trip from Cairo. Wadi Natrun became the centre of a series of monastic groups principally in the fourth century AD. Insecurity, the plague and attacks by Bedouin led to the decline of some scattered communities but also led to some centralization of Christians into monasteries, four of which remain populated to the present day.

Arriving in Wadi Natrun

Getting there   A taxi from Cairo for the day should cost around E£200-250, depending on your itinerary. You can hop on a **West Delta** bus to the village of Bir Hooker from Cairo's Turgoman station (hourly 0600-1800, E£5); from the village, you can either hire a taxi to take you around the monasteries (around E£50) or you can hitch a pickup bound to the monastery Deir Anba Bishoi (E£1). Alternatively, service taxis leave from Aboud Terminal and stop at the resthouses and petrol stations located at Km 105, where you will need to charter a taxi or you may be able to hitch a ride with Coptic pilgrims passing though.

   Note   Fasting days and feasts make the opening days of the monasteries rather erratic, and it is definitely best to check the website, www.copticpope.org, to see what is open and when. Deir Anba Bishoi is the only one of the four to open every day.

Visiting Wadi Natrun

The **Deir Abu Maqar** (Monastery of St Makarios) ⓘ *only open to visitors who have a letter of introduction from the Coptic Patriarchate in Cairo or Alexandria*, lies 3 km off the highway. Its significance is linked to the importance of St Makarios, the son of a village priest who arrived at Wadi Natrun in AD 330 and became the spiritual leader of the Christian hermits and monks in the area and was known for his rigorously ascetic way of life. He was buried at the monastery, and a further nine patriarchs of the Church are also interred at the site.

The site itself is made up of several **churches**, frequently destroyed and rebuilt. The main church, that of St Makarios, is basically a much-restored building on ancient foundations with some small survivals like the 11th-century dome and vestiges of the side chapels from the seventh to the ninth centuries. Those of St Benjamin and St John are among the most ancient of the original fabric. The main site contains the Cell of the Chrism, the fluid used to embalm Jesus Christ, and there is a belief that some of this original material was stored here at Deir Abu Maqar. A small bakery for making the host is located in a room still standing in its original form on the north wall. Behind the churches, there's an 11th-century three-storey defensive tower. Note the religious paintings in the tower's smaller chapels.

To the northwest lie two other living monasteries – **Deir Anba Bishoi** (Pschoi) and **Deir El-Suriani**. Deir Anba Bishoi was named after the patron saint who went to the wadi following a divine revelation and lived there in solitude. These two sites are easily reached and offer no problems for visitors who wish to walk around. The mainly 20th-century buildings at Deir Anba Bishoi are run by a thoroughly modern community of monks. The layout of the ancient church is cruciform, with a central nave leading to a choir, through doors to the altar sanctuary. Small side chapels (Chapel of the Virgin to the left and Chapel of St Istkhirun or Ischyrion to the right) lie on either side of the sanctuary.

Deir El-Suriani (Monastery of the Syrians) is thought to be an 11th-century foundation by orthodox monks who resisted a schismatic movement at Deir Anba Bishoi. The site was acquired by a devout Syrian Christian in the eighth to ninth centuries and thus took its now popular name since the schism had ended and the monks had returned to their centre at Bishoi. Built over the cave used by St Bishoi, the Church of the Virgin Mary, two main sections – the nave and the choir-sanctuary separated by buttresses and a doorway. The nave has a basin for the washing of feet, a stone screen and houses some religious relics, reputedly including hair from the head of Mary Magdalene, in a niche where St Bishoi lived in ascetic contemplation. In a semi-dome above the west door there is a picture of the Ascension. The altar is of very dark marble.

It is the choir that is most famous, however, for its wonderful 10th-century black, wooden doors with their ivory inlays. Note the paintings in the semi-domes, the death of the Virgin to the left and the Annunciation and the Nativity to the right. There is a library of over 3000 books and many valuable manuscripts. There is also a small museum on site which contains a large selection of 16th and 17th century icons. Check before visiting, as the monastery is closed to the public at times of important religious ceremonies.

Deir El-Baramous, also known as the Monastery of the Romans, is the fourth monastery of the group and the oldest of the sites. It is somewhat isolated to the north end of Wadi Natrun, among lush cultivation and orchards. Legend has it that Maximus and Domitius, two sons of the Roman Emperor Valentinian, died young of self-imposed fasting at this place and that St Makarios set up the new monastery to commemorate ●

them. The five churches are dedicated to the Virgin Mary, St Theodore, St George, St John the Baptist and St Michael. The church of St Michael is on the second floor of the keep, to which there is a drawbridge held in position by an unusual key/pin known as an Egyptian lock. The now unused refectory has a special 6-m-long stone table, carved all in one piece.

◉ Around Cairo listings

For sleeping and eating price codes and other relevant information, see pages 10-14.

🛏 Where to stay

Fayoum City *p145, map p146*
€€ Honey Day Hotel, 105 Sharia Gamal Abdel Nasser, T084-634 0205, T010-521 7090. A bit of a walk from the town centre en route to the Obelisk of Senusert, but a clean 2-star hotel that is small and friendly with its own restaurant. Rather blank carpeted rooms have a/c, TV and fridge, while public areas are a crazy hotch-potch of styles. Free Wi-Fi and use of the PC.

€€ Queen, Sharia Manshat Luftallah, T084-634 6189. Clean, carpeted rooms are comfortable if rather gaudy, with private bath, fridge, a/c and TV. Corridors and public areas are the most dimly lit of any hotel in Egypt. Breakfast included, restaurant with Egyptian dishes, free Wi-Fi and kindly staff. A quiet and pleasant place to stay, particularly if you're in town for a while.

€ El-Montazah, Manshat Lutfallah, T084-634 8662. Near the Bahr Sinnuris canal in a quieter area north of the town centre, run by Copts. A decent budget hotel and, though rooms have seen better days, they are clean. Cheaper small rooms share bathrooms (E£60), others have a/c and en suites (E£120).

€ Fayoum Youth Hostel, Flat No 7, Housing Block No 7, Hadaka, ask for 'Beit El-shebab' to find it. 46 beds, self-catering facilities. Breakfast included. Inconveniently located and often empty. Still, at E£12 per person, the price is the cheapest in town.

€ Palace Hotel, Sharia El-Horiyya, T084-631 1222. Good central location overlooking the Bahr Yusef. Reasonable and clean rooms,

older ones E£100 per double, or newly refurbished on the upper levels for E£200. All have private bath, TV, fridge and a/c. Breakfast included. Owner speaks English and is a good source of information. Cars, motorbikes and bicycles for hire.

Lake Qaroun and Tunis *p147, map p167*
€€€€ Helnan Auberge du Lac, Lake Qaroun, T084-698 1200, www.helnan.com. Built by King Farouk as a hunting lodge in 1937, most old black and white Egyptian movies were shot at the Auberge and King Ibn Saud and Winston Churchill met here in 1945 to carve up the Middle East. The Helnan have recently brought back some of the former glory, and rooms have been refurbished in a classical style including King Farouk's old bedrooms, which are now a duplex suite complete with jacuzzi. There are restaurants, bars, pool, facilities for the disabled and a fishing pier. The view from the more expensive rooms is blocked by the cheaper chalets built in the gardens beside the lake.

€€€ Panorama, Shakshuk, Lake Qaroun, T084-683 0746. 66 a/c chalet rooms with balcony and lake view, TV room, small pool, water sports, fishing, duck shooting, garden, restaurants inside and out – their speciality is seafood.

€€€-€ Kamariat, Lake Qaroun, Tunis, (Cairo office) T02-3302 5428. An environmentally friendly set-up with bright and simple rooms built mainly from natural materials, and including TV. You have to cook your own meals, but can also request a typical Fayoumi meal including duck or fish and *feteer*. Rooms at the back are E£100, or with a lake view E£300. They offer horse-riding as well as birdwatching trips.

€ Sobek, Tunis, T016-888 5423. A new little guesthouse with a distinctly hippyish vibe, has stone-built chalets of varying sizes and simplicity around a rustic garden. Some rooms share bathrooms, others are more comfortable and can sleep up to 4, There's a wicker gazebo for relaxing with views over olive groves and farmland towards the lake. Camping is possible for E£20. Traditional Fayoumi cooking is available, or guests are welcome to use the kitchen. Desert tours, boat trips and pottery workshops can all be arranged.

€ Zad Al Mosafer Ecolodge, Tunis, T084-682 0180, T010-639 5590, abdogobair@maktoob.com. Built from natural materials and encircling scented herbal gardens, appealing rooms have plastered walls, pottery lamps and rush – they are great value, but don't expect luxury. Some rooms share large bathrooms, other have en suites, plus there are chalets sleeping up to 5 persons. Rooms are E£80-150 for a double, or more for those with a better view and a/c. There are panoramic views of Lake Qaroun from the rooftop and the upstairs lounge, and lovely outdoor areas where you can slouch around. It is a short walk up the hill to Tunis village. Good restaurant, children's play area and little swimming pool (open to outside guests for a small charge). The owner, writer Abdou Gobair, also arranges bird-watching trips and excursions to Wadi Rayan, plus horse-riding (E£50 per hr) and camel-riding (E£40) is available. The gift shop has an excellent selection of crafts and pottery.

Restaurants

Fayoum City p145, map p146
There are several local eateries around the central Bahr Yusef canal and market areas, which tend to be better at grilled meats and chicken than *koshari* or *fuul*. None stands out enough to recommend.

€ Governorate Club, on the grounds of Nadi Al-Muhafzah, reached by *hantour* or minibus No 9. There's a small entrance fee to the club. Food is cheap and tasty, with kebab, chicken, and steak, spaghetti, and standard local *mezzas*.

Lake Qaroun and Tunis p147
€€€ Auberge du Lac, Lake Qaroun. Provides decent international food in attractive and historic surroundings.
€€ Café Gabal El-Zinah, Lake Qaroun. Play areas for children, boat landing, fish is main item on menu as well as duck from the lake.
€€ Lake Plage Café, Lake Qaroun. Has 1.5 km of beach, play areas for children, adequate but unimaginative.
€€ Zad Al Mosafer Ecolodge, Tunis. A lovely place for a decent dinner in the quaint restaurant, with Stella for E£18. As well as typical Egyptian grills and some international meals, they do Fayoumi pigeon and duck dishes and use organic produce from the garden.

Shopping

Fayoum City p145, map p146
Fayoum chickens, fresh fruit and straw baskets are available in the city Souk Al-Qantara.

Lake Qaroun and Tunis p147
The village of Tunis, a farming community transformed into an artist's haven, is renowned for its exquisite local pottery. Several small workshops can be visited, and it is a relaxing place to shop. The **Fayoum Pottery School**, T084-682 0405, T018-111 515, T1010-331 0813. Daily 1000-2000, are the most well established and teach local children (they also have a showroom in Cairo, www.nagada.net). **Rawya's**, T010-631 7840 is another good place to start, or just wander the lanes and see who is open.

Fayoum City *p145, map p146*

Bus

To **Cairo**'s Ahmed Helmi and Giza stations, buses leave every 30 mins between 0630-1830 from the main bus station (*'mowaf autobis'*) southwest of the town centre. There are also regular buses south to **Beni Suef** (from where you can change for onward journeys the to the Nile Valley and East Coast) from nearby Al-Hawatim terminal.

Microbuses to **Beni Suef** leave from a terminal 1 km north of the centre.

Service taxi

Service taxis are quicker than buses and leave the depot next to the bus station for **Cairo** to **Midan Giza** or **Midan Ramses**, 1-1½ hrs, E£10-12. To get to **Tunis**, services leave from *'mowaf Ab Shawai'* in Fayoum to Ab Shawai, from where you change to another service to Mafarit Tunis or Yousef el-Sedik.

Train

There are daily trains to **Cairo/Giza** at 0730, 1230 and 1700 and to **Al-Wasta** at 0520, 0830, 1600, 1900 and 2130, but the service is slow and limited to 3rd-class travel.

Fayoum City *p145, map p146*
Medical services Hospital: Sharia Saad Zaghoul, T084-634 2249.

The Nile Delta

Throughout the Delta, countless branches of the River Nile cut through cities, villages and fields that see few tourist visitors. The fertility of the area has enabled this scorched desert country, of which just 4% of the land is cultivatable, to support its huge population and to export large quantities of fruits and vegetables. Travelling around is easiest and quickest by microbus and service taxi.

Western Delta → *For listings, see pages 164-167.*

Across the wider Rosetta branch of the Nile is the Western Delta. The main attractions are the port of Rashid (Rosetta) and some of Egypt's biggest annual *moulids* held in and around Tanta and Damanhur. This route, like most in the Delta, goes through an interesting mixture of scenery: fields of cotton, sugar cane and patches of vegetables, tiny clusters of houses, and old-fashioned water-lifting devices. The area bustles with carts, donkeys, men perched on lawnmower-like contraptions chugging through the streets, and people working in the fields. It is an ever-changing scene of rural Egypt, yet most travellers rush straight on to Alexandria. The taming of the Nile in the late 19th century, allowing perennial irrigation, enables the cultivation of three or four crops a year in this extremely fertile region.

Tanta

This town maintains its rural atmosphere despite being one of the largest cities in Egypt and having a major university. Although it is an interesting and quite charming city, where you can enjoy a taste of contemporary Egyptian life without the glories of past eras and masses of tourists, there is little or nothing to see in Tanta itself for most of the year. Plenty of stunning neglected colonial-era buildings remain, but probably not for much longer as no one seems to recognize their beauty or historical value and modern high-rises are gradually replacing them. Tanta really comes alive, however, in late October at the end of the cotton harvest, during the eight-day festival or **Moulid of Sayid Ahmed El-Badawi** when the population swells to nearly three million as pilgrims pour in from throughout Egypt and the Muslim world. Until the *moulid* was forced into a decline in the mid-19th century because it was so overly riotous and dangerous it was the largest *moulid* in the Muslim world, and in the early years of the 20th century important officials from both the Ottoman and British hierarchy attended the celebrations. It is still the largest *moulid* in Egypt even though in recent years festivities have been further calmed down, and any local can tell you tales of their youth when the crushes in the streets resulted in death on a daily basis. The day after the Big Night (*Leila Kebir*), the *khalifa* which in the past was a riot of camels, drums and circuses as the mounted sheikh leads the procession, these days is merely a crush outside the mosque as the sheikh exits to his car.

Sayid Ahmed El-Badawi (1199-1276) was the founder of one of Egypt's largest Sufi brotherhoods/orders (*tariqas*), which is known as the Badawiya. Born in Fes, Morocco, he emigrated to Arabia and then travelled to Iraq where he joined the Rifaiyah brotherhood. After being sent to Tanta in 1234 as its representative, he received permission to establish his own *tariqa*, which soon flourished. Although the mosque built by his successor and

Moulids – festivals in the Delta

Officially, *moulids* are festivals in commemoration of a specific saint when pilgrims obtain their *baraka*, or blessing, by visiting their shrine. There is usually a parade of devotees, carrying banners and dressed in turbans and sashes in the colours of their saint, sometimes led by floats or camels. Chanting and dancing goes on for hours, led by charismatic singers (*munshi*). There is nothing more moving and uplifting than witnessing a *zikr* at a moulid. As the *munshi* sings and chants, he transports the swaying devotees into another realm and all inhibitions are lost as young and old, rich and poor, men and women, move together in praise of Allah. It's a real eye-opener to a side of Egyptian society that is hidden far beneath the layers of everyday life, a chance for people to cut loose and express intense spiritual joy. Women wearing *higab*, uniformed street cleaners, *felaheen* in *galabiyyas* and muscled T-shirted youths all sway and turn in harmony to the music making a truly hypnotic sight. In addition, the most important *moulids* are like a giant medieval fair where pilgrims meet their friends and eat, drink and celebrate. They stroll among the stalls and rides watching the magicians, acrobats, snake charmers, animal trainers, stick fighters, terrifying stunts on the wall of death and other traditional entertainments.

containing his tomb was demolished in the mid-19th century, a large, new, rather undistinguished one was built by pasha Abbas I (1848-1854) and is the focus of Badawi's annual *moulid*. Another *moulid* in July is held in honour of the female saint Sheikha Sabah.

El-Mahalla El-Kubra

The industrial city of El-Mahalla El-Kubra is 25 km northeast of Tanta and 120 km north of Cairo. It is a particularly scruffy and unattractive place that, unsurprisingly, sees few tourists. To the west of the hospital in the nearby riverside town of **Sammanud** lie the remains of the red and black granite **Temple of Onuris-Shu** ① *Sun-Thu 1000-1300*, rebuilt by Nectanebo II (360-343 BC) for Tjeboutjes, the capital of the 12th Nome of Lower Egypt. Now surrounded by apartment blocks, the small enclosure of dusty stone blocks, some adorned with hieroglyphs, is far from impressive. Further northeast some 10 km from Sammanud along the main H8 highway towards **Talkha** there is the modern town of **Bahbait Al-Hagar** and what little remains of the great **Temple of Isis** in the ancient town of **Iseum** (or **Pr-Hebeit** as it was known to the ancient Egyptians).

Damanhur

Midway between Tanta and Alexandria, Damanhur lies in the middle of the Western Delta, 160 km northwest of Cairo. This sleepy provincial capital and textile town, which was once the site of the ancient city of Tmn-Hor dedicated to Horus, has little to offer the visitor. In November, however, there is the **Moulid of Sheikh Abu Rish**, which follows the more important one in Tanta. Extending over two days in January is Egypt's only **Jewish moulid** at the shrine of a 19th-century mystic called **Abu Khatzeira**. For security, non-Jewish Egyptians are denied entrance to the festival; most attendees are Europeans and Israelis who bring sick relatives or bottled water to be blessed at the shrine.

The Hoopoe

The Hoopoe (*Upupa epopsis*) is like no other bird – it is the only one in its species. It is a resident breeder, fairly common especially in the Delta area. The sexes are similar, both 28 cm in length. You will see it on lawns and in parks and oases where it disturbs the ground searching for grubs. It also eats locusts, moths, spiders and ants. It nests in holes in old trees or ruins (plenty of scope in Egypt) laying up to six eggs.

In general the colouring is buff/pink with distinctive black and white bars in a striped pattern on the wings and tail. It has a long down-curving bill with a black tip, a square tail and broad rounded wings, striped with black tips. A distinctive crest runs from front to back of the head, the feathers having quite marked black tips. This crest is raised when it alights and is evident in mating displays. The call is a distinct 'Hoo-poo-oo'.

Rashid (Rosetta)

ⓘ *There's no direct transport from Cairo. The easiest way to arrive by public transport is to travel either via Damanhur or Alexandria, from where you can catch a service taxi to Rashid (1 hr, E£3.50).*

Rashid (Rosetta to Europeans), formerly known as 'the city of a million palms and dates', used to be the principal port in Egypt. Since ancient times its fortunes have been linked with the ebb and flow of those of its neighbour Alexandria, 64 km to the west. When one waxed, the other would wane. Mohammed Ali's Mahmudiya Canal project linking the Nile to Alexandria marked the end of Rosetta's significance as a port. And while Alexandria is now Egypt's second city, Rosetta is little more than a fishing village. However, its location on the brink of the Nile estuary is an especially scenic one and it's possible to hire bicycles to explore the outlying countryside (and take them across the river on the ferry to the rowdy villages on the east bank). There is still a medieval feel to the cobbled narrow winding streets, with *ahwas* on every corner and masses of horse-drawn carriages and donkey carts ferrying vegetables to market, while in terms of the number of Islamic monuments in town Rosetta is second only to Cairo. For most people, however, the town is synonymous with the 1799 discovery of the **Rosetta Stone**, the key to our understanding of hieroglyphics and, consequently, much of what we know of Egypt's ancient civilization. The stone is inscribed in Greek, hieroglyphics and demotic Egyptian with a proclamation by Ptolemy V Epiphanes. Today it rests in the British Museum of London.

There is some striking architecture in the town from the Ottoman period, recently renovated or under restoration, that offers a taste of Rosetta's splendid past. Many of Rosetta's 22 Ottoman houses are made of distinctive red and black brick and incorporate recycled stones and columns from earlier eras. Many too have delicately carved *mashrabiya* windows and screens. At the time of writing, the majority of these houses were not open to the public as much restoration work is still ongoing; however the exteriors are still impressive. Buildings which can be accessed include the **Beit Kili**, on Midan El-Gumhoriyya by the Corniche, which dates from 1879 and is now a museum ⓘ *T045-292 1733, E£25, students E£15, daily 0900-1700.* The building is noted for its delicately handcrafted woodwork, while on display are a few pieces of glassware, Ottoman period swords, manuscripts, costumes, tiles and armour. The upper rooms

Breaking the code

Jean-François Champollion was born in the village of Figeac in France in 1790. He was a precocious learner of difficult foreign languages and from an early age became involved with studies of Greek, Latin and the Coptic languages.

Like other scholars before him, in the 1820s he began deciphering Egyptian hieroglyphs and by 1822 evolved a virtually complete set of hieroglyphic signs and their Greek equivalent, using the information on the Rosetta Stone.

The Rosetta Stone was found near Rashid in 1799 by soldiers of Napoleon's expedition to Egypt. The huge, irregularly shaped piece of granite weighing 762 kg was embedded in the wall of El-Rashid fort, a piece of recycled fortification. It is thought to have been written by one of the high priests of Memphis in the ninth year of Ptolemy V's reign (196 BC) and is originally a decree of Ptolemy V declaring the benefits he, as a monarch, conferred on Egypt. Its importance was not in its content – though it did establish, among other things, that Ptolemy reunited the country – but in its presentation of three scripts: Greek script below and hieroglyphs; demotic and cursive Egyptian languages above.

The Swede Akerblad and the Englishman Thomas Young had made some progress in deciphering the Rosetta Stone but it was Champollion, using his knowledge of Egyptology, Greek and Coptic languages, who finally broke the code. He was the first to understand that individual Egyptian hieroglyphs stood for individual letters, groups of letters and even for entire objects.

Champollion undertook archaeological work in Egypt in 1828 with the Italian Ippolito Rosellini, recording a series of sites in the Nile Valley. He died in 1832 aged 42 years having been curator of the Egyptian collection of the Louvre and professor of Egyptian antiquities at the Collège de France. His brother Jacques-Joseph prepared and published his works after Jean-François's death.

---

contain some lovely inlaid furniture and the overall effect is pleasing. The museum ticket also gives entry to the Museum Garden opposite, although there is nothing to see save a few fragments of columns. The **Abu Shahim Mill** and adjacent **Amasyali House** ① *E£15, students E£8, daily 0900-1600*, are worth a visit. The mill was built in 1760 and contains two huge millstones that would have been turned by horses to grind flour and rice. The Amasyali House, dating from 1880, has an impressive facade with a fine mashrabiya doorway, painted ceilings and incorporates ancient columns into the building. This ticket also includes entry to the 19th-century bathhouse, **Hammam Azouz**, which gives a sense of the splendour of traditional marbled *hammams*. Some rooms have deteriorated, despite restoration, giving a quite spooky effect.

Of the 12 Ottoman mosques, a couple are worth a visit for their coloured tilework. The huge **Zaghloul Mosque**, built around 1600, a block north of the main road to Alexandria, is a double mosque. The brighter and smarter half to the west is noted for its arched courtyard while the other half, with over 300 columns, sadly suffers from partial submersion. The **Mohammed Al-Abassi Mosque** (1809) standing to the south of the town by the Nile, has a distinctive minaret. The **Ali Maladi Mosque** is being restored, and has many columns looted from Graeco-Roman sites and a beautiful doorway.

Herodotus: the historian

Herodotus lived in Greece in the fifth century BC. His great achievement was his history of the Greek wars against the Persian Empire. His origins are obscure but it is believed that he was a Greek born in Asia Minor in approximately 485 BC. He developed the great tradition of Greek historical research in which questions were asked and answers to them sought in the available written evidence. He became an avid collector of information – stories and travel data – which he eventually assembled into his *History*, writings on the wars against the Persians. He travelled widely in Asia Minor, the Black Sea region and the Mediterranean islands.

Perhaps his most famous journey was to Egypt. He began in the Nile Delta and voyaged to Memphis, Thebes and the first cataract. He was deeply interested in the topography of the Nile Valley and in the nature of the Nile flood. He is attributed with the saying that, "Egypt is the gift of the Nile". Like all geographer-historians of the early period, he mixed scientific evidence and serious observation with myths, fables and tall tales. His readers were given all the excitement of the grotesque and supernatural wonders of the world, though he rarely entirely gave up rational explanations for historical events. His works were widely accepted in Athenian society and today are regarded as an important development in the establishment of history as an academic study (he was a contemporary and companion of Sophocles). In his later life he moved to a new Greek city colony in Thurii, Italy, where he is buried.

Near Rosetta, there is the Mamluk **Qaitbay Fort (Fort St Julien)** ① *E£15, students E£8, daily 0900-1600 (closes at 1500 in Ramadan), 7 km out of town, most easily accessed by taxi (E£30-35 round trip) or taxi boat slightly more (E£50).*

The 18th-century mosque of **Abu Mandur**, 5 km upstream, is accessed by boat taxi or felucca (E£30).

Eastern Delta → *For listings, see pages 164-167.*

The branching of the Nile divides the Delta into three interlocking areas. The main Cairo to Damietta road (H1) runs north through the Central Delta via Tanta before striking northeast through El-Mansura, but there are more interesting routes. Turning east in Benha, a road goes through Zagazig and the ruins of Bubastis to the ancient sites of Nabasha and Tanis, from which a minor road continues north to El-Mansura. Damietta gives access along the coast either east to Port Said at the northern end of the Suez Canal or west to the coastal resorts of Ras El-Bar, Gamassa and even the isolated Baltim.

The main road is normally very busy with a mixture of agricultural traffic and vehicles bound for the ports. On Fridays and holidays it can be even busier with private cars. Shamut Oranges between Tukh and Benha is a very popular spot for picnics. Pigeon towers of varying designs are common in the Delta region, resembling enormous holey beehives and even crowning the roofs of multi-storey buildings in the centre of towns. The pigeons provide free fertilizer and are the main ingredient in 'pigeon sweet and sour', a speciality Delta dish.

Sacred cats

Cats were first domesticated by the Egyptians and it seems probable that the breed they domesticated was the Kaffir cat, a thin, striped, grey cat common all over Africa. Numerous tomb drawings and mummified bodies have been discovered which date from the very early Egyptian dynasties.

The cat was held in great awe and worshipped in the form of the cat-headed goddess Bast (or Pasht) from which it has been suggested the word 'puss' is derived. Egyptians believed that all cats went to heaven: there was a choice of two heavens, the more aristocratic creatures having a better-class destination. If a family cat died the household members would all go into mourning and shave off their eyebrows.

Benha

About 48 km north of Cairo, Benha is the first major town on the H1 highway. It's a stop on the Cairo–Alexandria train line, and accessible by bus every 20 minutes (0600-2100) from Cairo's Aboud terminal, where it's also possible to catch a service taxi. Close by lie the remains of the ancient town of **Athribis**, which was once the capital of the 10th Nome and associated with the worship of the black bull. Although it pre-dates the Greeks, its greatest importance was during the Roman period. Its orderly layout, like that of many Delta towns, was built around two intersecting roads. Little remains of the town today except traces of 18th to 26th Dynasty temples and an extensive Graeco-Roman cemetery. A cache of 26th to 30th Dynasty silver ingots and jewellery from the site is now in the Egyptian Museum in Cairo.

Zagazig

① *Reached by frequent buses or service taxis from Aboud Terminal in Cairo (E£4-6, 1½ hrs). Trains also run from Cairo each day, taking the same amount of time.*

The provincial capital, 36 km northeast of Benha, 80 km from Cairo, was founded in 1830 and its main claim to fame is as the birthplace of the nationalist Colonel Ahmed Orabi who led the 1882 revolt against the British. The town itself has little to recommend it, especially in terms of accommodation, but is lively due to the huge student population and very friendly to the rare independent traveller who winds up here. Most tourists come to Zagazig to see the jumbled ruins of **Bubastis** that lie 1 km southeast of the town, or (less frequently) to attend the **Moulid of Abu Khalil**, which happens during the month of Shawwal.

Bubastis

① *To reach the site, go through the underpass below the train tracks, then walk the km south along Sharia Farouq, or hail a taxi (E£1) or microbus (35 pt). A taxi from the central station square costs E£3. A museum and tourist bazaar are being constructed at the entrance to the site; daily 0830-1600, E£15, students E£10.*

Bubastis, also called **Tell Basta**, was the capital of the 18th Nome of Lower Egypt and was known to the Ancient Egyptians as Pr Bastet (House of Bastet). The name is derived from the worship of the Egyptian cat goddess Bastet who was believed to be the daughter of

The pied kingfisher

The pied kingfisher (*Ceryle rudis*) is very common in Egypt – wherever there is water. Like all kingfishers it is recognized by its larger than expected head with a rather insignificant crest, a long, sturdy, sharp beak and by its short tail and short legs. The bird, 25 cm long, is found in both salt and fresh water. It is a superb diver, fishing from a hovering position over the water or from a perch on a convenient branch. The sexes are similar in sizes in colouring, being black and white – a white band over the eye reaching to the back of the head, a mottled crest and a white throat and neck. The back is mottled, the feathers are black with white edges. The wings are mainly black with a white central band. It has a white breast and under surface except for two black bands (only one black band on the female). It nests in holes in the river bank.

the sun-god Re. During the Old Kingdom she was originally associated with the destructive forces of his eye and was symbolized as a lion. Later, during the Middle Kingdom, this image was tamed and she was represented with a brood of kittens and carrying the sacred rattle. The ancient Egyptians worshipped cats and mummified them at a number of sites including Bubastis because they believed that they would be protected by Bastet.

The town was begun during the Sixth Dynasty (2345-2181 BC) with the granite **Temple of Bastet**, which was enlarged over the centuries up until the 18th Dynasty (1567-1320 BC) and excavated in the 19th century. Herodotus described it as the most pleasing in the whole of Egypt but also criticised the antics of up to 700,000 pilgrims who attended the licentious festivals here and quaffed wine to great excess. Nowadays, the site resembles a field of rubble yet the lack of tourists, shadowy granite statues poking out of the grass, and blocks of masonry strewn about can make you feel like an early archaeologist piecing together a temple plan. Inspection of fallen blocks reveals hieroglyphs and hidden reliefs of Bastet, while hoopoes perch on top of the crumbled columns of the Hypostyle Hall. Look out for Ramses' torso – his decapitated head and feet and arms are scattered nearby. You won't miss the standing statue of Queen Meryut Amun, though her features are clumsy in comparison the beauty of her statue at Akhmim in Middle Egypt. An underground **cat cemetery** where many statues of Bastet have survived, lies beyond. You may (if you're lucky) get a guide to let you in, otherwise you can peer through the windows at the baby-sized remains.

Tanis

ⓘ *Daily 0800-1600, E£16, students E£5. Public transport from Zagazig involves changing at the villages of Faqos and Hassaneya before reaching San El-Hagar, from where you can take a tuk-tuk or walk 0.5 km to the site. It's a pretty lengthy process but incredibly cheap, totting up to just E£4.50. Bring a torch to explore the underground tombs.*

While most travellers from Zagazig head north to El-Mansura, those going east towards the Suez Canal might make a detour to the ruins of the Old Kingdom city of Djane, better known by its Greek name Tanis, located near the modern village of San El-Hagar 167 km from Zagazig.

High Noon at Damyanah – Martyrs' Calendar

Damyanah, who was the daughter of Rome's regional governor in the time of Diocletian (AD 284-305), chose celibacy rather than marriage and took refuge with 40 other virgins in a palace built for her by her father. When her father renounced the worship of the Roman gods and converted to Christianity both he and all of the women were executed on the orders of Diocletian. His persecution of the Christians was so great that the Copts date their era, known as the Martyrs' Calendar, from the massacres of AD 284.

The first shrine to Damyanah is believed to have been built by St Helena who was the mother of emperor Constantine (AD 306-337).

Until earlier this century it was believed that Tanis was Avaris, the capital of the Hyksos Kingdom during the 15th Dynasty, but Avaris has now been discovered further to the southwest at the modern day site of Tell El-Dab'a. French archaeologists are hard at work at Tanis, as they have been since the 1860s, and what they are establishing now is that it is in fact much newer than was previously thought, certainly post-21st Dynasty, one of three 'capitals' that existed in the area. Like other ancient Delta sites, the limestone blocks were pillaged and ground down to make lime leaving only the strong granite foundations, too big and heavy to be removed. What at first glance appears as a desolate wasteland dotted with ruins, broken statues and stone, inhabited solely by shimmering emerald birds swooping and beeping, becomes increasingly impressive close up. When confronted by countless immense stelae, some cleanly broken where they fell, and deeply carved sunken reliefs sharp in the sun, it is actually quite easy to imagine the grandeur that must once have been Tanis.

The layout of the city would have been very similar to Thebes, and in fact the temples to Amun and Mut found here exactly mimic those at Karnak. They are, of course, in a much more ruinous state, and only the remnants of the **Temple of Amun** are worth investigating. Tanis differed to Thebes, however, in that the **Royal Necropolis** was housed inside the Temple of Amun where six royal tombs have been uncovered, almost intact. Some of these can be entered, necessitating much scrambling and leaping as it's not very tourist-friendly. The Tomb of Usurkon II has remains of paint, portraying Nut and the Underworld in addition to various cobras, baboons, bulls and dogs. Sheshank III's tomb still contains his sarcophagus though his mummy is now in the Egyptian Museum.

Tell Al-Maskhuta

Another ruined site on the eastern edge of the Delta is **Tell Al-Maskhuta**, which lies just south of the main Zagazig (70 km) to Ismailia (11 km) road. It has been identified as the site of the ancient town of Tjehu which was the capital of the 8th Nome of Lower Egypt and was often known by its Biblical name of Pithom. Archaeological excavations have revealed the foundations of the ancient city, a temple structure and brick chambers for single and multiple burials together with children's bodies buried in amphorae. A well preserved sphinx and a statue of Ramses II were also uncovered and are now in the gardens of the Ismailia Museum.

El-Mansura

About 55 km north of Zagazig, El-Mansura is an attractive Nile city that was founded comparatively recently (AD 1220) by the great Salah Al-Din's nephew during the Siege of Damietta by the Crusader forces. Despite its name, which means 'the Victorious', the Crusaders reoccupied Damietta in 1249 and then, following the death of Sultan Ayyub (1240-1249), which was concealed by his widow in order not to demoralise his troops, the Crusaders recaptured the town. However, when the Crusaders were weakened by a vicious bout of food poisoning, the Muslims counter-attacked and captured not only El-Mansura but also France's King Louis IX.

Today Mansura is better known as the centre of the cotton industry. During harvest time it is interesting to see the activity in the fields, but the incredibly overladen carts bring road traffic to a standstill. If you do wind up here, visit the **Mansura National Museum** ① *on Sharia Bur Said, T050-224 3763, Tue-Sun, 1000-1800, E£3,* where Louis IX was held prisoner before he was eventually ransomed for the return of Damietta. The museum maps out the warring and bloodshed of the battles with the Crusaders and displays the odd bit of armour and weaponry from the time.

Monastery of St Damyanah

Continuing further along the H8 highway 25 km past Talkha, is the town of **Shirban**, which has a bridge to the east bank of the Rosetta branch of the Nile. Leaving H8 and travelling 12 km west along H7 is **Bilqas** where, 3 km to the north, is the Monastery of St Damyanah (Deir Sitt Damyanah). St Damyanah was put to death, along with another 40 maidens, under Diocletian's purges against the Christians. Normally it is isolated and difficult to reach except during the annual **Moulid of Damyanah** between 15-20 May, which is one of the country's largest Christian *moulids*. Thousands of pilgrims flock to the four 19th- and 20th-century churches on the site in the hope of being healed. Women praying for increased fertility and those who have lost young children are common visitors here.

Dumyat (Damietta)

Back near the Nile the easiest way north from El-Mansura is to cross the river to the Central Delta town of Talkha and head up the main H8 highway to the coastal town of Damietta (known to Egyptians as Dumyat). Furniture-making is a vitally important craft, with 'Louis Farouk' gilted chairs lining the streets and being exported throughout the Gulf from the new port, while production of confectionery and fresh fruit and vegetables adds to the economy.

The town is in many ways similar to Rosetta (see page 157), but has a much more modern facade and a significantly larger population. Damietta flourished as a trading port throughout the Middle Ages but suffered greatly during the Crusades. The Christian forces occupied the town in 1167-1168 and again in 1218-1221 when St Francis of Assisi accompanied the invaders. Worse was yet to come, for the Mamluks destroyed the city in 1250 and made the river impassable as a punishment for suspected disloyalty and to prevent further invasions. The Ottomans revived and rebuilt the town though, unlike Rosetta, many of their attractive buildings have been engulfed and you will be lucky to spot the occasional *mashrabiyya* balcony jutting from an otherwise modern edifice. The last Ottoman Pasha here surrendered to the Beys in 1801 before the time of Mohammed Ali, and the construction of the Suez Canal shifted trade to Port Said, 70 km to the east.

Though not unpleasant, being on a wide curve of the river lined with well-kept gardens, Damietta has little to attract visitors. Look out for remnants of the Ottoman buildings, and in particular the **Ma'ini Mosque** which has just been restored from utter dereliction. Microbuses can drop you at Midan Sorour very close to the mosque, which is now an active place of worship again, with a wonderful inlaid marble floor, *mashrabiyya* windows, octagonal, soaring internal arches and classic Delta-style brickwork. You may be allowed to climb the stairs to the roof and explore further interior rooms decorated with much *mashrabiyya*. Nearby, visit the **Greek Orthodox church of St Niklas and St George**, full of ancient icons and precious gifts from orthodox communities worldwide. Also close by is the new **Coptic church of St Mary** opened by Pope Shenuda in 1992, where the remains of the cleric Sidhum Bishai lie in a glass casket (reminiscent of the mummies of the pharaohs in the Egyptian Museum) plus a supposed relic of the true cross.

About 1 km from the bus station, the **Mosque of Amr Ibn el-Ars** has been rebuilt and revamped, with innumerable newly cut marble pillars filling the aisles around the central courtyard. Just outside remain fragments of the original ancient columns and the warden will be happy to show you the adjacent shrine of Abu Mouvy. Out of town is the huge **Lake El-Manzala** which in winter teems with migrating birds including flamingos, spoonbills and herons. On the other side of the branch of the Nile there are three beach resorts, **Ras El-Bar, Gamassa** and **Baltim** which, although technically in the Central Delta, are most easily reached from Damietta.

◉ Nile Delta listings

For sleeping and eating price codes and other relevant information, see pages 10-14.

🛏 Where to stay

Tanta *p155*
Unless you are visiting specifically for the *moulid* (when it is essential to book well in advance), there should be no problem in finding a room.

€€ Green House, Sharia El-Borsa, off Midan Gumhoriyya about 500 m east of the train station, T/F040-333 0320. 30 good a/c rooms with TV and fridge, restaurant, almost central location. Worth trying if **New Arafa** is full.

€€ Kafr Shishda village, past Mahala El-Kobra village, 17 km outside of Tanta. It's a pain to get to (you'll need to phone for directions) but this private residence which sleeps up to 18 people could come in handy around *moulid* time if you plan to attend for more than 1 day. 3 apartments, 2 very basic but 1 (that sleeps 4) with huge terraces and marbled bathrooms, is the attractive

get-away of the artist owner whose works decorate the walls. Orange and mango trees grow in the garden, the complex backs onto the river (though it's too near the bridge to be scenic), and you can self-cater or ask for meals to be supplied.

€€ New Arafa Hotel, Midan Al-Mahatta, T040-340 5040, F335 7080. Decent mid-range hotel with spacious rooms that have comfy beds, a/c, TV, fridge and adequate bathrooms. There's a restaurant, coffeeshop and alcohol available. Breakfast included. Directly outside the train station and only 250 m from the mosque at the centre of the *moulid* celebrations. Single/double E£260/380.

El-Mahalla El-Kubra *p156*
€€-€ Omar El-Khayyam, Midan 23 July, T/F040-223 4299. The only decent hotel in town has large good-value rooms with a/c, TV and clean private showers, plus some suites. The restaurant is OK and breakfast is included.

Rashid (Rosetta) p157
Rashid is just 45 mins from Alexandria, so you may be better of visiting as a day trip from there (unless you have a penchant for hanging out in traditional *ahwas*, of which Rashid is crammed).

€ El-Nile Hotel, on the Corniche, T045-2922382. The only place actually on the Corniche, some rooms are passable but others not (they won't even let you see them!), all are basic, a few have views of the river. Little English spoken, singles are E£50.

€ Mecca Hotel, just around the corner from the El-Nile down a lane off the Corniche, Cheaper rooms on the lower levels are often full, but the recently renovated upper floor is much preferable with fresh paint and new tiles. Pay more for private bath, though shared are about acceptable. No English spoken by the irritating manager.

€ Rasheed International Hotel, Midan Al-Horiyya, T/F045-293 4399, rasheedhotel @yahoo.com. Far and away the best hotel in Rashid, though that's not saying much. Rooms are spacious, with balcony, TV, fridge and small bathrooms. Expect curtains to be hanging off and the gloomy restaurant to be empty. However, breakfast is included and the staff kindly. Get a top-floor room for amazing views over the midan to the river.

Zagazig p160
You are better off venturing here from Cairo or Alexandria on a day trip. If you do get stuck in town, you can try:

€€ Marina, 58 Gamal Abdel Nasser, T055-231 3934. A 3-star option that is by far the nicest place to stay. Anyone who is not watching their purse-strings should immediately head here.

€ Opera, opposite the train station, no English sign, T055-230 3718. Out of the 2 budgets options, this fills up first, and it's not surprising as the **El-Zaf** next door is completely filthy, if marginally cheaper.

El-Mansura p163
€€ Marshal El-Gezirah, Sharia Gezirah El-Ward, T/F050-221 3000. About 2 km west of the town centre on the Corniche, it is the poshest in town. All rooms have balconies with nice views over gardens and the river, furnishings a bit gloomy in comparison with the marble lobby. Breakfast included. Single/double E£274/357.

€ Macca Touristic, 1 Sharia El-Abbasy, near the Corniche, T050-224 9910. 54 rooms, very decent for the price (doubles E£70), clean, good river views from top floors, TV, private bathrooms, pay extra for a/c, kitsch posters in the hallways, breakfast included. Bang next door to a mosque.

€ Marshal, Midan Mahatta il-Atr, T/F050-223 3920-2. 57 rooms that are very cosy if slightly old fashioned, with TV, fridge, a/c and little balconies, There's a nice patisserie and coffeeshop downstairs, with free Wi-Fi. A well above average buffet breakfast is included. Singles are E£90, doubles E£150.

Dumyat (Damietta) p163
€€ El-Manshy, 5 Sharia El-Nokrashy, T057-232 3308. Pinky-peach paint dominates in these 20 rooms, which have depressing carpets but are clean and comfortable, with TV, a/c and small bathrooms. Down a lane off Sharia Galaa, near the Corniche, There's no lift so it feels like a lot of stairs with heavy bags and the restaurant is not appealing. Single E£80, double E£120.

€€ Soliman Inn, 5 Sharia Galaa (just off the Corniche), T/F057-2377050. Old-fashioned but not unattractive rooms with fridge, a/c, TV and decent bathrooms. Balconies have good views, though it's on a noisy road. They also have 'suites' for a silly E£500. Breakfast included, worth haggling on the price.

🍴 Restaurants

Tanta p155

Besides the acceptable restaurants in the aforementioned hotels, there are cheap stalls around town. For fantastic stuffed pigeon (*hammam*), a Delta speciality, try **Um El-Mohamed** restaurant on Sharia Fatah. The best sweet shop in town is on Midan Sa'ha. During the *moulid* special sweets fill the shops and stalls around the central mosque and in abundance are dried chickpeas (*hummus*) sold by weight.

Rashid (Rosetta) p157

There are a few local eateries around the market area (Abu Youssef is good for *fuul*, *tamayia* and has OK *kushari*), plus a few stalls that grill the day's catch until the fish is positively blackened – yet delicious.
€€ Andrea Park, 2.5 km north along the Corniche, T010-709 8595. For somewhere more salubrious, take a taxi (E£1.50) to 'Andrea Bark' (as the sign says), where a fish meal (*bouri*, rice, salads) costs E£35 per 500 g. Meals are served lunchtime only (until 1500), but the cafeteria is open until late (0400 in season) and it's a pleasant location on the river.

Mansura p163

There's a **Metro** supermarket where Sharia El-Gomhoriya meets the Corniche, 2.5 km west of the town centre.
€€ Giardino, 117 Sharia El-Gomhoriya, T050-222 2097. Closes at 0100. The 'only' place to eat in town has a restaurant upstairs (open from 1300) and café downstairs with very reasonably priced fish and chicken dishes, sandwiches, and good juices. It's near the Gamat el-Mansura (university) about 2.5 km along the Corniche.
€€-€ Abou Shama, Sharia El-Sawra, T050-225 5811. Open 0730-0100. Lots of kebabs, chickens, clay-pots and *kushari*, in a modern and inviting fast-food/take-away restaurant.

Located half-way down Mansura's main shopping street, which links the railway station and Sharia Bur Said.

🎉 Festivals

Tanta p155
Oct Moulid of Sayid Ahmed El-Badawi. See page 155.

Damanhur p156
Jan Jewish moulid, at the Shrine of 19th-century mystic Abu Khatzeira.
Nov Moulid of Sheikh Abu Rish.

Zagazig p160
The **Moulid of Abu Khalil** takes place during the month of Shawwal (around Oct/Nov).

🚍 Transport

Tanta p155

Bus
Gomla bus station, 2 km north of the city centre, has hourly service (0600-2100) to all the towns mentioned in this section, plus 3 morning buses to **Port Said**. Buses to **Cairo** leave every 30 mins from 0600-2200.

Taxi
Service taxis run regularly from the bus station to **Cairo** and **Alexandria**, and to other Delta destinations. Leaving when full.

Train
There are 8 trains daily to **Cairo** calling at **Benha** and to **Alexandria** (1 hr) calling at **Damanhur**, preferable to the bus, and less frequent services to **Mansura**, **Damietta** and **Zagazig**.

El-Mallaha El-Kubra p156

Bus and service taxi
Superjet buses and service taxis for **Cairo** and **Tanta** leave from Midan Shown on Sharia 23rd July, while services for western

Delta destinations (**Kafr El-Sheikh, Disuq**) leave from Zahra station. Local minibuses which can take you to either Shown or Zahra are easily picked up from Midan 23rd July. Services to **Mansura**, **Sammanud**, **Alexandria** and **Dumyat** leave from Midan Talat Harb, which is close to the railway station.

Train

There are trains to **Cairo** at 0600, 0700, 0815, 1530, 1830 and 2130 (2½ hrs) and **Alexandria** at 0900 and 1800 (2½ hrs), plus trains to Mansura every hour.

Zagazig *p160*

Bus

Buses leave from the terminal on the far side of the train tracks for **Tanta**, **El-Mansura**, **Benha**, **Alexandria**, **Ismailia** and **Port Said**.

Taxi

Service taxis congregate by the railway station. They go all over the **Delta** as well as to **Cairo** and the **Canal region**.

Train

Trains from Zagazig run daily to **Cairo**, (26 daily, 1 hr), via **Benha** (45 mins). Also to **Ismailia** (13 daily, 1½ hrs), and **Port Said** (7 daily, 2½ hrs).

El-Mansura *p163*

Bus

Buses run hourly (0800-2100) to **Cairo** (E£10) and **Alexandria** from the bus station on the west side of Midan Umm Khalsoum. It's also possible to take a bus directly to the **Sinai** and the **Canal Zone** cities.

Service taxi

Service taxis for **Cairo** also leave from Talkha service depot, which is the hub for destinations such as Mahalla, Kafr El-Sheikh, Tanta, Dumyat, Port Said and Alexandria.

Train

From Mansura, there are trains to **Cairo** at 0530, 0630, 0730, 1500 and 1800 (2½-3 hrs, 1st class E£40), **Zagazig**, **Damietta** and **Tanta**.

Dumyat (Damietta) *p163*

Bus and service taxi

From the bus station (*mauwaff*) on Sharia Galaa, there are buses every 45 mins from 0630-1930 to **Cairo** either down the main H8 highway via **Tanta** and **Benha** or the east route via **El-Mansura** and **Zagazig**. Buses to **Alexandria** leave at 0630, 0800, 1400 and 1600 (2 ½ hrs, E£20) and buses for **Port Said** leave at 0730, 0800, 0830 and 0900 (1 hr, E£3). Nearby, service taxis to **Port Said** go when full (E£3.50), as they do for **Cairo**, **Alexandria** (E£16), **El-Mansura** and other Delta towns.

Train

Although they are slower, there are trains to **Cairo**, **Alexandria**, **Tanta** and **Zagazig**.

Contents

Footnotes

Basic Egyptian Arabic for travellers

It is impossible to indicate precisely in the Latin script how Arabic should be pronounced so we have opted for a very simplified transliteration that will give the user a sporting chance of uttering something that can be understood by an Egyptian.

Greetings and farewells

Hello	*ahlan wasahlan/*
	assalamu aleikum
Goodbye	*ma'a el salama*
How are you?	*Izayak?* (m); *Izayik?* (f)
Fine	*kwayis* (m) *kwayissa* (f)
See you tomorrow	*Ashoofak bokra* (m)
	Ashoofik bokra (f)
Thank God	*il hamdullil'allah*

Basics

Excuse me	*law samaht*
Can you help me?	*Mumkin tisa'idny?* (m)
	Mumkin tisa'ideeny? (f)
Do you speak English?	*Bitikalim ingleezy?* (m)
	Bitikalimy ingleezy? (f)
I don't speak Arabic	*Ma bakalimsh 'araby*
Do you have a problem?	*Fee mushkilla?*
Good	*kweyyis*
Bad	*mish kweyyis, wahish*
I/you	*ana/inta* (m); *inty* (f)
He/she	*howwa/heyya*
Yes	*aiwa/na'am*
No	*ia'a*
No problem	*mafeesh mushkilla*
Please	*min fadlak* (m)
	min fadlik (f)
Thank you	*shukran*
You're welcome	*'afwan*
God willing	*Insha'allah*
What?	*Eih?*
Where?	*Fein?*
Where's the bathroom	*Fein el hamam?*
Who?	*Meen?*
Why?	*Leih?*
How?	*Izay?*
How much?	*Bikam?*

Numbers

0	*sifr*
1	*wahad*
2	*etneen*
3	*talaata*
4	*arba*
5	*khamsa*
6	*sitta*
7	*saba'a*
8	*tamenia*
9	*tissa*
10	*ashra*
11	*hidashar*
12	*itnashar*
13	*talatashar*
14	*arbatashar*
15	*khamstashar*
16	*sittashar*
17	*sabatashar*
18	*tamantashar*
19	*tissatashar*
20	*'ayshreen*
30	*talaateen*
40	*arba'een*
50	*khamseen*
60	*sitteen*
70	*saba'een*
80	*tmaneen*
90	*tissa'een*
100	*mia*
200	*miteen*
300	*tolto mia*
1000	*alf*

Dates and time

Morning	*el sobh*
Afternoon	*ba'd el dohr*
Evening	*masa'*
Hour	*sa'a*

Day	yom
Night	bil leil
Month	shahr
Year	sana
Early	badry
Late	mit'akhar
Today	inaharda
Tomorrow	bokra
Yesterday	imbarah
Everyday	kol yom
What time is it?	E'sa'a kam?
When?	Imta?

Days of week

Monday	el itnein
Tuesday	el talaat
Wednesday	el arba'
Thursday	el khamees
Friday	el goma'
Saturday	el sapt
Sunday	el had

Travel and transport

Airport	el matar
Plane	tayara
Boat	markib
Ferry	'abara
Bus	otobees
Bus station	mahatit otobees
Bus stop	maw'if otobees
Car	'arabiya
Petrol	benzeen
Tyre	'agala
Train	atr
Train station	mahatit atr
Carriage	karetta; calesh
Camel	gamal
Donkey	homar
Horse	hosan
Ticket office	maktab e'tazakir
Tourist office	makta e'siyaha
I want to go…	a'yiz arooh (m)
	a'yiza arooh (f)
Does this go to…	da beerooh
City	madeena
Village	kareeya

Street	shari'
Map	khareeta
Passport	gawaz safar
Police	bolice

Directions

Where is the…	fein el …
How many kilometres is …	kem kilometers el …
Left	shimal
Right	yimeen
After	ba'ad
Before	'abl
Straight	doghry; ala tool
Near	gamb
Far	bi'eed
Slow down	bishweish
Speed up	bisora'
There	hinak
Here is fine	hina kwayis

Money and shopping

25 piasters/a quarter pound	robe' gineih
Bank	benk
Bookstore	maktaba
Carpet	sigada
Cheap	rikhees
Do you accept visa?	Mumkin visa?
Do you have…	'andak … (m); andik … (f)
Exchange	sirafa
Expensive	ghaly
Gold	dahab
Half a pound	nos gineih
How many?	kem?
How much?	bikem?
Jewellery	seegha
Market	souk
Newspaper in English	gareeda ingleeziya
One pound	gineih
Silver	fada
That's too much	kiteer awy
Where can I buy…	fin ashtiry…

Food and drink

Beer	beera
Bread	'aysh
Chicken	firakh

Coffee	*'ahwa*
Coffee shop	*'Ahwa*
Dessert	*helw*
Drink	*ishrab*
Eggs	*beid*
Fava beans	*fu'ul*
Felafel	*ta'ameyya*
Fish	*samak*
Food	*akul*
Fruit	*fak ha*
I would like...	*a'yiz* (m); *a'yza* (f)
Juice	*'aseer*
Meat	*lahma*
Milk	*laban*
Pepper	*filfil*
Restaurant	*mata'am*
Rice	*roz*
Salad	*salata*
Salt	*malh*
Soup	*shorba*
Sugar	*sucar*
The check please	*el hisab law samaht* (m) *samahty* (f)
Tea	*shay*
Tip	*baksheesh*
Vegetables	*khodar*
Vegetarian	*nabaty*
Water	*maya*
Water pipe	*shisha/sheesha*
Wine	*nibeet*

Accommodation

Air conditioning	*takeef*
Can I see a room?	*Mumkin ashoof owda?*
Fan	*marwaha*
Hotel	*fondoq*
How much is a room?	*Bikam el owda?*
Is breakfast included?	*Fi iftar?*
Is there a bathroom?	*Fi hamam?*
Room	*oda*
Shower	*doush*

Health

Aspirin	*aspireen*
Diarrhea	*is hal*
Doctor	*dok-tor*
Fever	*sokhoniya*
Hospital	*mostashfa*
I feel sick	*ana 'ayan* (m) *ana 'ayanna* (f)
I have a headache	*'andy sod'a*
I have a stomache ache	*'andy maghas*
I'm allergic to	*'andy hasasiya*
Medicine	*dawa*
Pharmacy	*saydaliya*

Useful words

Church	*kineesa*
Clean	*nadeef*
Cold	*bard*
Desert	*sahara*
Dirty	*wisikh*
Hot	*har*
Less	*a'al*
More	*aktar*
Mosque	*gami'*
Mountain	*gabal*
Museum	*el mathaf*
River	*nahr*
Sandstorm	*khamaseen*
Sea	*bahr*
Summer	*seif*
Valley	*wadi*
Winter	*shita*

Dodging touts

You'll get hassled less and respected more if you learn a bit of Arabic.

no thank you!	*La'a shocrun*
I told you no!	*U'ltilak la'a*
I don't want; I'm not interested	*Mish ay-yez* (m) *mish ay-zza* (f)
enough	*Bess*
finished, that's it	*Khalas*
'when the apricots bloom' (ie 'in your dreams')!	*F'il mish mish*

Index

Titles available in the Footprint *Focus* range

Latin America	UK RRP	US RRP
Bahia & Salvador	£7.99	$11.95
Buenos Aires & Pampas	£7.99	$11.95
Costa Rica	£8.99	$12.95
Cuzco, La Paz & Lake Titicaca	£8.99	$12.95
El Salvador	£5.99	$8.95
Guadalajara & Pacific Coast	£6.99	$9.95
Guatemala	£8.99	$12.95
Guyana, Guyane & Suriname	£5.99	$8.95
Havana	£6.99	$9.95
Honduras	£7.99	$11.95
Nicaragua	£7.99	$11.95
Paraguay	£5.99	$8.95
Quito & Galápagos Islands	£7.99	$11.95
Recife & Northeast Brazil	£7.99	$11.95
Rio de Janeiro	£8.99	$12.95
São Paulo	£5.99	$8.95
Uruguay	£6.99	$9.95
Venezuela	£8.99	$12.95
Yucatán Peninsula	£6.99	$9.95

Asia	UK RRP	US RRP
Angkor Wat	£5.99	$8.95
Bali & Lombok	£8.99	$12.95
Chennai & Tamil Nadu	£8.99	$12.95
Chiang Mai & Northern Thailand	£7.99	$11.95
Goa	£6.99	$9.95
Hanoi & Northern Vietnam	£8.99	$12.95
Ho Chi Minh City & Mekong Delta	£7.99	$11.95
Java	£7.99	$11.95
Kerala	£7.99	$11.95
Kolkata & West Bengal	£5.99	$8.95
Mumbai & Gujarat	£8.99	$12.95

Africa	UK RRP	US RRP
Beirut	£6.99	$9.95
Damascus	£5.99	$8.95
Durban & KwaZulu Natal	£8.99	$12.95
Fès & Northern Morocco	£8.99	$12.95
Jerusalem	£8.99	$12.95
Johannesburg & Kruger National Park	£7.99	$11.95
Kenya's beaches	£8.99	$12.95
Kilimanjaro & Northern Tanzania	£8.99	$12.95
Zanzibar & Pemba	£7.99	$11.95

Europe	UK RRP	US RRP
Bilbao & Basque Region	£6.99	$9.95
Granada & Sierra Nevada	£6.99	$9.95
Málaga	£5.99	$8.95
Orkney & Shetland Islands	£5.99	$8.95
Skye & Outer Hebrides	£6.99	$9.95

North America	UK RRP	US RRP
Vancouver & Rockies	£8.99	$12.95

Australasia	UK RRP	US RRP
Brisbane & Queensland	£8.99	$12.95
Perth	£7.99	$11.95

For the latest books, e-books and smart phone app releases, and a wealth of travel information, visit us at: www.footprinttravelguides.com.

footprinttravelguides.com

Join us on facebook for the latest travel news, product releases, offers and amazing competitions: www.facebook.com/footprintbooks.com.